Customers Are People . . . the Human Touch

John has tapped into the importance of treating customers with respect and attention. He clearly shows how every customer transaction is a chance to build trust. John has demonstrated an uncanny knack for communicating what is obvious, yet difficult, for many companies to attain. Keeping promises and building trust must become the centerpiece of all financial services organizations in the future.

Michael Coomer, Group Executive
Business & Technology Solutions & Services

John McKean clearly articulates the logical evolution of customers as consumers to customers as people. However, few companies know how to do this, or have the capabilities within their organizations to culturally make this happen. This insightful book gives real world examples as to why this is critical for a business's survival and how to actually implement these powerful but critical approaches.

Rob Strange, Change Director
Legal & General

John McKean's inspiring book dispels the myth that CRM is the retailers' panacea by providing us with a timely reminder that sustained profitability results from every employee being focused on serving the customer, not just with products, but with integrity and respect for the customer as an individual. This was a common occurrence for our grandparents but a rare event in today's shopping experience.

Trevor Dukes, Project and Systems
W.H. Smith

Customers Are People ...

The Human Touch

John McKean
Executive Director, Center for Information Based Competition

"70% of our decision to buy is based on how we are treated as people ..."

JOHN WILEY & SONS, LTD

Published 2003   John Wiley & Sons Ltd, The Atrium, Southern Gate, Chichester,
West Sussex PO19 8SQ, England

Telephone (+44) 1243 779777

Email (for orders and customer service enquiries): cs-books@wiley.co.uk
Visit our Home Page on www.wileyeurope.com or www.wiley.com

This publication is designed to provide accurate and authoritative information in regard to
the subject matter covered. It is sold on the understanding that the Publisher is not engaged
in rendering professional services. If professional advice or other expert assistance is
required, the services of a competent professional should be sought.

Other Wiley Editorial Offices

John Wiley & Sons Inc., 111 River Street, Hoboken, NJ 07030, USA

Jossey-Bass, 989 Market Street, San Francisco, CA 94103-1741, USA

Wiley-VCH Verlag GmbH, Boschstr. 12, D-69469 Weinheim, Germany

John Wiley & Sons Australia Ltd, 33 Park Road, Milton, Queensland 4064, Australia

John Wiley & Sons (Asia) Pte Ltd, 2 Clementi Loop #02-01, Jin Xing Distripark, Singapore 129809

John Wiley & Sons Canada Ltd, 22 Worcester Road, Etobicoke, Ontario, Canada M9W 1L1

British Library Cataloguing in Publication Data
A catalogue record for this book is available from the British Library

ISBN 0-470-84889-8

Project management by Originator, Gt Yarmouth, Norfolk (typeset in 11/13pt Plantin)
Printed and bound in Great Britain by TJ International, Padstow, Cornwall
This book is printed on acid-free paper responsibly manufactured from sustainable forestry
in which at least two trees are planted for each one used for paper production.

Contents

For my young daughter Jessica,
who is growing into a beautiful human being

Preface

THIS BOOK WAS WRITTEN TO HELP BUSINESS ENTER THE NEXT COM-
petitive era of customer fulfillment – customers as people. Its
approach builds a human touch competency that creates the more
profitable reaction in the person inside every customer – a feeling of
acknowledgement, respect, and trust.

This book was written so that any business, large or small, can start
applying basic human touch principles across its entire business
easily and quickly at the scale and sophistication of its choosing.
The power of these human touch principles is that any business can
start implementing each principle in its simplest form immediately
with noticeable impact on customers. As a business desires more
consistency, depth, unanimity, and scale to its human touch, more
rigor will need to be applied. The simplicity of the principles does
not change with the size of the business, only the scale of implementation. These principles are drawn from learnings of the
world's most successful early practitioners of the human touch.
The insights focus on the human touch behaviors that have the
biggest impact on a customer's decision to buy, and keep buying.

Acknowledgements

I AM HONORED BY AND APPRECIATIVE OF THE FOLLOWING FRIENDS, colleagues, and advisors whose time and insight shaped the ideas contained in this book.

Thanks to Brian Schwady, Marilyn Lindsay, Norman Mayne, Ryan Disher, John Higgins, Kim Yedlowski, Julie Gregory, Steve Albright, Raj Grandhi, Pat Mene, Dave Talbot, Jackie Ashburn, Jane Manfrie, Julia Trusty, Dave Schardt, Tim White, John Pelligrino, Peter Ferras, Joe Mrochek, Jonathon Cole, Alex McHaikhi, Jerry Clarkson, John Voss, Rick Viszantz, Dr Stephen Levitt, Cornelius Martin, Dick Lange, Dennis Gruber, Ken Miller, Norm Kern, David Briggs, Jo Ann Brumit, Roger Quayle, Don Evans, Adrian Horwood, Steve Jones, Shawne Howells, Paul Telford, Mike Dace, Vince Morgillo, Arcona Devan, Richard Jung, Jeff Deneen, Steve Wells, John Goodman, Rick Hinger, Frank Scmermancic, Joni Newkirk, Joe Ruszkiewicz, Glen Kaiser, Bob Barker, David Overton, Jaimie Pickles, Bruce Clark, Jim Bauer, John Peterson, John Parolisi, Simon Wood, Stephen Ciombrone, and David Curby.

Several people listed above helped shape my thinking, but corporate sensitivities required their firm names and specific references be withheld.

Special thanks to Ray Kordupleski for his groundbreaking work. He was and continues to be an inspiration to me. Also, a special thanks to Ilmar Taimre under the visionary leadership of Steve Jones for sharing the leading edge innovations at Suncorp. Ray's current work can be found in his book *Mastering Customer Value*

Management (Cincinati, OH: Pinnaflex Educational Resources, 2002, www.pinnaflex.com/cvmbooks). The material in Chapter 7, "Human Touch as a Series of Interactions", contains Ray's and Ilmar's important contributions.

Special thanks to Horst Schulze whose unquestionable vision and leadership ability created the pinnacle of "The Human Touch" – Ritz-Carlton. The material contained in the chapter "Human Touch as a Process" is from Horst Schulze and the Ritz-Carlton Hotel MBNQA (Malcolm Baldrige National Quality Award) Application Summary.

Special thanks to a new-found colleague and sounding board, Wendy Eggleton, whose insight and clear thinking helped immeasurably in sharpening this book's ideas, structure, and delivery.

Special thanks to my research assistant Terri Vanderberg whose hard work, dedication, and sensibilities in research and editing enabled this book to be clear and understandable.

Special thanks to the wisdom of Jim Howland, Chairman Emeritus of CH2M Hill, whose *Little Yellow Book* ideas are interspersed in the leadership chapter (Chapter 2).

Special thanks to Don Peppers for his unwavering encouragement and guidance, and for being there when I needed him.

1

Customers as People

Customers are People – "The simplest explanation for some phenomenon is more likely to be accurate than more complicated explanations."   OCCAM'S RAZOR

Current Situation

CUSTOMERS WANT THE BEST PRODUCT AT THE BEST PRICE FOR THEM and want to be treated well in the process of buying and owning that product. In a market where competitive product and price offerings exist, customers will choose the business that best treats them like a "human being". An emerging body of evidence verifies the intuitive notion that a customer's decision to buy is based more on how human his or her interactions are and less on subtle product and price differentiation. The latest research reveals that up to 70% of a customer's decision to buy is based on interactions and only 30% based on product attributes. It is the "human touch" that stands out in the mind and memory of the customer. Although many businesses advertise they treat customers as "relationships", ironically less than 10% of their resources are invested in how human they treat their customers. Over 80% of customer initiatives are focused on how to "sell the customer better" through matching products to customers rather than investing more resources in "treating customers better". The resources applied to "selling the customer better" for specific customer initiatives have little impact on a customer's future decision to buy during subsequent campaigns whereas resources applied to "treating the customer better" have a strong annuity effect on successive campaigns. Resources invested in "selling the customer better" have little or no impact on the customer's future buying decisions whereas resources applied to "treating the customer better" have a significant influence on future buying decisions. Matching customers with products only addresses 30% of the factors influencing a customer's decision to buy in the competitive market. This 30% best indicates which product the customer will buy. It fails to provide an adequate framework to influence where the customer will buy it. Sales and marketing efforts based on this attribute approach often create equal demand for the product among competitors. This is the common downfall of most Customer Relationship Management (CRM) initiatives. In this scenario, the more competitors in a marketplace, the worse traditional customer initiatives fare. In this environment, customers will continually substitute competitive product offerings because they can perceive no difference between products or the companies that offer them. Only the business with the "human touch" that consistently demonstrates, "you're a real person and we genuinely care" will stand out as noteworthy in the eyes of the customer. Product and price is easily copied; a business's "human touch" competency is not.

The "human touch" competency should not be confused with the popular but misconceived notion publicized by most businesses that they have customer "relationships" or seek customer "intimacy". The truth is that most customers don't want what the word "relationship" or "intimacy" implies – a certain degree of closeness or meaningfulness regarded by most as offensive and intrusive. Customers want and need something more akin to an "understanding". An understanding has certain emotionally based expectations and exchanges without the implied closeness and meaningfulness suggested by the word "relationship".

Research has shown that this "understanding" is based on three primary human needs of customers and the resulting expectations:

1   Acknowledgement

2   Respect

3   Trust

How and why customers choose to buy, both initially and follow-on customer purchases, is eloquently simple. Here is a snapshot of how customers buy as "people" (through their eyes):

1   Build trust in me so I feel buying your product is the best decision for me.

2   Acknowledge me and my importance to you.

3   Respect me and my needs.

Initial trust is either confirmed and strengthened or is disproved and decreases based on the customer's experience.

Why Hasn't a Business-wide Human Touch Been Addressed Sooner?

There are many reasons why business is only now beginning to realize that a customer's buying behavior has more to do with human behavior than "consumer" behavior. In fact, it could be said that consumer behavior only explains 30% of why people buy, whereas people's behavior explains 70% of why customers buy. First, it is a simple matter of the evolution of understanding and approach to customers. When reviewing the evolution of customer approaches, it is clear that business has been evolving toward Human Behavior – the DNA of business – for decades. Table 1.1 represents this evolution.

Pre-1980s was characterized by a general view of customers as a homogeneous group of consumers. The beginning of this era was dominated by the large industrialists' views of consumers. This view is captured by Henry Ford's famous pronouncement that customers could have any color of Ford they wanted, as long as it was black. Today, research shows that roughly 40% of automobile buyers say they would switch core brands if they could not get the color they wanted.

Table 1.1   Customer evolution

Era	Mantra	Approach	Type
Pre-1980s	Consumers	Customers as a group	Product-based
1980s	Customer focus	Customers as important	Product-based
1990s	CRM	Customers as individuals	Product-based
2000+	People focused	Customers as people	Interaction-based

The 1980s was characterized by the recognition that an external focus on customers was becoming increasingly important. Applying resources toward an external customer focus instead of a predominantly internal operational focus became necessary. Concepts such as "reengineering the business" toward customers became popular during this era.

The 1990s was characterized by the recognition that customers are individuals with distinctive attributes. Once business realized this, they made the leap of faith that fostering a "relationship" with customers would somehow compel them to buy more products. While the popular term CRM was used to describe this approach, most of the actions focused less on what the word "relationship" implied and more on how to sell more products by matching product attributes with customer attributes. Although this approach provided initial gains, returns are diminishing because it fails to adequately address why people buy a product from a particular company in a competitive market.

2000+ is characterized by a growing set of early "human touch" practitioners who are raising the bar on their competitors by not only recognizing their customers as individuals but creating a primary focus toward treating their customers as human beings in every customer interaction.

This evolution is the result of several decades of "peeling back the onion" on the real reasons why and how customers buy as people. The most significant factor in understanding and verifying the importance of human interactions has been business's very recent openness to engaging behavioral scientists. This openness has grown out of frustration with conventional customer approaches that continue to yield only moderate improvements in the attempt to create consistent profitable buying behavior by customers. Interestingly enough, during the time business was evolving its understanding of customers, the underlying human needs, which determine how people buy, have not fundamentally changed. It is only the cause-and-effect relationship between customer expectations and the ever-rising bar of competition that has created the illusion that customers' buying behavior has fundamentally changed.

Throughout this management evolution, the "human touch" has been practiced intuitively at an individual level. Top business professionals in marketing, sales and service have discovered this truth through personal experience and practice this intuitive art at varying degrees of conscientiousness. Most brilliant moments in business can be traced to the practice of this art. Despite this, most firms have not established the art of humanness as a firm-wide science to create a unanimous and consistent human touch across every interaction. It has not been until recently that its importance has begun to be explicitly recognized and funded; and once again the competitive bar is raised.

What Are the Challenges of Actually Doing It?

The following questions and how well a firm answers them, and implements their answers, represent the major challenges a firm will have when evolving its human touch:

+ What needs do customers have as people that will most influence their decision to buy?

+ What leadership behavior best creates a firm and its culture to fulfill those needs?

+ What types of employees best fulfill those needs?

+ What employee behavior best communicates and fulfills those needs?

+ What training best enhances those employees' innate abilities?

+ What communication methods and skills best deliver the desired messages?

+ What employee treatment best enhances both employee and customer fulfillment?

+ What approaches best create human touch consistently across each interaction?

+ What processes best deliver a consistent human touch?

+ What technology approaches maximize humanness, and do not dehumanize?

Where and How to Start

Any business can begin the journey to develop its human touch with small and simple actions that cost nothing yet have immense and immediate impact on customers. This journey could begin with the simplicity of a smile, direct eye contact, and the words "please" and "thank you". Encouraging employees to use these simple behaviors with customers more often and with genuine warmth will make all the difference in what the customer remembers about the business.

These simple actions communicate the message "you're a real person and we care". Customers remember these little human touches because that's what is important to them as a customer and as a person. These human touches satisfy the three primary human needs that impact the customer's decision to buy – Acknowledgement, Respect, and Trust (ART).

A higher degree of consistency and unanimity in the desired humanness of a business requires increasing levels of focus and dedication in order to achieve greater business impact. The primary human needs of Acknowledgement, Respect, and Trust provide a common thread that helps keep efforts focused and aligned through any level of rigor a business wants to pursue. The implementation complexity is determined by the scope and scale of the business and its customers.

There are eight major areas on which business should focus:

(a) Leading the Human Firm.

(b) Acknowledging Customers.

(c) Treating Customers with Respect.

(d) Building Trust with Customers.

(e) Communicating Humanly.

(f) Implementing the Human Touch Consistently across Interactions.

(g) Understanding and Applying the Human Touch as a Process.

(h) Implementing Technology to Humanize (not Dehumanize).

(a) Leading the Human Firm – leading the human firm is about selecting, developing, and fulfilling employees so they can fulfill the three primary human needs that make the biggest impact on a customer's decision to buy.

(b) Acknowledging Customers – understanding how best to fulfill the human need for acknowledgement. Activities should focus on acknowledging the customer's existence, importance, characteristics, and feelings. It is also important to focus on eliminating behaviors (intentional or unintentional) which create feelings of being ignored and anonymous.

(c) Treating Customers with Respect – understanding how best to fulfill the human need for respect should center on their dignity as human beings. Sending messages of respect start with basic common courtesies and extend into such areas as respect for the customer's time, privacy, personal space, home, and diversity. Equally important is focusing on eliminating behaviors that convey disrespect.

(d) Building Trust with Customers – understanding the role of trust is key because customers don't buy without trust. Actions to build trust in customers should be focused on honesty, ethics, integrity, openness, educating customers, and most importantly operational excellence. It is also important to focus on eliminating behavior which creates distrust.

(e) Communicating Humanly – understanding and developing the skills to create the most human communication between employee and customer. This involves becoming a better listener as well as a better communicator to customers both verbally and nonverbally.

(f) Implementing the Human Touch Consistently across Interactions – businesses should view their interactions with customers as a series of interactions that must be consistently "human". The "human touch" of each interaction of the series should be

consistently measured by a hierarchy of human needs, their weighted importance, and linked to the supporting business processes.

(g) Understanding and Applying the Human Touch as a Process – each human touch can be viewed as one step linked to many other interdependent steps to make up an entire process. Businesses should focus on human touch as a process that not only enables a high degree of consistency in delivering their humanness but also helps to isolate activities that dehumanize.

(h) Implementing Technology to Humanize (not Dehumanize) – Currently, the implementation of technology in customer interactions humanizes and dehumanizes in equal proportions. The areas in which technology has the greatest impact on making interactions more human are in enabling: convenience and control, anonymity, simplicity of life, and the sense that the business truly "knows" them. Technology should also set employees free from task execution to focus on the human elements of the interaction.

To leverage the awesome power of the human touch is to recognize the genius behind every successful business transaction. Now there is a body of documented evidence and experience that will enable businesses to explicitly and purposefully implement the science of the human touch across an entire organization consistently.

2

Leading the Human Firm

E MPLOYEES ARE SNOWFLAKES. THEY ARE MAGNIFICENT. THEY ARE
people. Their strengths are their differences, not their similarities. When they are nourished with acknowledgement, respect, and
trust, they perform extraordinary feats for their firm and its customers. When they are not, they fulfill expectations but that's all.
And when pushed too hard and too long, they melt.

The following verse summarizes the main points presented in this
chapter of what creates the best environment for employees to fulfill
themselves and customers:

Verse for Human Leaders

So, take care leaders ...

Select them Well

Develop them with Care

Create a Caring Culture for them

Acknowledge, Respect, and Trust them

Fulfill them as people

And their performances will astound you.

(Copyright © 2002 John McKean)

The following "Leader's Promise" summarizes responses to countless interviews asking employees what leadership behaviors best
enable and fulfill them as employees and people.

Leader's Promise to Employees

I'll ACKNOWLEDGE you – recognize your worth

I'll be ACCOMMODATING – change things for your needs

I'll be ACCOUNTABLE – take ownership of my decisions and their outcome

I'll be COMMUNICATIVE – openly exchange ideas/information with you

I'll be CONSIDERATE – think of you first

I'll be COURAGEOUS – bold and tenacious, even when it's tough

I'll be EMPATHETIC – sensitive to your feelings

I'll be ETHICAL – do what is right

I'll be FAIR – balance your needs with others

I'll be FLEXIBLE – open to alternatives

I'll be GENEROUS – give more than expected

I'll be HONEST – tell the truth

I'll have HUMILITY – give credit and avoid self-importance

I'll be INSPIRING – provide enthusiasm toward a goal

I'll be LOYAL – always there for you

I'll be PERSONABLE – easy to be with

I'll be RESPECTFUL – recognize your dignity as a person

I'll be SUPPORTIVE – provide help and remove barriers

I'll be TOLERANT – accept you without judgment and forgive mistakes

I'll be TRUSTING – believe in you

I'll be TRUSTWORTHY – do what I say and what needs to be done

Human Leadership Makes Cents ($)

There is a strong correlation between employee fulfillment, customer fulfillment and fluctuations in share price. Figure 2.1 below illustrates this powerful cause and effect relationship. The trendline for share price has been manually shifted to the left on the chart by one quarter to more easily illustrate the relationships without the inevitable lag between customer fulfillment and share price fluctuations. In this particular example, the lag time between customer fulfillment changes and share price fluctuations was one quarter. This can be as short as one-week and as long as several quarters, depending on how fast the market changes, e.g. sales cycles, speed of competitors.

These three elements represent the classic behavioral business cycle, i.e. happy employees tend to create happy customers, which positively affects share price and profitability. This particular telecommunications firm actively tracked employee and customer satisfaction for 2–3 years using quarterly summary measurements. The correlation between customer satisfaction and employee satisfaction was 0.75 during eight measurement periods. The correlation was stronger than coincidental while the conclusions were intuitive and statistical. The study covered six business units that contained 75 000–80 000 employees. Actual responses for the employee survey totaled roughly 50 000 employees. The number of customers who responded from the six business units totaled 50–75 large corporate customers.

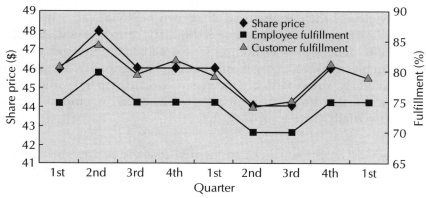

Figure 2.1   Employee = customer = shareholder fulfillment

Select Them Well

Match employee values to business values

In order for a firm to achieve its cultural and value objectives, it is critical to hire employees with a personal value system consistent with the firm's cultural and value objectives. From the employee's perspective, if the firm's culture (value system) is out of sync with the person an employee believes himself or herself to be, the employee will be less effective, less productive, and less committed. In addition, the firm will be creating undue stress and possible emotional damage to its employees as human beings. More specifically, if the firm's objective is to deliver humane and kind service to its customers, employees who are treated in the same fashion will be more likely to create this environment for customers.

The people who happen to be working as an associate for some business do not go through a miraculous transformation when they walk through the doors of that business. They are the same human being they always were. Employee stress arises when associates are hired because of their personality of wanting to please customers and yet the business has many restrictions that inhibit their ability to please customers. If an associate is empowered to please their customers, they will be a happier and a more content associate.

Whether the employees are conscious of it or not, they usually make a choice of employment based on their sense of personal values relative to the firm's value systems. In this regard, this is dependent on how clearly they understand their own personal value system as well as how accurately they understand the firm's espoused value system. In general, firms should hire for personal human characteristics such as self-respect, genuine caring, and empathy. Empathy is a particularly important characteristic because many times it is more important to a customer to be listened to empathetically then to actually have a problem fixed.

A Wal-Mart store manager commented that the reason she came to work for Wal-Mart was their culture of customer focus. She had an innate desire to help people. The reason she stays with Wal-Mart is the never-bending culture of "do the right thing for the customer" above all else. As she says, "What I love about this company is that we put our customers before the numbers". She adds, "but we do need to make our numbers". This attitude is the perfect balance of "customers first", with the supporting realization of business imperatives. It is this balance that Sam Walton professed from the first day his first store opened in Bentonville, AR. The human approach to business has propelled this small-town retailer to become the largest retailer in the world. Wal-Mart are currently the second largest employer in the USA, next to the US government.

Integrity first and last

Integrity is the all-important prerequisite to employment. The person must be honest with themselves and others or there is no foundation on which to build.

LITTLE YELLOW BOOK

Match employees to target customers

Every business interaction is ultimately between two people – an employee and customer, or the employee who designs the customer interface and that customer. Most high-performance business relationships are heavily influenced by emotional compatibility. Therefore, the employee selection process should begin with carefully selecting employees who will first best match the targeted customers, then the company. Although we lack understanding of the emotional state of the customer at the beginning of an interaction, it is possible to hire for and then match emotional predispositions of employees, e.g. sales, service to particular customers. This entails matching employee human attributes with customer human attributes. After a firm segments their customers by human need, it can then match the emotional attributes of employees to emotional attributes of customers. One of the ways to accomplish this is through applying classic personality typing during employee screening. The firm can then hire "personalities" who best match how the firm delivers its value to a certain segment of customers. When employee and customer human attributes are not matched, it is stressful to the employee and increases the chance that the customer will not be satisfied. In many cases, management will end up chastising the employee for apparent performance shortcomings when in fact it is simply a mismatch of emotional attributes between employee and customer. Matching can be accomplished by creating customer needs profiles and employee needs profiles for particular customer "need" segments and employee roles respectively. The critical component of matching employee to customer is the first focus on what emotional end state the customer desires; next is hiring employees whose natural ability is to create such an end state. This goes far beyond the conventional job description of roles and tasks. When customer/employee emotional matching is embedded into core hiring practices, not only does customer and employee fulfillment increase but so does employee efficiency and effectiveness.

Ultimately, employees' ability to fulfill customers is determined by their inherent human characteristics. Below is a comparative table of people with high self-esteem versus low self-esteem illustrating this principle.

Employees with high self-esteem are:

1   Likely to think well of others.

2   Expect to be accepted by others.

3   Evaluate their own performance more favorably than people with low self-esteem.

4   Perform well when being watched: not afraid of others' reactions.

5   Work harder for people who demand high standards of performance.

6   Inclined to feel comfortable with others they view as superior in some way.

7   Able to defend themselves against negative comments of others.

Employees with low self-esteem are:

1   Likely to disapprove of others.

2   Expect to be rejected by others.

3   Evaluate their own performance less favorably than people with high self-esteem.

4   Perform poorly when being watched: sensitive to possible negative reaction.

5   Work harder for undemanding, less critical people.

6   Feel threatened by people they view as superior in some way.

7   Have difficulty defending themselves against others' negative comments; more easily influenced.

(Adapted from Don E. Hamachek, *Encounters with the Self*, 2nd edn (New York: Holt, Rinehart & Winston, 1982), pp. 3–5)

Better emotional fit upfront creates a more content employee

Each employee role requires a certain emotional predisposition. For example, if a business needs a genuinely caring employee for a particular customer-facing role, it is critically important that the person chosen has an innate genuine caring personality. If not, both the business and the employee will go unfulfilled. In some cases, even the best screening efforts will not detect a mismatch of emotional requirements and employee emotional predisposition. This is why it is important to understand the emotional requirements of each type of job so employees can be moved, without the "stigma" of failure, to a better emotionally matched job. A business that freely cycles employees to different jobs creates an environment that minimizes any such stigma. Almost all employees have an innate desire to be competent, and competence is best achieved when there is an emotional match. For example, in the Internet startup community, hiring employees with a high tolerance for ambiguity is of the utmost importance. Not addressing this emotional trait could be terminal to both company and new employee.

Have 'em do what they love, and the money will follow

The hidden benefit is that if the employees are doing what they love, your clients will love it, and the money will follow. Good work should be done because they like the work, not for the compensation. If the employee is more interested in the compensation than the work, maybe they're in the wrong position. The compensation comes as a result of all the good things your business has done for your customer (source: Norm Kern).

Nothing is really work unless you would rather be doing something else.   JAMES MATTHEW BARRIE
                    (1860–1937; Scottish dramatist and novelist)

The Law of Least Effort – Nature's intelligence functions with effortless ease with care freeness, harmony, and love. When we harness the forces of harmony, joy, and love, we create success and good fortune with effortless ease.   DEEPAK CHOPRA

An integral being knows without going, sees without looking, and accomplishes without doing   LAO TZU

Match personality types to desired brand "emotions"

Land Rover centers attract customers who associate with the brand image that the Land Rover Way represents: individualism, authenticity, freedom, adventure, guts, supremacy, and courage. Many potential Land Rover customers are corporate executives, sports celebrities, and environmentalists who simply enjoy the outdoor lifestyle. This requires the employees who interact with these customers to communicate with a wide range of demographics. These interactions must be done across every aspect of Land Rover's sales and service. Communications and teamwork crackle across the Land Rover center.

Hire for interpersonal skills and personality type first, then technical knowledge, skills, and experience. In most cases, it is easier to train employees to acquire technical knowledge and skills than it is to increase an employee's interpersonal skills. Therefore, most businesses should seek to hire for interpersonal skills as the primary job prerequisite for customer-facing employees and commit to train them sufficiently for the acquired technical knowledge of the job. Employees with a high degree of interpersonal skills and a small amount of technical knowledge many times will succeed beyond someone with great technical knowledge and few human interaction skills.

"People" people like people

"People" people like people (customers) and customers are more likely to like them in return. Employees who genuinely enjoy human interaction are increasingly being valued and sought after. The competition is increasing for employees who both have the mentality and ability to treat customers with friendliness. A business's screening process should include as a central characteristic an upbeat and outgoing personality with the ability to be comfortable approaching and communicating approachability to customers.

Even inherently shy employees can work well if they are considered to be a "people person", i.e. enjoy being around people and helping them. Employees should have a natural, innate desire to help customers, as this desire is the foundation for service excellence. Once the "people pleasing" employees are in place, the humanizing culture grows stronger and is more immune to erosion. Almost all other product and service attributes can be quickly copied.

Hire attitude over experience

A good attitude will enable an associate to readily learn and gain great experience. A bad attitude will typically negate the ability to utilize an associate's great experience. Norman Mayne, chairman and CEO of innovative Dorothy Lane Market, prefers to hire associates for attitude rather than "experience". He has historically steered away from hiring associates whose knowledge was gained from the training of his competitors. He prefers to hire for "attitude" and then provide that special brand of DLM knowledge in terms of its specialty products and "style" of customer service. Norman comments, "experienced people often bring bad habits and all kinds of cultural legacies to DLM that are contrary to what we believe in". Norman characterizes the strategy to hire employees primarily based on attitude and personality characteristics as being able to start with good "seed stock". The top three personality traits Norman looks for in potential DLM employees are human friendliness, compassion, and honesty. For every five applicants, Norman will only hire one of them. DLM's hiring process begins with a three-minute screening interview. If the prospective employee seems to fit their humanizing culture, they are brought in to take a one-hour Scantron test which offers a glimpse into human characteristics, personality, and behavioral history. If they do well in the Scantron test, the prospective employee will have a 30-minute interview with an employee who reports directly to Norman. When Norman ultimately gives his personal consent to hire 10 new associates, it represents 50 screened prospective DLM employees. Norman also believes that in order to end up with the right mix of special employees, above-average wages need to be paid. His competitors have an average payroll expense of 9% of sales whereas Norman's payroll percentage is 14% of sales. Norman observed that this percentage differential in payroll costs is easily made up from the number of new customers gained from his competitor's less rigorous approach to hiring humanizing employees. Once hired, the employees are first placed in a DLM store to learn the basic mechanics of store operations for a two- to three-week orientation period. After this initial store operations introduction, the associate has a personal meeting with Norman to talk about the culture and history of Dorothy Lane Market and how their customers' needs have changed over the years.

The longer I live, the more I realize the impact of attitude on life. Attitude, to me, is more important than facts. It is more important than the past, than education, than money, than circumstances, than failures, than successes, than what other people think or say or do. It is more important than appearance, giftedness or skill. It will make or break a company ... a church ... a home. The remarkable thing is we have a choice every day regarding the attitude we will embrace for that day. We cannot change the inevitable. The only thing we can do is play on the one string we have, and that is our attitude ... I am convinced that life is

10% what happens to me, and 90% how I react to it. And so it is with you ... we are in charge of our Attitudes!
CHARLES SWINDOLL
(on "Attitude"; with thanks to Roger Wright)

Certain flaws are necessary for the whole. It would seem strange if old friends lacked certain quirks.   GOETHE

Nobody can be exactly like me. Sometimes even I have trouble doing it.   TALLULAH BANKHEAD

To be nobody-but-yourself – in a world which is doing its best night and day, to make you everybody else – means to fight the hardest battle which any human being can fight; and never stop fighting   E.E. CUMMINGS

Develop Them with Care

After employees have been carefully selected, it is just as important to develop those attributes for which they were so carefully selected.

Help "caring people" care better

Enhance the innate ability for human interaction. Once a business has carefully screened for the most "humanizing" employee, the next step is to enhance this innate ability. A significant part of this enhancement is to help them understand the customer value of their abilities, i.e. personality predisposition. For example, a person whose human interaction courtesies come very naturally and intuitively may not realize the full value of this to a customer's perception of the business. As simple a behavior as a smile may be taken for granted and as a result the employee may have a tendency to smile in more limited situations. Employees should be taught that a smile is the most universal method of making another human being feel comfortable and should be encouraged beyond their functional roles or responsibilities. When an employee smiles at a customer, the customer will likely return the smile. Neither training nor innate ability by themselves can create a sustainable and consistent human experience; they must be joined together.

Coaching helps determine genius from joker

There is a fine line between a genius and a "joker". Which side of the line a person comes down on, can depend on the coaching received from the group leader and the quality of the peer support.   LITTLE YELLOW BOOK

Flaunt flamboyance when thinking or dreaming

Encourage people to be flamboyant when it comes to dreaming and thinking but conservative in their personal habits while doing interesting, innovative things inside and outside the firm.   LITTLE YELLOW BOOK

Do not fear to be eccentric in opinion, for every opinion now accepted was once eccentric.   BERTRAND RUSSELL

Every child is an artist. The problem is how to remain an artist once he grows up.   PABLO PICASSO

First humanize employees, then customers

Treat employees well and they will treat customers well. Norman Mayne of Dorothy Lane Market believes strongly that focusing on employees first as special human beings will ultimately enable them to treat the customers as special human beings. To help employees humanize their customers, Norman conducts a personal session with the employee explaining his philosophies on treating customers as special human beings. The employees are then trained in a four-hour workshop with a university professor, focusing on human communication skills for customers. This human communication session is a program purchased by DLM many years ago and evolved over the years to suit their customer communication needs. Much of the session involves role-playing of human communication skills between associates and customers. After the program, the associates are awarded a diploma for graduating from DLM's training program.

Focus 25% of development on emotional transfer of pride and enthusiasm

Most companies view training as largely knowledge transfer with a supporting element of pride and enthusiasm. For the training to be most effective, the transfer of pride and enthusiasm should encompass at least 25% of the training activity as an employee's behavior is driven by emotion, not facts. This "pride and enthusiasm" transfer should take place as soon as possible in the new employee's exposure to the business's humanizing culture. A charismatic leader can most effectively infuse a deep sense of commitment and humanism to both employee and customer. It is clear that "pride breeds pride", which makes it critical that new employees be teamed with seasoned employees who have a deep sense of commitment and pride in their work. In this type of training, the focus should be for employees to "absorb the pride and then become the pride". The next challenge is to help employees sustain their pride and enthusiasm. This role falls largely on the shoulders of management. It is therefore important for leaders to understand the day-to-day conditions that humanize or dehumanize their employees. It is only then they can effectively perpetuate the pride and enthusiasm in each employee every day. Every day leaders should attempt to spend as much time with employees as possible to accomplish such things as increased understanding of employees' human condition, create formal employee feedback opportunities, assimilate this feedback while in the front lines, keep the employees engaged, and help break down some of the barriers.

This is a business that's basically driven by people. If you look at the market capital of Pfizer – I think we're the fifth most valuable company now – it's $250 billion, some mind-boggling number. Our balance sheet assets the number is less than 10% of that. And so the delta is basically our intellectual property and the expectations of what our people can do.   ROBERT NORTON
(Senior Vice President,
Corporate Human Resources, Pfizer Inc.)

Respect movements up and down the organizational chart

Respect should follow those who voluntarily move down or sideways on the organization chart. One reason so many kings and emperors met violent deaths is that their jobs were for life; thus the only way to get a change at the top was to eliminate the top man.   LITTLE YELLOW BOOK

Create a Human Culture

There are many ingredients to making a truly human culture. Much of the effort should be focused on freeing, not controlling, employees to give the best of themselves. This requires effective "human" leaders not to seek to control the behavior of employees but instead lead the behavior of employees. A leader must understand, acknowledge, and manage their own strengths and weaknesses in order to take the first critical step in leading people. The second step is providing an active example of the desired behaviors that support the business's strategy.

OMI, Inc.'s "OMI University" aids this process by providing training to help people to get in touch with their own behaviors. The next step is to help employees realize that while they cannot control the behavior of others, they are responsible for and control their own behavior.

In addition, creating a human culture from the top down will only be effective if it reaches sufficient strength where employees will make decisions on culture-supporting behavior without question. At a cognitive level, they know what behaviors support the culture. At the emotional level, they know in their heart what actions are the "right thing to do" without question. At an organizational level, they have been given the responsibility and the authority to "do the right thing" without having to "ask" for permission or approval.

Create a culture of dignity and worth with approachability and humility

Any organization has layers of reporting structures that inherently create a feeling of subordination among human beings. Anytime one human being is subordinate, i.e. livelihood (survival) is dependent on this person, natural anxiety and fear is inevitable. Leadership must constantly work diligently to minimize the natural anxiety that builds up between different layers in an organization. One way to help reduce this anxiety is for executives to practice humanizing activities. Another approach is to practice approachability at all levels of the organization.

Communicate. This is enabled by communicating as much as possible using every means possible, e.g. videos, meetings, letters, notes, conference calls, personal cards.

> *Bravo for brevity. When communicating, brevity is best. A five-minute speech will win over the longer variety. Few points are made or souls saved after the first five minutes of a monologue. Short communiqués are the most effective form of written communication, i.e. the number of communiqués set aside and lost increases by the square of the number of pages.*
>
> LITTLE YELLOW BOOK

> *The most interesting information comes from children, for they tell all they know and then stop.*   MARK TWAIN

> *When ideas fail, words come in very handy*   GOETHE

> *Park the perks. Avoid position perks such as parking spaces reserved for individuals, thick rugs, swivel thrones, and oversized offices. Smaller offices and more conference rooms provide better use of space. Excessive perks trap the receiver. Conscientious perk receivers knock themselves out to justify the perks.*
>
> LITTLE YELLOW BOOK

Leaders should be "customer for a day" ... constantly

Making the transition to a highly human and interactive business requires cultural change for both employees and executives. An important activity to break down the traditional barriers between executives and customers is to actually have the executive go through the process of buying a product and having the experience of a service call themselves. The traditional business-to-business executive visits to a client's executives are often too removed from the real issues of day-to-day interactions.

Humanness and approachability

Los Alamos National Bank (LANB) regularly offer executive level functions that help add a sense of humanness and approachability to the executives. One activity sponsored by LANB's CEO, Bill Enloe, is referred to as "Breakfast with Bill". In these sessions, employees have an opportunity to eat breakfast with the CEO and discuss, informally, any issues they feel are important. LANB's president Steve Wells sponsors "Snacks with Steve" with a similar format providing an excellent sounding board for both the employees and the executives. LANB also hold an employee appreciation day for all employees instead of such traditions as "secretaries day". For employee appreciation day, the CEO and the President serve hamburgers on the balcony to all of the employees. In addition, executive parking is the furthest away from the bank. This makes another clear statement that customer's have priority parking, followed by employees, followed by the management and executive team – in that order of importance.

Norman Mayne practices a very humanizing leadership style at Dorothy Lane Market. He is affectionately known as the "BOSS". This is a title of endearment bestowed on him initially by one of his loyal employees. It happened one day when one of his employees candidly reacted to his seemingly long-winded official executive title and responded, "you're not Chairman and Chief Executive Officer, you're the boss". From then on, this affectionate title stuck and his business card was forever changed to his current official title of "BOSS". Every day Norman constantly challenges himself to humanize employees as he walks through the stores and thinks, "I want to treat each associate the way I would want to be treated if I worked here". This awareness of his human employees has led his employee loyalty figures to far exceed industry standards. Norman also has the same high expectations with regard to fulfilling customers' needs. He prioritizes his accessibility to customers over other business activities. He recalls one situation: "I was in my office working on an important real estate purchase with my attorney and stopped the meeting to receive a customer call".

John Higgins, President of a leading Lexus Dealership, is highly visible and interactive with the employees at his dealership. John makes sure that each technician feels recognized and cared for by ensuring that he is physically present in his dealership's service garage several times a day. His presence is not seen as a monitoring activity but rather as an interactive involvement. A recently hired technician revealed that he had never seen the head of the dealership he had previously worked for in person. This segregation of organization levels has negative effects on how employees feel about themselves as "special" or "valued" human beings.

Jo Ann Brumit, CEO and Chairman of Karlee, an award-winning manufacturer, holds an annual team member appreciation day. At this event, executives serve hamburgers, hot dogs, Mexican food around the clock (with little sleep) to all three shifts, e.g. first shift (12.00 p.m.), second shift (7.30 p.m.), third shift (3 a.m.). In a small, subtle way, this activity demonstrates how much the executives appreciate, i.e. care for and love their employees. Seemingly insignificant gestures by the executives such as asking the team member whether they would like mustard or ketchup on their hotdog "touches" the human being in the team member. Karlee actually use the word "love" in a business setting, which is typically considered "taboo". Karlee define "love" in the way it is defined in Christian values as "love and care for each other", i.e. spontaneous desire moving a person to self-giving for the benefit of the other. Jo Ann's leadership philosophy is very much based on treating their customers as human beings. These philosophies are underpinned by Christian values, or faith-based values as they sometimes refer to them. This value system embraces the following characteristics: genuinely caring for each other, sense of respect and responsibility, honesty and trust, and integrity. These values create the guidelines by which they treat people both inside and outside their organization, e.g. suppliers, customers, community, and all people they do business with. It is the expectation of employee behavior. Negative human behaviors such as internal bickering, dictatorial management, and hierarchical behavior are not tolerated. Karlee's humanizing approach with the highest of ethical and Christian values has brought them from one used machine garage funded by a $1100 loan to $80 million in sales volume with 560 team members.

Dick Lange manages one particular Land Rover Center where he has empowered each employee to "Send the BOSS home" if he is having a bad day. Also, each employee is encouraged to send anyone home if they are in an emotional state that will create a negative effect on customers. Every employee occasionally experiences exceptionally "bad" days where it is probably better for the employee to stay home to avoid negative interactions with other employees and customers. Employees are encouraged to keep a vigilant eye out for any employee who is having such a bad day that they would be detrimental to other employees or customers. They are encouraged to try raising the fellow-employee's spirits, if possible. If this is not possible, they are empowered to send any employee home, including the general manager. For example, if the general manager comes in and is not smiling or is greeting other employees or customers in a less than friendly fashion, one of the employees may ask him, "What's wrong?" or, "Is there something we can do that will make your day better?" If it appears that he is not receptive, they may suggest that he take a "long lunch" for a necessary attitude adjustment. In order to avoid tension or additional negative feelings, it is best to establish this policy as part of the culture, as well as interjecting humor in its execution. This is particularly critical for any business with a smaller number of customers because upsetting even one of those important customers may have a devastating impact on the company's business.

One Wal-Mart store's management holds charity days where they create lighthearted contests to dress up managers in an embarrassing fashion (within reason). The team who dressed their manager in the most embarrassing fashion was awarded prize money to be donated to the local charity of their choice, e.g. Children's Miracle Network. This game was played on all three shifts of the store. These activities serve many purposes:

1   Uplifting for associates.

2   Communicate humility from the manager's management.

3   Stress relief for any hierarchical structure.

4   Satisfying both management and associates for the betterment of the community.

These games not only uplift associates but also help relieve the underlying stress created between management and the employee who is subordinate. Human beings reporting to human beings typically causes stress. Most people feel some level of anxiety when "reporting" to another human being. In order to alleviate this anxiety, engaging in lighthearted games will allow venting of frustrations or anxieties that build up between the associates and the management team.

Culture starts with strong leadership

Wal-Mart's very "human" culture came from Sam Walton. Wal-Mart haven't changed in their basic beliefs since day one. The only slight modification has been to Wal-Mart's five customer commitments in 1996 by Tom Collins who worked one-on-one with Sam Walton during his whole career. Sam Walton's book, *Made in America*, espouses most of these beliefs. The following is from Wal-Mart's website: He was always ambitious and competitive, and by the time he reached college at the University of Missouri in Columbia, Sam decided he wanted to be president of the university student body. In his words, "I learned early on that one of the secrets to campus leadership was the simplest thing of all: speak to people coming down the sidewalk before they speak to you ... I would always look ahead and speak to the person coming toward me. If I knew them, I would call them by name, but even if I didn't I would still speak to them. Before long, I probably knew more students than anybody in the university, and they recognized me and considered me their friend. I ran for every office that came along." Not only was Sam elected to just about all of those offices, but he also carried his philosophy into the world of retail, where you can see it practiced every day by Wal-Mart associates throughout the world. (Sam was president of the senior men's honor society, QEBH, an officer in his fraternity, president of the senior class and captain and president of Scabbard and Blade, the elite military organization of ROTC.)

An excellent example of Sam Walton's human philosophy is Wal-Mart's culture of associate respect, customer service, and operational excellence. A major part of Wal-Mart's cultural strategy is ensuring that no one associate is in charge of executing any one particular piece of it. Wal-Mart's culture is based on three simple commitments upon which Sam Walton built the company (source: Wal-Mart's website):

1   Respect for the individual.

2   Service to our customers.

3   Strive for excellence.

All three of these commitments are based on the customer being the most important aspect of the business. These commitments are "beliefs" which manifest themselves in specific actions every day.

The first belief, "Respect for the individual", is practiced every day, in every store, and in every Wal-Mart.

> *"Our people make the difference" is not a meaningless slogan – it's a reality at Wal-Mart. We are a group of dedicated, hardworking, ordinary people who have teamed together to accomplish extraordinary things. We have very different backgrounds, different colors and different beliefs, but we do believe that every individual deserves to be treated with respect and dignity.*
>
> DON SODERQUIST
> (Senior Vice Chairman of Wal-Mart Stores, Inc. (retired))

One of the unique ways Wal-Mart show respect for their associates is by featuring employees and the family members of employees in print advertisements for Wal-Mart merchandise. This creates tremendous pride, acknowledges the importance of the employees to the business, and shows respect for these employees by acknowledging them in a very public manner.

The second belief, "Service to our customers", is defined as a combination of the trust that Wal-Mart have built up about consistently delivering the best value (lowest prices of high-quality products) with the best possible human-oriented service. The underlying understanding behind these two promises is that "We're (Wal-Mart) nothing without our customers".

> *Wal-Mart's culture has always stressed the importance of Customer Service. Our Associate base across the country is as diverse*

as the communities in which we have Wal-Mart stores. This allows us to provide the Customer Service expected from each individual customer that walks into our stores

TOM COUGHLIN
(President and Chief Executive Officer, Wal-Mart Stores division)

The third belief, "Strive for excellence", is the fact that associates should never stop trying to find new and innovative ways to achieve excellence for their customers in terms of value and human-oriented service.

Sam was never satisfied that prices were as low as they needed to be or that our product's quality was as high as they deserved – he believed in the concept of striving for excellence before it became a fashionable concept.

LEE SCOTT (President and Chief Executive
Officer of Wal-Mart Stores, Inc.; source: Wal-Mart website)

Communicate culture through behaviors, not structure and control

There is a direct cause and effect relationship between how a leader behaves and how the employees behave. If employees hear "words" and see no supporting behavior, they will be less likely to change their behavior. If they hear the words, and see those words supported by the leadership's behavior, they will take both the words and behavior to heart. Examples of behaviors that stand out are such things as commitment and punctuality. This communicates respect for other's time. Therefore, every meeting should have an agenda and a time schedule.

Businesses should also communicate humanness through behavior, and human processes will follow, i.e. lead with humanizing behaviors, processes will reflect behaviors. Jo Ann Brumit of Karlee believes that companies are based on humanizing behavior, not such things as organization structure or company policy. If you lead a company by behavior, you can influence what actions you want these behaviors to produce. Once the behaviors are in place, all else will follow. Jo Ann illustrates this point by suggesting that if you ask a child, "Would you steal from a store?" The child's response may be: "No, because I would get in trouble". If the child understood the underlying values and desired behavior, his response would be: "No, because it is the wrong thing to do". If the underlying value or behavior was not successfully taught to the child and the child felt they would not get in trouble if they stole – they would steal. It is to this end that employee training is focused at teaching the Karlee values so the employees clearly understand what behaviors are expected of them. Ultimately, it becomes simply a way of life that is constantly reinforced in the workplace. The training reinforces the importance of the behaviors as well as Karlee's identity as a human company.

It is easier to fight for one's principles than to live up to them.
ALFRED ADLER

Our deeds determine us as much as we determine our deeds
GEORGE ELIOT

Honesty is the best policy

Taking the direct approach with honesty builds trust. In many industries, there is still a legacy of fear that businesses are inclined to be dishonest with employees in implicit or explicit ways. To counteract some of these legacy biases, it is important to take a direct and honest approach.

Create a culture of "it's OK to be human"

The emotional benefits of creating an "it's OK to be human" environment are significant to the employee and ultimately the customer. This environment creates increased positive emotions, enhancing trust, confidence, accountability and esteem. It also reduces the negative emotions of anxiety and fear, thereby reducing the tendency for dishonesty and shirking of responsibilities. John Higgins's Lexus Dealership establishes the "it's OK to be human" environment for his dealership in the first meeting he has with his technicians. He reviews his top directives and expectations for the dealership. One of his main expectations is that his employees are expected to be "human", i.e. make errors as a human being. He also clearly communicates that they can expect to be forgiven as human beings as well, i.e. to err is human, to forgive divine. This does not imply that John expects them to consistently make mistakes. In fact he has put in place a series of processes to ensure the highest degree of "mistake avoidance". If all of these processes fail, and the employee makes a "human" mistake, they will be forgiven – no judgment. A typical scenario: if a technician is in the midst of troubleshooting a Lexus service issue and is either (a) stuck with a service problem, (b) is not sure they have fixed the service issue completely, or (c) is unsure whether the repair is correct, the technician is expected to ask for assistance from another more experienced technician. The fact that this less-experienced technician asked for assistance carries no judgment about the technician's ability to perform his job. John supports this "no judgment" position by communicating that the final objective is not about one technician per service appointment but about creating the highest probability that when the customer picks up the automobile following service, it is repaired correctly the first time. The second major expectation is that "to err is human, to forgive divine". John communicates that if a technician accidentally makes a mistake, e.g. nick, scratch, dent, dropping a wrench, they are instructed to report the incident immediately to the service director. John makes it abundantly clear that the service technician is not financially responsible for the accident nor will the mishap ever be deducted from any future compensation. At this point, the main responsibility of the technician is to communicate any problem to the service director so the customer can be contacted about any possible delays in picking up their car. In the pursuit of total honesty, the customer will be contacted to explain the incident and will be shown the damage prior to it being repaired. Customers sincerely appreciate this level of integrity at the dealership. The customer will be given a free loaner automobile while the repairs are being completed. In many dealerships, if a technician damages a customer's car or breaks a tool, the cost of replacing or fixing the damage will be deducted from the technician's paycheck. These dealerships somehow believe that punishing the mechanic teaches a sense of responsibility when, in fact, it prompts the mechanic to cover up an incident that could possibly be discovered by the customer at a later stage and cause even more damage.

John previously ran another automobile dealership where he instituted a fumble board for his mechanics. The idea behind a fumble board was that every time an automobile came back for the same problem, the mechanic would get a football placed on the fumble board representing something that wasn't done right the first time. The mechanics with the smallest number of footballs on the fumble board were awarded a nice dinner for two plus a cash bonus. This fumble board accomplished two things – it created competition among the mechanics to repair the automobiles correctly the first time and made it fun.

The wisest of the wise may err.   AESCHYLUS

The greatest of all faults, I should say, is to be conscious of none.   THOMAS CARLYLE

Create a "human" customer culture for the non-customer-facing employees

Businesses should regularly give both employees and executives who don't have frequent customer interactions a "taste" of high customer interaction roles. In every business, there is the group of employees who interact with customers on a daily basis and those who seldom interact with customers. Those employees who seldom interact with customers usually support the more frequent customer-facing employees in some fashion. They should be given quick refresher experiences, reinforcing that their customers are living, breathing people, on a regular basis – a role of high customer interaction because this is virtually the only way they can execute their supporting role with first-hand insight. All levels of the organization should be included, particularly the executives. This does not mean having one executive complete an extremely well-planned customer visit to another executive. This means having an executive answer the helpdesk phones for three hours every month. Four Seasons have a program allowing them to rotate different managers to high customer interaction areas to continually remind them what it means to deal with a high volume of real customers with real issues. They refer to this program as their "Lobby Lizard" program. This program entails managers coming from different departments to spend time working at the front lobby at peak times with high guest interaction.

Give employees the confidence and freedom to "run their own business"

Norman Mayne of Dorothy Lane Market employs roughly 50 managers among his 500 total associates. Norman instills a great deal of confidence in each one of these 50 managers by allowing them to run their department as their own business. Norman refers to these 50 managers as "leaders". He treats them as leaders to symbolize his confidence in them as individual human beings. He also gives them the freedom to lead, at their discretion, in areas other than their designated departments. For example, the "leader" behind his computer initiatives is a department manager for his meat department.

This enables the employee to be the leader, and the customer to be their boss. It is very difficult for employees to truly serve their customers as human beings if their overriding objectives and measurements are biased toward pleasing management, instead of customers. The first step toward customers becoming "boss" is accomplished by having a clearly articulated promise and a commitment to employees as to their roles and expectations. This is just as important as clearly articulating a promise to customers. Employees must be empowered to make the customer "boss". This also requires the right tools and technology to enable them to actually focus on the customer. The litmus test here is whether employees are more concerned about what the boss thinks or what the customer thinks in any given situation.

Create a culture with the caring of a family

Create a sense of belonging to a family or community with common goals and values. Human beings have the social need to belong to a group or family. Also, most human beings enjoy being part of a group that has emotional connections beyond just a working relationship.

Norman Mayne of Dorothy Lane Market truly views his longtime employees as "family". A significant percentage of Norman's associates have been with them for over 25 years with a portion of them having worked at Dorothy Lane for over 40 years. As Norman states, "When you've (associates) been here for that long, guess what ... you're family". He feels that great customer relations are a direct result of great employee relations. In the early 1990s when the great "customer focused" mantras became popular, Norman began contemplating whether the customer truly was the most important part of the business. He finally decided that the employee was the most important part of the business. It is only after the employee is fulfilled as a human being that the customer can then be treated in a human and personal manner. Norman focuses on making sure that each employee is well taken care of, with strong training and a creative, fun work environment. He provides department heads and their families' use of the company condominium every other year. For the non-department heads, there is a drawing for the use of the condominium every other year. One significant aspect of creating a sense of family is the acceptance of life's emotional traumas and the added emotional toll these traumas can inflict. An emotional trauma Norman sees occurring with greater frequency is divorce. As a result, he has negotiated with a local psychologist to provide free counseling for the first three or four visits of any DLM associate who is grappling with the roller coaster emotions caused by divorce. The deep sense of family at DLM is reflected by the demographics of his employees. The employee who runs DLM's web page works in his produce department as he earns his way through college. Another employee, who manages the Dorothy Lane club card (Club DLM), worked at Dorothy Lane during high school. She initially wanted to become a teacher until the warm, humanizing environment drew her to Dorothy Lane as a career.

One Wal-Mart store regularly schedules activities to create a sense of "community" or "family" with associates about the business. This store regularly sponsors activities such as pizza parties, family picnics, and fun dress-up days to enhance the feeling of "community" or "family" surrounding their store. On family picnic days this Wal-Mart store will invite all of the associates and their families to come into the store and have a picnic-like atmosphere around the store including a "cookout in the backyard". During these picnics, managers and associates and their respective families have a great opportunity to mingle with each other in a very family-oriented atmosphere. These activities have been so successful that the associates in the store playfully refer to the male and female store co-managers as "Mom and Dad".

Create a culture where employees and their families come first

Promote a culture that explicitly demonstrates that associate needs and their family needs are a higher priority than short-term business needs. One of Wal-Mart's key philosophies is that not only do they put associates' needs ahead of the business, but they also put their families' needs ahead of it. For example, an associate's grandchild was having surgery on a day she was scheduled to work. That associate was granted a day off without question to be with her grandchild during the surgery. Wal-Mart will actually encourage the associate to put their family's needs first. There is awareness that, periodically, there will be special family situations during which special allowances must be made without question.

Many typical businesses will have strict human resource rules and regulations for associates regardless of their family's needs. This is typically because there is an unreasonable "fear" that such leniency will create slack work ethics. More "humane" human resource policies create a sense of belonging beyond simply being employed by a business. Ultimately, this more humane approach creates downstream benefits such as increased associate loyalty and improved productivity.

Create a culture of "we're here for you in good times and bad"

Create specific avenues for associates to easily handle emotionally challenging life events. Most associates will have several emotionally draining life events that will affect their productivity. Many employers' first reactions to these events is to assume that the associate should continue work uninterrupted and that the responsibility for these personal problems rests squarely on the associate's shoulders. Wal-Mart address these emotional needs by creating the culture of a true "open-door policy". It is important that a business that professes an open-door policy have the supporting processes and policies in place to actually implement it. Wal-Mart do so by allowing an associate the opportunity to present frustrations or concerns in a closed-door session with a manager. Any subjects or issues discussed behind these closed doors are kept between the manager and the associate. If the associate's issues extend beyond the ability of the manager and associate to adequately deal with at that time, an external agency equipped to handle these events is engaged. They corporately retain this agency as a resource for associates to handle the more challenging life events. This agency is essentially a professional counseling agency that conducts an initial counseling session by phone. The associate then has the choice whether the manager is present during following counseling sessions. Professional assistance not only helps the associate handle problems better, but also adds to the productivity of the Wal-Mart store.

Encourage sharing personal or professional issues

Give employees the opportunity to share personal or professional issues that preoccupy them before meetings. The personal lives of employees consciously or unconsciously affect each business relationship and performance. It is a common presumption by both management and employees that employees can and should "hide" all emotions from their personal life (good or bad) in a business setting. This is not possible for most human beings. In every business environment, business associates and customers are interacting with the employee's "whole" person, i.e. personal and professional self. Most employees have vibrant lives that ebb and flow continually. The issues affecting their personal lives pre-occupy the employee at some level in each business meeting. This makes it important to offer an avenue for employees to purge this preoccupation before business meetings whenever poss-ible. Because he believes that business and personal lives cannot be completely separated, OMI's president, Don Evans, will ask his employees to share events that are going on their lives. He finds that this helps the dynamics of meetings both in productivity and effectiveness.

Create an unquestionable culture

Create an environment in which employees automatically know that if they unquestionably "do the right thing for the customer", they will have done the right thing as an employee – every time. This "do the right thing for the customer" expectation should exist regardless of short-term cost and ownership of cost. This unquestioned employee response to fulfilling customer needs can only be accomplished through clear and consistent communication to employees. It is this overriding edict that John Higgins believes is the key to long-term profitability for his Lexus dealership. John makes it clear that if any employee is uncomfortable with this humanizing approach, that employee is encouraged to find happiness elsewhere. This approach establishes a great sense of employee "pride" in working for John's dealership. This stems from John's pride in how his employees conduct themselves with their customers and out in the community itself. John Higgins is personally active in the community and would find it extremely distasteful to be confronted with subtle innuendoes that his dealership was inherently dishonest or unfair to customers. Nor does he want his employees to be out in the community and be embarrassed about working for his dealership. John wants his employees to be proud about where they work and feel a genuine sense of self-esteem when they talk about their place of employment. John wants this feeling of pride to be with them throughout their workday. He believes this pride radiates transparently to the customers. His service people are unfettered by any idea other than the core objective of treating customers like human beings.

Acknowledge Them

Acknowledge the good, not the bad

Businesses should focus on directing their employees down the right path, not concentrating on what path "not" to take. This supports the underlying human motivational theory that positive reinforcement is much more effective than negative reinforcement. This creates an overall positive approach to implementing the business's strategy and direction.

Catch 'em in the act ... of doing good stuff

Catch employees "in the act" of good behavior, not bad behavior (carrot vs. stick). One of the ways Norman Mayne of Dorothy Lane Market maintains this very positive, human employee environment is to perpetuate a culture where the positive side of employee behavior is rewarded and recognized. In other words, much more effort is expended on looking for good behavior rather than looking for bad behavior. Norman comments, "We at Dorothy Lane have a culture where we try to catch people (employees) doing something right". It is expected that every day management will look for examples of "exemplary" employee behavior to fuel their program known as "Munch money". This munch money is Dorothy Lane "currency" with Norman's picture displayed on the front of the award. Displayed on the back of the award is a description of what exemplary behavior prompted the award. The employee with the most "munch money" awards will win the "Employee of the Month" award, which then makes them eligible to win the "Employee of the Year" award. Another humanizing program that rewards people for being "caught in the act" of exceptional human compassion for customers is the "legend letter". This letter was specifically instituted to highlight any employee who has shown exceptional compassion for any DLM customer. There is the story of a DLM customer who bought a boneless leg of lamb that she intended to cook the next day. She was going to put the leg of lamb in her crockpot and let it cook while she was at work. That evening at midnight, she noticed that the leg of lamb was "bone in" instead of boneless. She phoned the store's butcher shop at midnight to explain the situation. After listening carefully to the woman's story, the butcher asked for the woman's home address and within fifteen minutes was at her house boning out her leg of lamb. Two very important human dynamics happened in this situation. The first was that the butcher had the confidence in DLM to know that his decision to do the extraordinarily human act of physically driving to the customer's house to help her would be the unquestioned "right thing" to do. Secondly, the customer had the human trust in DLM and its employees to allow a 6 ft 6 in, 275-pound butcher into her house at midnight wielding a large carving knife. Another example is a woman who arrived home after shopping at Dorothy Lane and noticed that the case of Coca-Cola that she had purchased was not in her car. The DLM associate who received the call immediately responded by asking for the woman's address and promptly delivering the case to her home. This approach to dealing with customer or employee humanness is so ingrained in DLM's culture that it is not perceived as heroics, but as Norman states "just what we do here at Dorothy Lane". DLM employees are all trained that a human mistake that affects a customer is a wonderful opportunity to demonstrate exemplary service in the process of making amends.

Better to light a candle than to curse the darkness.
                                                    CHINESE PROVERB

If we all did the things we are capable of doing, we would literally astound ourselves.   THOMAS A. EDISON

Give light, and the darkness will disappear of itself.   ERASMUS

Note how good you feel after you have encouraged someone else. No other argument is necessary to suggest that you never miss the opportunity to give encouragement.   GEORGE ADAMS

The spirit, the will to win, and the will to excel are the things that endure. These qualities are so much more important than the events that occur.   VINCE LOMBARDI

Be generous with generosity

Being generous is especially important for those at or near the top of the heap, be willing to spread the returns around in dollars and recognition. The gymnast on top of the human pyramid is dependent on all those solid people who support him..
                                                    LITTLE YELLOW BOOK

Make acknowledgements extraordinary

Sponsor "out of the ordinary" employee celebrations that cause employees to take notice. At Dorothy Lane Market, employees mean so much that they go "out of business" for one day every year. Norman closes all of the DLM stores for a day to hold the annual employee party. He makes sure that he communicates to the customers that although the customers mean a great deal to him, it is important for the customers to give this important day to the employees. He is also known for publicizing that DLM's competitors will be visited by a lot of very nice people that day. During this party, Norman ensures that there are plenty of "off the wall" prizes and surprises for the employees.

In order to keep his employees feeling important and "human" John Higgins's Lexus Dealership routinely surprises them with special activities. Recently, he flew them all to Florida to Arnold Palmer's Bay Hill Country Club for a weekend of golf. On Saturday night, John brought them to dinner at an exclusive restaurant where they celebrated with fine wine. These unexpected surprises send a signal of John's commitment to communicate how important his employees are as special human beings to his business, as well as creating an incredible employee loyalty through recognition and respect. One of the special ways that John helps his people feel emotionally involved and proud of their employment is that they are given the chance to lease brand-new Lexus automobiles for a substantially discounted rate ($200 per month). Lexus call this program the "senior certified program" that entitles many different positions within the Lexus dealership to lease a Lexus car for one-third of the lease price. Under this program, the dealership pays one-third, the manufacturer pays one-third, and the employee pays one-third of the lease. When many employees at the dealership experience the quality of Lexus automobiles firsthand, they become an extension of the sales force. Driving this new Lexus automobile also adds to the employee's sense of personal accept-ance, belonging, and camaraderie because they drive a beautiful luxury automobile that they could not ordinarily afford. Ultimately, John believes that it is basic human nature for employees to want to do their jobs correctly, to be proud and conscientious of their work. They also want some kind of reward or acknowledgement and to know that someone notices and appreciates them – very similar to what customers fundamentally want. John believes that the human treatment of employees creates a one-to-one correlation to the human treatment of customers and the resulting financial rewards that follow.

Excess on occasion is exhilarating. It prevents moderation from acquiring the deadening effect of a habit.
                                                    W. SOMERSET MAUGHAM

Acknowledge them in the way they need, not as you think they may

Be sensitive to how and what employees need for acknowledgement. Sometimes a leader will assume that employees need recognition in a manner and degree similar to the person giving the acknowledgement or recognition. Most people have different ways in which they prefer to be acknowledged or recognized by their firm. A good example of this is in the humility and humanness that Don Evans of OMI showed when reviewing employee feedback regarding his leadership.

Don found, through employee feedback, that his employees needed to celebrate success beyond his personal need to celebrate success. As a result, Don supports and encourages more frequent celebrations causing his employee's respect for him to grow. OMI has also moved away from just having a Christmas party and a summer picnic to having a company celebration every month. At these parties several awards and acknowledgements to employees heighten the feelings of camaraderie and success. These special awards include the "Longevity" award celebrating extended years of service by loyal employees; there is the "Soaring Eagle" award celebrating any incredible accomplishment either personal or professional; and the "Golden Apple" award for great service to either community or family. One rather unusual award is a peer-to-peer award called "Tag-you-win". Anyone can give anyone else a "Tag-you-win" award for something they did that benefited somebody else in the organization. This Tag-you-win award can be given to a truck driver or a high-level executive. There is also a "Teamwork" award that entitles a team to a $250 gift certificate.

Acknowledge the team, avoid "Michael Jordan" rewards

Most of the outstanding "day-after-day" performances in business come from the least-celebrated employees. It is very important when setting up compensation and bonus programs that every employee is rewarded. Los Alamos National Bank (LANB) have implemented a profit-sharing program where everyone benefits, not just management. Once an employee has worked for LANB for 18 months, their "inoculation" ends and they began participation in the profit-sharing program. Last year, LANB paid $1.1 million to the profit-sharing pool for roughly 130 employees. LANB also decided to eliminate "employee of the month" programs because they feel these types of programs go against the grain of their philosophy of "when the company wins, everyone wins". This philosophy also extends to avoiding such things as "employee of the month parking space". LANB believe that bigger "wins" are possible when all of the supporting players around the "Michael Jordan" are rewarded equally for passing the ball to Michael Jordan for the big score, i.e. a team benefit. LANB also do not have "Secretary's Day" any more because it made other supportive employees feel unimportant, "why isn't my position celebrated as well?" In reality, there is equal emotional fallout from compensating employees too little or too much. Compensating employees insufficiently creates feelings of not being appreciated, whereas overcompensating employees creates feelings of insecurity as they wonder, "How long is this job going to last?"

Pat peers on the back

Create immediate, genuine, peer-to-peer recognition rituals. For employees it is important to create regular, immediate feedback on a peer-to-peer level, i.e. human-to-human. Promoting simple but genuine "on the spot" recognition keeps the function of recognition personal and deeply rewarding. In such programs, any employee can recognize another peer based on certain criteria set up by the business. The most important caveat is that it is genuine recognition.

Build acknowledgement for individuals and the team simultaneously

A major challenge in supporting individuality is to have individuality work within a team environment. The key is to create an environment that builds acceptance and awareness for individuals and the team simultaneously. Creating recognition programs where peer-to-peer, management-to-team, and management to individual awards coexist accomplishes this.

Employee Fulfillment

By nature, most employees want to do a good job and many want to do a great job. One of the keys to improving the probability that they will to a good and even great job is to believe in them. Belief in employees will put them on the road to accomplish extraordinary things for themselves, the business, and ultimately the customer. As well as performing well at their jobs, they want to lead meaningful lives. Leaders can help them be excited, happy, and productive by showing them how their lives will be better and how the company will be better. There are certain requirements for creating true employee fulfillment.

Contrary to popular belief, what creates fulfilled employees is not predominantly the size of their paycheck but rather it is the feeling of acknowledgement, respect, and trust. Very simply, it comes down to knowing what's expected of them, being supported to actually accomplish what is expected of them, having the abilities to accomplish them, and doing it all in a socially rewarding environment:

1   Understanding the objectives.

2   Having support in accomplishing the objectives.

3   Having the ability to accomplish the objectives.

4   Healthy interpersonal relationships at work.

1. Understanding the objectives

Communicate objectives – knowing the objectives is critical to any employee who has a desire to do a good job. Without knowing the goals, the employee is severely hampered from deriving esteem from completed tasks. The linkage is: understand objectives – complete task – derive self-esteem.

Help employees understand the "why" behind objectives. Many businesses create business strategies and objectives that are never fully explained to employees, and still expect employees to execute them with passion and conviction to their customers. The chances of success in this scenario are minimal. For example, if a business sets its objectives to sell premium products at premium prices without educating its employees as to why these prices are premium but still fair and good value to customers, the ability to achieve these premium prices will be lessened. Helping employees help customers understand pricing models is key to most business objectives, yet it is a typical downfall for many businesses who believe that the subject is somehow taboo and needs to remain a mystery to employees. Businesses need to explicitly communicate the pricing model to employees for their own understanding as well as being able to communicate with the customers effectively. A good example of this is Dorothy Lane Markets (DLM) which have strategically placed themselves on the higher end of the grocery market with many specialized items at slightly higher prices than competitors'. DLM's "boss", Norman Mayne, spends a good deal of time educating his employees about the added value customers will experience by paying slightly higher prices for DLM's exceptional customer service and specialized products. It is important that the employees understand why these premium prices exist and are comfortable communicating the logic to customers for their trust and comfort. This is especially important when so many of Norman's competitors are promising to deliver the impossible – the cheapest prices, the best service, and the best quality. In reality, delivering all of these three promises is virtually impossible. A business can typically only achieve two out of three of these promises. Norman's focus has several core value dimensions. The first is that DLM are reasonably competitive with other discount retailers on household brand items, e.g. Tide, Clorox, Charmin. This is a message that needs to be proactively communicated to customers to avoid the stereotyping that all of their products are higher margin and specialized. The second dimension is that DLM will always provide an exceptional level of humanizing customer service. This added level of customer service must be funded by additional margin in some aspect of the business. Norman jokingly comments that if DLM chose to have similar service and prices as their competitors it could easily be achieved by "simply laying off 40% of our workforce". The third is that he provides specialized products that justify slightly higher prices. DLM do command a premium price for such items as hand-picked specialty olive oils imported directly from Italy. Developing this specialized product repertoire does require added investment and therefore added prices. Norman must first educate his employees in a fair amount of detail about the reasons for these value dimensions. To understand these value dimensions, the investment and resources behind developing the specialty products must be understood. Every year, DLM send seven or eight employees to Italy and France to research and select special food items that the team feels the customers would value and, as a result, would be happy to pay for the extra value. DLM's cheesemonger regularly travels to Switzerland to select fine cheeses for their cheese departments. Norman also funded a trip for the associate who runs DLM's meat departments to a little town in Italy to work alongside the Italian butchers to learn about creative ways to cut as well as combine different meats. DLM's meat manager has applied this learning by offering customers a specialized blend of breast of veal, sausage, poultry products and select spices wrapped in pancetta to create a wonderful new product. This cooperative working arrangement with other European butcher shops came about from a previous trip in which a DLM employee noticed how beautifully one Italian butcher shop's meat was displayed – "The meat looked like diamonds displayed in the case". Another good example of DLM's highly valued specialty items is their ultimate pursuit for the finest virgin olive oil from estates in Italy's Tuscany region. Offering their customers the finest virgin olive oils can be contrasted with their competitors' offerings of olive oil in bulk from places where the olive oil is mixed and blended in varying degrees of quality. For DLM's fruit spreads, Norman provides his customers with exceptionally healthy fruit spreads without adding sugar. Employees are educated about the quality of their fruit spreads by actually being sent to the processing plant to watch the fruit spreads being created. These specialty items are typically branded as special DLM products. DLM also provide Coleman's natural beef, which comes from cattle raised from birth without antibiotics and without added growth-stimulating hormones, and being given feed that is free of pesticide residues. In addition, because there is no growth-stimulating hormone added, the cattle take longer to "finish", i.e. develop more naturally and slowly from conception to steer. This more natural process costs more but is healthier than cattle raised "fast" and mass-produced using drugs to speed up the animal's growth. When the customers understand this value clearly, they have no problem paying slightly extra for this natural beef. In addition, this specialty beef is not cut with a meat saw as most beef is, but is cut by hand by DLM's trained butchers. Norman's deli manager has stopped buying most of the national brands of lunchmeat and has switched almost exclusively to buying Boar's Head delicatessen products. Boar's Head products are still made the old-fashioned way without the use of artificial colors or artificial flavors, extenders or fillers, which other delicatessen manufacturers discovered make products appear better than they really are. As a result, the cost of this lunchmeat is higher and a certain segment of DLM customers are willing to pay more because they value a healthy delicatessen product. Norman also sent their head baker to France to learn how the French make their breads in order to enhance DLM's bakery selection. On a recent trip to France by DLM's baker, they bought a $70 000 Paviller oven. Six months after the purchase, two people flew over from France to build this special oven in one of DLM's stores. One of the unique features of this European oven is that opening the doors causes only a two-degree loss of heat, whereas a typical American baking oven loses roughly forty degrees of heat. Heat loss during baking significantly changes the process of baking fine breads. This specialized oven allows DLM to bake great breads in their store that the customers value highly. As a result of having the oven, they sold more French baguettes than they did the popular household brand, Wonder bread. DLM also prepare their own salad makings for its deli rather than taking the typical path of buying salad makings from a factory. In the prepared food sections, the chefs only use real butter or clarified butter, not margarine. Norman also uses their fine DLM Tuscan virgin olive oils in their prepared foods rather than factory-processed olive oils. These specialized DLM products are never aggressively marketed to customers but simply displayed alongside other household-brand grocery items. The customers make the determination whether DLM's specialty products warrant the slight price premium.

Promote understanding objectives by employee involvement in planning. A fundamental weakness of many company's strategic planning process and the resulting strategic plan is the fact that most employees feel little or no involvement in a plan only communicated to them after the fact. It is critical that a company create a planning process that not only helps employees understand the resulting objectives but also creates a "feeling" they helped create the objectives themselves. As a result, they are more likely to believe that the vision is valid and therefore more likely to actually execute it. Los Alamos National Bank's (LANB) strategic planning process brought involvement from internal organizations to create a strategic plan for six years from today that addresses future visions and possibilities. It is very difficult for a firm to execute a vision that is solely the idea of executives; however, there is tremendous buy-in from employees when they have had a part in the decision-making process because they then feel, "I helped shape that".

2. Having support in accomplishing the objectives

First, give employees both responsibility and authority. It is only when they have both, can they fulfill objectives. They will also act with increasing independent and creativity which will likely extend what both business and employee may have thought possible.

Second, provide them the right tools. This human desire is very much linked to self-esteem. If the right tools are unavailable to an employee, this directly affects his ability to take pride in a job well done, and thus feel satisfaction as a productive employee. Ninety percent of what causes an employee to fail at his job is the lack of timely and accurate information. It is important to note that, statistically, having the right tools is more important to an employee than general happiness on the job. This has to do with self-esteem being a deeper and more powerful emotion than a general sense of happiness. In many cases, tools and materials rather than information are what is necessary to complete a job. However, it still holds true that these tools and materials must be accessible and in top working order for an employee to feel growth in self-esteem.

Tools also create the human expectation and competency for great results. Providing the right tools for employees has a multidimensional impact on employee esteem. On the front end, providing the employee with excellent tools increases their esteem because it makes them feel as though the employer cares enough about them as human beings to provide them with the best tools available. They also feel that by being given these great tools, their employer expects great results. Using these tools, they feel an inherent sense of pride and productivity. When they have completed tasks efficiently and effectively, they feel a tremendous sense of accomplishment and pride.

One telecommunications firm focused on the critical questions of how well they were supporting their employees in fulfilling their objectives. One critical question they asked their employees was: "Do the services provided by our company make you more functional?" They also drill down into this employee satisfaction analysis to determine which specific processes could potentially make the employees more confident or help them "feel" more confident, e.g. information systems, support infrastructure, human resource support infrastructure, and operational support infrastructure, such as payables. One of the processes they examined was the process to submit a voucher, or a purchase order. Then they analyzed how these processes could be made more user-friendly and less onerous. They also analyzed how an increase in web utilization could add to the ease of managing human resource issues, e.g. being able to update personnel records online. One way to improve employee job satisfaction through operational efficiencies was to enable HR personnel to submit vouchers or purchase orders online instead of physically filling out a form, then faxing or sending it as an inter-office memo. This focus on improving operational efficiencies through improving their company's customer support infrastructure enabled employees to achieve a higher likelihood of fulfilling customer needs, and therefore to feel a higher degree of self-esteem and social acceptance. One challenge was to measure the return on the investment from the capital expenditures on the human resource systems to enable these online efficiencies. Another challenge was accounting for improvements in one area when the company had to transfer resources from another area whose process was previously manual. Another analysis that was done focused on investments made in employee satisfaction and the gross impact on retention of customers, as well as any resulting changes in the company's economic status and customer satisfaction.

John Higgins's Lexus Dealership ensures that his service department has the latest, most efficient, and safest equipment that is available today. He does not expect his service people to work with worn out or outdated equipment because he realizes that not only does it make them inefficient and put them at risk, it also makes his service people "feel" like they are not valued as human employees. In addition, John believes that the proper tools make them feel "wanted" and "respected" – two critically important human needs. Feeling respected heightens their own perspective of their technical abilities and thus usually enhances those abilities. Naturally, the quality of their work increases after being shown that they are needed and respected as human beings. An important aspect of having the right tools is having the right technical knowledge to perform the task. This is where training plays a critical role in an employee's ability to self-actualize the need for competence in their job. John has found that his passion for advancing his technicians to the highest level possible has allowed him to retain his employees longer than his competitors. Lexus categorize technicians as A, B, C, and D level technicians. The D level technician is an entry-level technician who starts out performing oil and filter changes while learning other basic aspects of Lexus service. John's objective is to advance all his D level technicians to A level as quickly as possible and his high aspirations for his technicians cause them to have high aspirations for themselves as technicians and human beings. Almost every single one of John's technicians today is an A level Lexus technician. John's service technicians are sent to the Lexus training facility in Chicago to become proficient in Lexus repair systems. Lexus then rate these service technicians on these repair systems. The higher the technician moves in the rating category, the further up the pay scale they climb. As a technician climbs the ladder of rating and pay, there is a continuously growing sense of pride and accomplishment and, therefore, a deeper feeling of fulfillment.

3. Having the ability to accomplish the objectives

A good example of this is the ability to respond to a customer in a timely fashion. Any human employee who is relating to a human customer is driven by social forces to either please them or garner acceptance from them. If an employee cannot respond in a timely manner to a customer request this highly motivating connection of social acceptance cannot be achieved and both customer and employee are left unsatisfied.

4. Healthy interpersonal relationships at work

Employees need good personal relationships with people at work because that is how they derive much of their human satisfaction while at work, i.e. do I have a good friend at work?

Create "fun" at work. Regularly schedule "fun" activities to best enhance positive emotions and reduce negative emotions.

Keeping associates happy in the pursuit of keeping customers happy requires activities that defuse, release, and uplift associate's emotions. One fun and uplifting activity is a scooter contest that a Wal-Mart store put on for its managers and associates. They began with all the associates, department managers, and store managers having coffee and donuts in the morning, and then they formed teams to scooter down the store aisles. Other similar emotion-releasing games were contests in which associates competed by hula-hooping down the store aisle. Whoever could go the farthest would win a $25 gift certificate from the store. One Wal-Mart store manager will announce a time for "zoning munchies" during more mundane activities, e.g. zoning (restocking shelves) or late-night store cleanup. Zoning munchies typically consists of candy that is handed out to help make the activity of cleaning up a store more fun, particularly for the younger associates. These "zoning munchies" also boost the energy level of the associates.

Reduce employee unhappiness. Reducing employee unhappiness is just as important, if not more so, than focusing on enhancing employee happiness. It is the best for the employee as well as business. The impact of unhappy employees on the interactions with customers as well as overall company image and brand is many times underestimated. Disgruntled employees are a major source of bad "word of mouth" information for customers. In most countries, a significant percentage of how a customer forms an opinion of the firm is how the company treats its employees. This makes sense because employees spend more time with the customers than the chairman or top-level management spend with customers.

Be proactive against "emotional burn-out". Businesses that are insensitive to emotional burnout of employees pay a hidden price from the employee, other associates, and customers.

Allocate time, training, and space to help associates emotionally "recoup" from serving difficult customers. Sometimes, associates must engage in conversation with a customer who is venting some intense feelings. In a small percentage of cases, they will intentionally, or unintentionally, release their anger on store associates, which transfers that anger to the associate. The associate will then need an avenue to vent their anger or have a physical place removed from customers to go to cool down. In this scenario, the associate's frown will have to be "turned upside-down" as well. There are some truly frustrating situations for associates who are sincerely making every effort to give a customer the best advice or information when that customer instead expresses anger or disbelief that the associate is acting on their behalf.

Sensitive employees become desensitized to common customer inquiries – employees whose job it is to respond to customer inquiries often get desensitized due to the repetitiveness of customer inquiries and questions. It is easy for call-center employees to appear uncaring because they have heard the same question several hundred times that week. What is a boring, repetitive question to the call-center many times has created significant anxiety for the customer. The customer's problem may be something they will only deal with once in a lifetime and that often determines their emotional reaction.

Create emotional "time and space" for employees besieged by stress from aggressive management, "unkind" customers, and operational issues.

Two realities of a customer-oriented business:

1   Some customers are unkind.

2   Employees have an emotional limit to what they are able to endure.

The general manager of one Land Rover Center has observed that there will always be a certain segment of the population who are never satisfied and these customers can cause significant morale damage to any employee with their behavior. As a natural aspect of human emotions, when one person is unkind to another person, the negative feelings created must have some avenue for venting. Otherwise, there is a likelihood that the employee may transfer or vent those negative emotions onto either another customer or another employee, perpetuating the negative emotional cycle. An environment that makes it "okay" to take the time away from business to resolve negative emotions is the key to stopping the negative emotional cycle.

In one example, a gentleman entered a Wal-Mart store responding to an ad in the previous day's newspaper for a special on futons. The gentleman came to the Wal-Mart store to purchase the futon and found that they were out of stock for the sale. He was very angry and aggressively approached the manager. These out-of-stock situations occasionally occur because Wal-Mart are reliant on local vendors to supply the right goods, at the right time, and at the right place. The manager did a product search using Wal-Mart's item locator, which scans a 150-mile radius to find which stores have a particular item in stock. The manager found that no store within a 150-mile radius had these futons in stock, so she told the customer that the best thing that she could do for him at that time was to issue him a rain check for the sale price of the futon. He refused to believe that this was the best that could be done to solve the situation, even though he actually witnessed the manager perform the item locator function and saw the actual results of the search. The customer continued insisting that he wanted the futon "right there, right then". He was very angry, unreasonable, and rude. Continuing her best efforts to be courteous and friendly the manager offered the customer an additional 10% discount off the sale price. Eventually, though still unsatisfied, the disgruntled customer grudgingly accepted the rain check with the 10% additional discount. Maintaining a "good attitude" is often a challenge for managers and associates. In this case, the manager took some time to remember the many positive and humanly rewarding experiences she had in her job to help put this negative in perspective.

Arcona Devan, owner of The Arcona Studio, an exclusive health spa in Los Angeles, California, observed that when her employees interact with the occasional negative client, they absorb a portion of that client's negative emotions. When they absorb too much negative emotion, e.g. tension, anger, they deplete themselves and quickly become unproductive. To overcome this, Arcona applies the principle of chakras and the directional flow of personal and universal energies to keep both her employees and clients happy. She encourages her employees to visualize the positive emotions or energies that they give to their clients as not being their own but coming from inexhaustible universal energies. Her employees are encouraged to visualize pulling energies in one direction from the universe, through their crown chakra (head) and pushing the energy into the client. When employees visualize giving to their clients in this manner, they feel they can give more to clients for a longer period of time because they are not depleting their own energies. They also are not absorbing negative energies because the energy flow is only in one direction. While these principles may seem too ethereal for mainstream business, emotional burnout of employees is common for employees in roles that serve customers who have a steady stream of negative comments or reactions. Burnout has a significant impact on employee productivity and customer fulfillment. Experimenting with more innovative approaches such as these may be worthwhile in high employee burnout environments such as call-centers and customer service operations.

Effective human leadership begins with an understanding of the strengths and weaknesses of self. From there, knowledge of the marketplace and the dynamics of human interaction in that marketplace enable the selection of the right people to fulfill customers. Developing those carefully selected people with care and providing them the freedom to be the best they can be for themselves and their customers is an essential element of human leadership. For both employee development and the execution of business objectives, an environment should be created where employees feel clearly directed and unquestionably empowered with responsibility and authority to fulfill customers as people. The nourishment of this environment centers on the employee's need for acknowledgement, respect, and trust. When these three essential human needs are fulfilled, employees will perform in extraordinary ways with customer's responding in kind.

3

Acknowledging Customers

ONE OF THE MOST IMPORTANT NEEDS A CUSTOMER HAS IS TO BE acknowledged. The customer will react most favorably to the following types of acknowledgement:

1   Acknowledge my existence and importance (and my companions).

2   Acknowledge you know me.

3   Acknowledge my feelings.

Acknowledge Their Existence

Most businesses don't consider whether or not they are effective at acknowledging their customer's existence, much less their importance, because they assume they are proficient at this acknowledgement. The very thought that they do not seems absurd; so it is assumed. At the most basic level, customers continue to feel dehumanized by businesses that do not sufficiently acknowledge their existence.

In a recent research study, 77% of customers have felt that "too often I see salespeople acting like I'm not there".

Research has also shown that in the area of financial services one critical factor behind customer defection is that they feel unwanted and neglected. Whether a customer feels a sense of respect and

Figure 3.1   Customers' feelings ignored
(data from *Aggravating Circumstances*, 2002 Public Agenda, used with kind permission)

value is determined by how things are handled when customers have questions and problems.

The Abercrombie & Fitch Co. example referenced in Chapter 6, "Communicating humanly with customers", illustrates what a significant impact not acknowledging your customers has on those customers. The powerful negative reactions by customers to the previous manager's instructions to employees not to talk to customers first is clear evidence that lack of acknowledgement is one of the most damaging effects a retail business can have on its customers. For customers to label employees as rude, lazy, and aloof for the simple fact that employees did not initiate a warm simple greeting illustrates the powerful impact of acknowledgement or the lack thereof.

Wal-Mart address the acknowledgement problem by training their employees in their "ten foot rule" as referenced in Chapter 4, "Treating customers with respect". Sam Walton would tell his employees "I want you to promise that whenever you come within 10 feet of a customer, you will look the customer in the eye, greet the customer and ask the customer if you can help him or if there is anything you can help him find."

Wal-Mart are also renowned for their "door greeters" who strive to acknowledge each and every customer who walks in their doors. The irony of Wal-Mart's famed store greeters was that this type of human greeting was commonplace a hundred years ago. The small corner shop 100 years ago didn't have to institute specific customer greeters. It was simply a normal and natural function of any business day. The effectiveness of these customer door greeters has much to do with how naturally personable they are as human beings. Not only do these door greeters acknowledge customers as they walk in the door, they pass out stickers, giving directions for finding a particular product in the store, and pass out shopping carts. The door greeters who excel at their position are the people who truly feel passionately and compassionately about their customers. One door greeter named Ruth who was 85 years old embodied Wal-Mart's passion for treating each customer as a special person. Most customers who came through the door when this person was working would receive a warm smile and handshake. If she witnessed any customer who appeared even remotely to be having a bad day they would receive a big, warm, human hug. In most cases, the people who experienced this woman's warm, human, friendliness remembered little else about the Wal-Mart shopping experience beyond the warmth of this woman's personality. To the customers who experienced this special door greeter, she "was" Wal-Mart. When Ruth finally left this particular store and moved to another location to be with her family, a large number of customers were more concerned about where "Ruth" was as opposed to any other aspect of their shopping that day. Wal-Mart try to instill this compassionate intensity for customers in all of their store greeters. It is a true challenge, because new store greeters who didn't have Ruth's natural gregarious and passionate nature tend to be slightly more cautious in their humanizing approach to customer greeting. Wal-Mart strive to hire door greeters who are inherently warm, cheerful and have a natural, genuine smile. The litmus test for how well a door greeter is doing is when customers will consistently come in and say hello to the door greeters by name without even looking at their nametag.

Acknowledge medical patients through availability, affability, and ability

The medical industry has been traditionally extremely weak in acknowledging their patient's existence and importance. The Hippocratic Oath written by Hippocrates in 400 BCE refers to the "practice of the art" for the "benefit of my patients", not the practice of the science for the benefit of the doctor. Somehow many in the medical industry have forgotten that. This offers a tremendous opportunity for those who haven't forgotten. It is a common perception that in any given area of specialty in the medical industry, 10% of the doctors are the "cream of the crop" with many of them being at university medical centers, 10% of doctors are not very well trained, and the balance of the 80% are layered out in the middle. This necessitates that most doctors who are the "middle 80%" of this proficiency graph must somehow differentiate themselves to patients. In addition, the sheer size of this middle 80% is growing because of the tremendous supply of doctors available today. In other words, patients have more choices in many respects today, in terms of which doctors they choose. One of the most effective ways to compete in such an environment is through service-oriented medicine. This involves conducting warm, caring interactions between every employee in the doctor's office and the patient to create a welcoming environment for the patient. It starts from the initial phone contact with the receptionist for an appointment and continues until the receptionist bids the patient farewell.

Over 80% of the patients' perception of the quality of medical care is determined by the doctor's art of availability and affability, yet 95% of a doctor's training and subsequent focus is in applying the science of their medical knowledge and ability. It is essential for doctors to realize that the major determinant of their patients' perception of them is more in the art of interaction rather than applying the science of their profession, i.e. the art of medicine is how a physician interacts with their patients. The ex-chairman of Louisville's School of Medicine stated that, in order to be successful, a physician must focus on the "3 A's" – Availability, Affability, and Ability – in that order. Availability refers to a physicians' accessibility to patients. Affability refers to a physician's friendliness toward patients. Ability refers to a physician's skill in practicing the science of medicine. Dr Levitt pursues the first of the "3 A's", i.e. availability, by keeping hours in tune with his patients' personal schedules. He pursues the second of the "3 A's", i.e. affability, by continuously interacting on a friendly and personal level with his patients. The pursuit of the third of the "3 A's", i.e. ability, is more of a prerequisite obtained through medical school and residency to ensure a basic "ability" to practice medicine as well as continuing to keep up-to-date on the latest medical advances. The ex-chairman went on to point out that while most, if not all, physicians qualify in ability, it is the first two "A's" which will distinguish them as exceptional physicians.

In the medical field, one successful dermatologist, Dr Levitt, uses eye contact and touch to communicate to his patients that he has acknowledged their existence. It is a common weakness in the medical profession that a physician's interaction with patients is clinical, removed, and impersonal. This weakness is being driven by the insurance industry's insistence that doctors spend less time with patients.

He has found that physicians who practice more physical touching and maintain eye contact increase the patient's perception that the physician is spending more time attending to their needs. This is due to the fact that these basic elements of communication, i.e. physical touch and eye contact, are communicating to the patient that the physician is acknowledging them as a person, and consequently acknowledging their medical condition. In Dr Levitt's case, if a patient wants him to look at a skin mole, he will touch the mole to signify that he truly recognizes their emotional concern. He also makes sure that he looks them directly in the eye as frequently as possible. He does both the physical touch and eye contact with little or no productivity consequences as he continues to treat a high volume of patients. The end result is that the patients "feel" he has spent more time with them and there is an increased perception that he has recognized their medical ailments adequately and done so with a higher medical competence. He has noticed that whether he spends five minutes or twenty minutes with the patient, if he has taken the time to look into their eyes, his patients feel cared for and acknowledged.

Acknowledge customer companions, e.g. pals, parents, pets

Businesses should be treating a customer's companion as an honored guest rather than a potential inconvenience in the buying process. Simple gestures, such as offering a beverage, or asking their opinion, are usually all that is needed. While it is important to acknowledge a customer's existence, it can be equally important to acknowledge the customer's companions and employees should be trained to focus on both. In many cases, a business will only focus on the person who is "paying the bill" and not on the other people traveling or shopping with the customer. The customer's companion wouldn't be with the customer if they didn't personally value them. The most common oversight is treating children as a "necessary evil" and not as a key to the customer's fulfillment, i.e. heart. Interacting with a customer's children takes special communication and entertainment skills, e.g. eye contact at their physical height, acknowledging precious toys, providing self-service entertainment items. In particular, restaurants and retail stores sometimes view the children as a bother rather than an opportunity to greatly increase the customer's human fulfillment. In particular, as adults will perceive the wait in a line longer if it does not move, children have a heightened sense of impatience. Therefore, it is often helpful to seek ways of entertaining children during periods of waiting. The benefits are twofold: (a) Customers can focus on the check in or out process, which yields a more efficient process; (b) Customers are more content because their children are more content.

Four Seasons hotels have a special program to acknowledge their guest's pets. They are a pet-friendly hotel that allows guests to bring pets weighing up to 30 pounds. Once the guest arrives with their pet, the staff sends up a package of pet amenities, e.g. doggie biscuits, bowl of water as an added personal touch.

Land Rover have set performance standards by which their centers (dealerships) acknowledge the existence and importance of their customers. One standard is simply the common courtesy of answering the telephone within three rings. This quick customer response is possible because all employees carry portable phones. Another Land Rover acknowledgement standard is that customers should be greeted or acknowledged within one minute of entering the center. It is a standard courtesy for the service department to schedule a customer for service within 48 hours of the desired service day to minimize the customer's wait time and communicate their importance. Other standards include cleanliness standards for the showroom, bathrooms, and grounds. Land Rover send unannounced auditors into the centers four times a year to determine how well they are complying with these standards.

Have fun with them

One of the highest acknowledgements of humanness a business can bestow on its customer is to have fun with them. There is a multitude of ways that the business can create an atmosphere of merriment with customers. These periodic extra-joyful customer atmospheres can be created simply for an extended moment of customer appreciation or in conjunction with almost any business activity, e.g. advertising campaign, sale, marketing blitz, service milestone. These types of activities can either be planned as known, scheduled activities or as surprises.

Fun days

Businesses can easily and inexpensively create "fun days" that customers will happily anticipate, plan on, and participate in. Wal-Mart regularly have lighthearted activities called "dress-up days", which are typically done in conjunction with a product promotion. During one of Wal-Mart's "rollback days", which is where the store reduces the price of a product below the normal selling price, they encourage the associates to dress up as Zorro, if they wish. To add an additional sense of humanness during these "rollback days", the store mascot, also dressed as Zorro, walks around the store to participate in the physical act of "slashing" the prices. On a "beach party" day, the mascot dresses up as "sunshine". During these beach party days, associates dress up as if they are on the beach, wearing such items as straw hats and sunglasses. During another dress-up day with the theme of the old West, the associates were encouraged to dress up as cowboys and cowgirls, with the mascot dressing up as a cowboy as well. These dress-up days are typically done in conjunction with a product promotion and increase the emotional engagement of both the customer and the associate during these promotional activities. This feeling of emotional engagement increases the associate's emotional involvement with a particular business activity rather than leaving him an unemotional participant. It is important to point out that the store's approach to product promotions are more a product "celebration" than simply another advertising campaign. The approach of a "celebration" promotes the sense of an emotionally positive event rather than an activity dedicated toward "selling more product".

A good example of a fun day is from Tudor Day Spa. They create certain business days with outlandish themes such as "pajama days" or "funky hair days". On "pajama day", the staff come to work in their favorite pajamas. On "funky hair day", the staff create an outrageous hairstyle for themselves and wear that hairstyle the entire day in the shop. Clients enjoy participating in these fun days because of the added connection and human feel to them despite the fact that the themes have little or no connection to Jane Manfre's (the owner of Tudor Day Spa) product or service. These fun days have the potential of engaging both customer and employee beyond almost any other business activity. They also dramatically increase the level of communication between client and employee. Jane observes that these days "wake up everyone, and get their juices flowing". One of her clients flies in from Chicago to get her hair done specifically during one of these fun days. Jane schedules regular customer appreciation parties, which combine paying tribute to her clients with simultaneously benefiting charitable causes. This is just one of the ways that Jane lavishes attention and affection on her clients. The parties are an explicit acknowledgement that she appreciates their patronage and loyalty. She also holds regular seasonal parties dedicated to helping homeless children, as well as charity walks for the cancer society.

Delight in the delivery

Business can enhance the customer's emotional fulfillment and have fun by focusing on creating specific emotions during the actual delivery of the product. There are special emotions surrounding the act of taking possession of a special product that can easily be made into an enjoyable celebration. One Land Rover center goes to exceptional efforts to turn the ordinary delivery of a car into a customer "celebration" of the delivery. The delivery is truly a celebration because almost every employee in the center is partially involved in delivering the customer's Land Rover. When a customer purchases a new Land Rover, the center reviews every technical detail (including safety) of the automobile with the customer. This detailed partner view is not necessarily to bestow extensive knowledge to the customer but to create a great sense of importance in the customer, i.e. the attention received. The Land Rover center has found that customers will remember less than 50% of the vehicle's technical details during the delivery process but forever remember the personal "manner" in which it was presented or delivered. Customers anticipating their first off-road excursion will not remember how to shift into a particular low gear but will remember the small human courtesies at the time of delivery, e.g. how courteous the sales and service people were, special refreshments offered, and was the delivery timely and problem-free. At the conclusion of each delivery, the customer is asked to fill out a survey, which is returned to Land Rover. Land Rover will then send the completed forms to the center with the comments section referred to as "celebrations". When the center receives these "celebrations", a meeting is called for everyone who was involved in the sale and delivery process to review the customer's comments for potential improvements for the next celebration, i.e. delivery.

Fun for all

This same Land Rover dealership transforms any marketing and advertising activities into entertaining and cost-effective media days. Because this Land Rover center (dealership) was competing against much larger dealerships with significant advertising budgets, they chose to create this cost-effective, highly personalized and fun-targeted marketing event that was rich in media coverage. This activity targeted two specific segments of their customer base, viz. government and non-government customers. Grand openings are more personal and more cost-effective than running full-page ads or television commercials that are more appropriate for larger dealerships. This Land Rover center also held a "Media Day", which meant inviting all television, radio, and print media in the community. Each media organization competed against the others in a Land Rover driving competition. The object was to drive a Land Rover Discovery across the off-road course behind the center without spilling water from the fishbowl perched on top of the hood. Sixty-eight media people completed the course that day with over a hundred in attendance and four radio stations with live broadcast coverage. The winner of each media group was able to drive the Land Rover Discovery for a weekend with the overall winner having the Discovery for an entire week. In addition, the Land Rover center donated one thousand dollars to the winner's favorite charity.

Make the sales process fun

This Land Rover center has embedded "extreme" fun as an integral part of its sales process. During the time when the customer is getting to know the car, they will be offered an opportunity to drive the Land Rover over a specially designed course that demonstrates its off-road capabilities. Customers walk away from the sales process with five distinct emotional memories:

1   This is the most unusual place I've ever been.

2   They are all very nice people (employees).

3   I can't believe the Land Rover didn't turn over on the off-road course.

4   They gave me a free Land Rover T-shirt.

5   They didn't ask me to buy, even once.

This Land Rover center also encourages casual visitors who have simply walked into their center out of curiosity (possibly while waiting for a table at a local restaurant) to take a test drive on their center's track. The center does this in hopes that when these casual visitors return to the restaurant, they may talk about their exciting experience on the test track and encourage potential customers to visit.

Go play outside

This Land Rover dealership also fosters deeper human relationships outside the traditional business environment. They regularly sponsor free outings for their customers to local places of interest. They sponsor one off-road excursion and two "point of interest" road excursions. One road trip started with coffee and donuts then a tour of the local Air Force Museum followed by a movie at the IMAX theater and a buffet lunch. Off-road excursion fun means four days of challenging off-road driving at a local 100-acre farm. Land Rover invite a professional off-road driving instructor to join a group of customers on a specially constructed course through woods, across rivers and even a large hole deep enough to totally cover the vehicle. There is also a trials course built for customers to compete against each other and the clock. Entertainment (like a climbing wall) is also provided for the children, so the customers have complete freedom to enjoy themselves.

Surprises ... use with care

Surprises are a very powerful tool to create wonderfully fun experiences with customers most of the time. However, surprises have their own set of risks as well as being an emotional "double-edged sword". Surprises can be unpredictable, reduce the customer's sense of control, and can result in creating negative emotions rather than positive emotions.

Surprises tend to make many customers feel "out of sync" with the comfortable rituals of doing business with a company. The degree to which the customer feels as if they have lost control ties into how powerful their innate desire is to control their environment, and this varies significantly from customer to customer. Some people feel "excitement" is exciting while others feel "excitement" is emotionally threatening to their sense of security. People have many reactions, including feeling afraid, threatened, unnerved, or panicked, as if they need to do something. Other people just don't want to have to respond to events that are exciting or "different". This is partially due to the fact that they are uncertain "how" to respond to this excitement. It is the degree to which a firm can predict a customer's reaction to a surprise that determines whether they can safely utilize surprises as a technique to enhance the customer experience or interaction.

Sometimes the simplest, little surprises on a day-to-day basis have the greatest impact on a customer's perception of the business's service level. The simple surprises can be offering a soft drink or glass of water to a customer.

A good example of a situation in which a good surprise worked very well is when Wal-Mart were in the process of remodeling their housewares and stationery departments. At the conclusion of a remodeling effort, the manager found there was a tremendous amount of leftover merchandise and no practical way to dispose of it. The store manager decided to have some fun with the customers and took a tremendous markdown on the items. Essentially, the manager "blew" the merchandise out the door at unusually deep discounts. The customers were ecstatic with emotion. They ended up getting unheard of values as well as feeling special that they happened to be in the store at the time of this impromptu sale. Wal-Mart have a specific policy with regard to the bad surprise of incorrect pricing. They will reduce the price of many items by $3 as compensation to customers. If the item's price is under three dollars, the customer will be given the item free of charge.

A good example of a surprise that didn't work is when a respected executive sent a box of "goodies" to thank a customer not knowing that the company had a strict policy against gifts. The intention was to show goodwill, but it backfired and instead created stress. Therefore, it is always a good idea to follow up in order to make sure not only that the desired surprise/activity happened but that it happened in a manner desirable to the recipient. Most of the time attention is focused on the surprise itself rather than on how it will affect the recipient.

Most firms will create good surprises for customers, whereas other firms will avoid them due to the uncertain nature of the emotional outcome. When proactive surprises are done well and in appropriate situations, surprises can create very positive reactions from customers. When done poorly or in inappropriate situations, surprises can create anxiety, fear, and embarrassment. When unexpected "negative" surprises occur, there is usually an initial negative emotional reaction from the customer. Having said that, there is almost always the opportunity to create a positive outcome from a negative surprise. This is dependent on how the negative surprise is handled.

Acknowledging Their Importance

It is a true irony that a customer's patronage determines a firm's existence yet few take the time to communicate this importance and few customers feel it.

One of the best ways to communicate the customer's importance is to give responsibility and authority to employees to own a customer's request until completion.

Follow-up with customers to communicate "we're thinking of you"

Conducting regular follow-ups with customers is a good way to communicate the business is "thinking of them" even when they are not engaged in purchasing activities. The business is also communicating that they truly desire to make the customer's next experience a little bit better from the knowledge they gained during the follow-up.

Dorothy Lane Market telephone five different customers, five nights a week at each store to ensure that they were happy with DLM. Norman Mayne commented that they got this idea from a local dentist who called his customers after each visit. The telephone survey of DLM's customers is very simple: "We noticed that you visited Dorothy Lane today and just wanted to know about your experience". The positive customer comments are recorded and the negative comments are addressed each weekend. Norman's employees personally hand out 10 customer service grading cards each day to customers for the customer to fill out. Just the fact that there is a real human being handing out customer survey cards makes this process much more effective with customers because the customers take the survey more personally. Norman also has a "Mayne line" form, which is a feedback form targeted directly toward Norman for customers either to mail in or get feedback via DLM's website. Separately, DLM interview 400 households each year and asks, "What would you like us to do?" The review process takes roughly half an hour. The interview questions cover a wide range of topics that compare department by department with their competitors. The responses range widely, from being able to simply cash a check to being able to have a wedding cake made from scratch ingredients rather than the typically frozen wedding cake. Ultimately, Norman believes that it is time better spent understanding what negative human reactions are causing them to lose customers rather than dedicating money to acquiring new customers. Most of the negative human reactions that cause grocers to lose customers are related to a human being's need for attentive and genuine caring service or cleanliness and inherent food quality (both emanating from a human's sense of self-preservation).

Communicate importance one at a time

For luxury car dealerships such as Lexus, it is critical to provide top-quality automobiles to its higher-end clientele. As with most dealerships, there is a concerted effort to accomplish the cliché of customer satisfaction, i.e. exceeding customer expectations. While many dealerships strive for this level of customer satisfaction, few dealerships actually attain it. One dealership, headed by John Higgins, is currently ranked No. 1 in customer satisfaction in the United States and has achieved this status in five out of the last nine years. John has accomplished this in the face of overwhelming odds as a dealership which represents the Japanese manufacturer, Lexus, in a predominantly GM-based town. His success is almost completely based on John's human approach to both customers and employees. John's philosophy is that treating customers as individual human beings is accomplished one at a time. Lexus has a very strong customer service philosophy and as a result is very selective about choosing dealers. Initially, John competed against 50 other existing dealerships for the Lexus dealership in his geographic area. The Lexus credo states, "Make every customer feel as if they are a guest in your own home". This superior level of human comfort, consideration, and sensitivity to feelings is supported by the Lexus customer service philosophy. It was this philosophy that not only helped create the dealership but also ultimately resulted in exceptional business performance statistics. The essence of his approach is that you cannot interact with 100 customers at a time –

just one human customer at a time. As a result of this philosophy, John's Lexus dealership has the highest repeat-buying statistics in the United States. Seventy percent of John's customers will buy their next car from John's dealership. The national average for repeat customers of domestic car-buying is 28%. Another indicator that John's human approach is extremely successful is his employee retention. Over the past 10 years, John has had only one service technician leave his dealership's employment and that particular person left to work for the Lexus manufacturer. The statistics for John's turnover of salespeople also is significantly better than industry standards. John's average salesperson turnover rate is six years, compared with a one-year average for many car dealerships. In addition, John has a growing number of customers who have bought over twenty Lexus automobiles from him.

Follow up, but don't stalk 'em

While follow-up activities are critical to understanding whether customers "feel" they have been taken care of, uncoordinated and insensitive "follow-up" activities can quickly damage customer fulfillment. John Higgins's Lexus Dealership ensures personal follow-up with his customers through a retired nurse to ensure sensitivity. She calls every service customer to inquire if his car was not only fixed on time but also repaired properly. She also makes sure that the customer understands the bill as to "what they paid for" in their automobile repair. For his customers who have purchased automobiles, John has a mandatory follow-up procedure to ensure that every customer receives a follow-up call from their respective salesperson to ensure that the customer had all their questions answered satisfactorily. The Lexus manufacturer have their own customer follow-up procedure which includes following up directly with the customer as well as monitoring John's follow-up. John periodically receives customer letters saying that the customer "loves the service, loves the car, but quit calling me". John will then place these customers on his list not to be called as often. On the other hand, if the dealership stops calling the customer completely, then the customer may feel unimportant or ignored as a human being. In essence, the customer is saying, "I know you want me as a customer but I don't want you to want me that much". Beyond phone calls, many times John follows up with gifts of appreciation. Occasional gifts, such as a beautiful Orvis leather briefcase for longtime customers are not uncommon. John estimates that appreciation gifts are given away roughly ten times a month.

Own the customer response

Personally and physically handle each request from a customer, or remain with them until they have reached the appropriate destination to fulfill their request. Respond correctly the first time; make it timely, and with caring. This is important because currently customers are becoming increasingly fed up with their requests being delegated, put off, placed on hold, transferred, etc. The underlying behavioral message every time a customer is "put off" is, "I am not important enough".

Businesses can acknowledge their customer's importance by owning customer requests without passing them onto another employee or department.

Ritz-Carlton have empowered all their employees with the responsibility and authority to own the requests of their customers (guests). Each employee has the authority to spend up to $2000 to alleviate any problem for any customer. Typically, in most businesses, if a customer approaches an employee with a problem outside their normal job responsibility, the employee will respond by saying, "I'll tell someone about it". The customer responds with the feeling that the employee doesn't care about him or his problem because it was delegated to someone else and he often believes that nothing will ever be done about the problem. Making these discoveries has energized Ritz-Carlton to explore every possible avenue of what their guests truly need as human beings, as well as what type of human beings are the best employees to satisfy the guest's needs.

Wal-Mart always strive to have the customer "feel" like they are the most important entity in the store. This philosophy emanated from Sam Walton's challenge many years ago that all Wal-Mart associates practice what he referred to as "aggressive hospitality". He said, "Let's be the most friendly – offer a smile of welcome and assistance to all who do us a favor by entering our stores. Give better service – over and beyond what our customers expect. Why not? You wonderful, caring associates can do it and do it better than any other retailing company in the world . . . exceed your customers' expectations. If you do, they'll come back over and over again." In an excellent example of this, one of Wal-Mart's managers noticed that a woman was frantically searching for a particular item in the store's toy department the week of Christmas. The woman's face was filled with stress and anxiety. The Wal-Mart manager walked up to this anxiety-filled customer and asked whether she could be of help. The woman explained that the week prior she had been in the store with her six-year-old daughter who spotted an African-American version of a newborn baby doll. The daughter had told her mother that the only present she wanted for Christmas was this particular doll. The little girl was scheduled to enter the hospital the following morning for a leukemia bone-marrow transplant and she had not purchased the doll earlier because she wanted it to be a special surprise. By the time the customer came back to purchase the doll, the toy department was sold out. At that point, the Wal-Mart manager started calling every Wal-Mart within a 150-mile radius to try to find this doll. The manager finally found the doll an hour away and drove to that Wal-Mart to pick the doll up and returned to personally give it to the young girl. The store manager did not charge the mother for the doll but instead gave it to the little girl as a gift from Wal-Mart. This tremendous gesture of human kindness not only made a child very happy but also made an incredible statement to the mother about how important her feelings as a human being were to Wal-Mart. Other stories include a Wal-Mart employee named Sheila who risked her own safety when she jumped in front of a car to prevent a little boy from being struck. Another Wal-Mart employee named Phyllis administered CPR to a customer who had suffered a heart attack in her store. Another employee named Joyce threw a plate on the floor to assure a young mother that a set of dishes was truly unbreakable and Annette who gave up the Power Ranger she had on layaway for her own son so that a customer's son could have his birthday wish. These experiences will be forever etched in each customer's mind. It is important to remember that there is a delicate balance between reacting to a customer's immediate need and the normal activities that are temporarily put on hold to serve the customer's immediate request. A Wal-Mart store manager was working on remodeling the store's hardware department while also coordinating a new product promotion sponsored by major soft drink vendor which happened to be sponsored by the local police department to benefit the local Children's Hospital. During the time that this manager was juggling these two simultaneous tasks, a customer approached her and asked for her immediate assistance. As is the culture and behavioral expectation of Wal-Mart, the manager immediately placed the customer's need above the other activities she was performing. This clearly increased the probability that her other work would not only take a longer period to complete but also increased the probability for mistakes. This is one of the costs of placing immediate customer needs above other non-customer tasks. Another example is one in which a store manager was doing price changes in one department and then was called away to help a customer. While helping this customer, several other customers required her attention and by the time she returned to continue pricing the items, she had forgotten exactly where she had stopped. As a result, she missed changing the prices on several items. This resulted in these items being incorrectly priced at checkout adding additional processing time for the cashier to adjust prices and handle special pricing offers to the customer because of the policy of offering special discounts for incorrectly priced items. Wal-Mart has made the wise and strategic decision that the cost of added time and price adjustments to several items is worth keeping their directives of "customer's first" while they are shopping in their stores. If the situation is analyzed, each customer is pleased with the retailer, i.e. several customers receive a significant price break and the customers who require attention receive it immediately. The end result is customers feeling like they were treated as individual human beings. They also assure their commitment to correcting mistakes; it will be settled within 24 hours of the mistake.

John Higgins's Lexus Dealership have clearly communicated that if any customer approaches any employee with a question or issue, that employee must follow through with the customer to the conclusion of the request or issue. John has taken the position that any customer problem or issue transcends any department or role in his dealership. The employee who was initially approached by the customer, regardless of the department he works in, bears the responsibility for following up to ensure the customer is satisfied.

In the banking industry, research has shown that customers want recognition and acknowledgement that the money they have entrusted to the bank is still the customer's money – the only assets the financial institution has is not theirs: it belongs to the customer.

Businesses can add the "little" human touches to communicate that customers are important. It is especially important to make sure that the little human touches are present in what are typically perceived as unpleasant experiences, e.g. car repairs. Most businesses have some processes that have been historically dehumanizing to customers. One major challenge is to humanize an inherently unpleasant experience such as going to a dentist to have a tooth pulled, or, in this case, non-routine automobile service. Non-routine service appointments generate negative emotions from the beginning. Even normal maintenance service activities are an inconvenience, costly, and create fear that other service issues will crop up. Any time a customer has to write a check for $500–$1500 for unexpected automotive expense, it is not a pleasant experience. This underscores the necessity to execute every step of the service efficiently, with a human touch, and, most importantly, to correctly set expectations. Even if the repair was done 100% correctly, if the expectations were not set correctly, e.g. inaccurate estimate, time to repair, discourteous service staff, the customer will experience a series of long-lasting negative emotions which will not easily be forgotten. At the Land Rover Center after scheduling an appointment, they prepare a loaner Land Rover for the customer. When the customer arrives, he is offered a beverage and then reviews the specific problem with the service person. All pertinent customer contact information is collected, such as cell phone, beeper, and personal phone numbers. Once the service is completed, each customer receives a free carwash and vacuuming. If any small service items such as light bulbs need to be replaced, this is done at no charge as a gesture of human kindness. The manager of this Land Rover Center has made it clear that all service orders will contain some free service item explicitly written on the bill in addition to the free carwash. This symbolic goodwill gesture is simply an act of human kindness to send the message that this Land Rover Center cares more about people than multiplying service revenues.

In Chapter 8, "Human touch as process", there are many detailed examples of how Ritz-Carlton communicate to their customers how important they are. This is enabled by a directive to prioritize any customer request regardless of an employee's role or any task in which they are currently engaged. Examples are a bellman who assisted a handicapped racing team member with a wheelchair, to renting a metal detector to recover a precious ring on the beach. Ritz-Carlton's reputation is so well-known that a married couple with one partner recuperating from surgery made the decision to recover at a Ritz-Carlton instead of going home.

Los Alamos National Bank (LANB) have a similar directive to own the customer's request – every LANB employee is trained that if a customer asks a question of one employee that must be answered by a different employee, the original employee must physically escort the customer to the other employee. This particular aspect of the LANB experience yields the highest number of compliments by customers.

Give "a little more" vs. "a little less"

There is little else that signals the importance of a customer to a business as clearly as delivering "a little more" than expected. Conversely, the business that is constantly trying to figure out how to give "a little less" will communicate a message of customer unimportance. In many cases, businesses naively believe that the customer will not notice – they almost always do (source: Norm Kern).

Lagniappe (lan yap')

(French Creole, chiefly in the New Orleans area). Definition: a little something extra; a bonus; something unexpected; a small gift of appreciation given a customer by a merchant at the time of a purchase, e.g., the thirteenth donut in a baker's dozen. Lagniappe breeds good will, friendship and most importantly, return business.

Doing the "little things" to win the big things

There is a fine line between failure and success both in winning a project/sale and doing a project. Little things like getting the report in a day early, taking special care to keep the client informed, and going back once more on our own time to check on something or with somebody can be the critical ingredients. Each one is important. An extra phone call or meeting him/her at the airport are the kinds of things which, in addition to outstanding work on their behalf, can keep clients in our camp.

For a business, the difference in expenditure or savings between giving "a little more" and "a little less" is minimal, but to a customer's perception of being well served it is significant. Customers have an uncanny ability to "feel" the difference between striving to "give a little more" and trying to "cut corners". A business can gauge whether the business is delivering a little more or a little less by being sensitive to the customer's reactions. In other words, "it will always cost less to give a little more". One efficient approach to achieving this is to look for highly valued customer benefits that are relatively easy and cost-effective to deliver. Often, these are "little things" intertwined in the overall product or service delivery. As an example, a video production company was delivering an expensive video production to a client. Being experienced with these projects, the project manager knew that the client would sometimes ask for sample VCR copies of the project to take with them.

As a general practice, Kern Video produce VCR copies for the client at no charge as a gesture of kindness and goodwill. The customer will remember this small gesture of kindness far beyond some of the larger attributes of the project itself, i.e. giving the customer something they had not expected, but valued at no charge. This small gesture also creates positive customer feelings and loyalty for the production manager, not just Kern Video, and adds a subtle degree of increased confidence that helps the customer want to do business with this person again. The customer will feel as if the production manager is truly concerned for them being happy, not just charging for every little item they can. An added benefit of this strategy is that when a business is generous with their customers, they may be willing to extend that generosity back to the business. These types of give-and-take, conscious or unconscious processes, signify when a relationship between the business and customer actually becomes more trusting and "human". In a good example of this, one of Kern Video's clients contracted them to capture market research videos. This client was a market research company who wanted market research interviews videotaped in different cities around the United States. They asked the production manager to create a summary of the videotaped interview highlights from 15 hours of videotape. The normal process is for the VCR tapes to be brought into the studio where they are dubbed onto a digital format with special time codes that time stamp the entire videotape. This allows the business to look through the entire tape and pick out specific sections to highlight by referencing the time code. The new time-coded videotapes are called "window dubs". In order to accomplish this, one of the client's staff is required to review the entire 15 hours of tapes to compile a list of highlights. This is a long and tedious task. The client hired a new employee who was designated to review the 15 hours of tapes. This person was going to be forced to use a simple TV/VCR unit to review these tapes with no "jog shuttle" controls, which allow easy manipulation back and forth between tape segments. This function is critical in a tape mechanism because the person will have to search back and forth three or four times to get the exact time code numbers for the exact highlight sequence. Realizing the predicament, the production manager lent the client a VCR with a jog shuttle feature to make this task infinitely faster and more effective. This simple act projected a distinct touch of human kindness, compassion, and empathy. The cost of lending the VCR was negligible but the client and their employee will always remember the kindness. To lend out a VCR on a regular basis, the rental price would be roughly $250. For the insignificant cost of $250 the client experienced a tremendous value in time-savings alone plus gained sense of humanity and trust for Kern Video. The same amount spent for a newspaper ad may only yield one or two new customers who may or may not be profitable, but the positive word-of-mouth testimonials resulting from the loaned VCR can reap untold long-term benefits.

John Higgins's leading Lexus Dealership takes this philosophy a step further by encouraging his employees to keep their eye out for the "little things" surrounding the customer's automobile both on and off the job. If an employee observes that a customer's car has a brake light out, the employee is encouraged to write down the license plate number and inform the service manager. The customer is then given a courtesy call asking them to bring the car in to have the brake light bulb replaced. In many cases, John will replace the light bulb in this situation free of charge. It is these "little things" that customers never forget. John's total cost to do this "little thing" that the customer would never forget was roughly $25. John Higgins also makes sure that his salespeople are given enough time to attend to the "little things" that customers notice and appreciate, such as acquiring license plates for automobile purchases. Even though this is usually the customer's responsibility, John makes sure that this ancillary, time-consuming activity is taken care of for his customers. His dealership orders the customer's license plates and contacts the customer when the license plates are in hand. The salesperson personally installs the license plates for their customer either at the dealership or at the customer's home – the human touch.

Don't cost-cut the "little things"

Most customers do notice when businesses cut back on the "little things". This communicates a message that their importance has been lessened in the eyes of the business. John Higgins's leading Lexus Dealership has bucked the trend of other dealerships that have decided to reduce their operating expenses by examining the cost of pencils, the cost of maintaining the blacktop, how little they can pay employees, how little insurance to provide employees, and hiring the maximum amount of minimum wage employees. These myopic cost-cutting activities are telltale signs that a dealership is not striving to place employee and customer needs first. John is outspoken about his belief in attending to the human needs of his customers: "If you spend an inordinate amount of time attending to your customers' wants and needs, the rest of the crap that makes a business successful just falls into place". He continues: "You don't have to spend all your life going over financial statements and looking for nickels and dimes and pennies and quarters and ways to squeeze stuff out of here – worry about keeping your customers happy, and they will in turn bring repeat business themselves as well as bring other customers, which will constantly refurbish your business". John takes as much care in hiring the employees who wash the cars as he does in hiring his salespeople. His reasoning is that both employees will ultimately have close contact with human customers on a one-to-one basis. He can then be very confident that both his carwash employees and his salespeople have an equal ability and understanding of the importance and dynamics of treating customers like human beings. The incremental cost to the dealership of having a real human answering the phone is minimal compared to the negative feelings created when having to navigate unfriendly voice-response systems. "Little things" such as never forcing a customer to "deal" with a voice-response system is very important to John's strategy of a humanizing dealership. John emphasizes his human approach to communication with customers by stating, "If I have to have 11 incoming phone operators, you'll never have to talk to a machine at this dealership". There is nothing that magnifies an automobile service problem more than being placed on hold or into a nonhuman voice response system. He comments, "If a customer is mad when they first call in, how mad are they when the customer finally gets through to a real person?" Having multiple "real human beings" to answer calls from customers is unimportant if those call-center reps are dehumanized because of overwork and harsh call statistic objectives. John could also decide to stop his airport shuttle service because of the added costs of a driver and vehicle. He will not do this because he knows how precious his customers' time is and how much his customers appreciate the convenience of this service. John provides this airport shuttle service if a customer needs to have their car serviced at the same time they also need to make a business trip. The customer simply drops off the car at the dealership and then is shuttled to the airport. The customer tells John's service people what day they will be back from the business trip and the customer's freshly cleaned and repaired car is waiting for them at the airport when they arrive. Not only is John's airport shuttle service a tremendous convenience to the customer but it also minimizes any parking fee that the customer would otherwise incur from leaving the car in airport parking for the entire business trip. From the customer's human perspective, they feel incredibly pampered. When a customer feels so extremely well cared for, that pampered feeling will be remembered far beyond any detail of product or price.

Fix it fast

One of the best ways to acknowledge a customer's importance is to respond to customer problems quickly. A critical component of resolving any uncomfortable experience is the degree to which it is resolved at the time the problem occurs. If the problem cannot be resolved at the moment it occurs, the next best scenario is that it be resolved before the customer physically leaves the business premises.

Quick problem resolution is also the key to minimizing negative emotions with customers. It also is a unique opportunity to create higher customer fulfillment than if there had been no problem in the first place. Key to quick problem resolution is maintaining a friendly but professional attitude during the process. An effective approach is to reduce volatile emotions by careful listening and then discussion of the problem from both the customer and business perspective. If this is ineffective, it is natural to involve a management person. This sends a message to the customer that the customer's emotions are valid and that the problem is important enough to warrant a management employee. In addition, physically writing down the incident with a customer present also sends a message that the customer's emotions are valid and that this problem merits special attention. These are all aspects of addressing the emotional issues related to a customer problem. Follow-up to problems, which cannot be resolved immediately, should be done within a certain standard response time and with a personal touch.

Acknowledge You Know Them

In order for a business to acknowledge they know the customer, they must first have knowledge of that customer. The sophistication of information, which can serve to send an adequate message to the customer that the business "knows them", can range from simply being able to refer to them by name all the way to very sophisticated analysis of their lifestyle preferences and buying patterns. Most business does capture and analyze customer information with varying degrees of sophistication. Ideally, each business should strive to have a single view of customer interactions supported by modeling and database technologies.

Show them you know them

One of the simplest ways for a business to communicate to a customer that they know them is to address them by name. Ninety percent of customers appreciate some level of recognition whether it is a simple smile or the pleasing sound of their name. Four Seasons have implemented a program called "Show me you know me" which involves collecting simple information from guests who desire to be personally recognized. If the guest is amenable, staff will take a photograph of the guest for their records to enhance Four Seasons' ability to serve the guests better through visual recognition. This information is then reviewed prior to the beginning of each shift so that if the guest is encountered during their shift, the staff can address the guest by name and ask about any personal needs that were indicated during the earlier information-gathering process.

This program is a reflection of the exceptionally strong culture Four Seasons have with their guests which emanates directly from the company's founder, Isadore ("Issy") Sharp. His guiding principle is simply "treat people well". This simple business principle has led to an incredible array of awards captured in the following accolades: "Like all world's greatest hotels, Four Seasons feels like a second home in which you are never a stranger".

Another program Four Seasons implemented is their "Repeat guest" program for guests who frequent their hotels. This program is focused on understanding their needs and then exceeding those needs based on information gathered from previous visits, e.g. a certain treadmill, prefers certain types of bottled water, certain television station, certain number of towels. Other informal observations can be just as effective in the process of acknowledging guests. An alert staff can easily notice personal items which guests may be particularly proud of such as driving a certain luxury automobile or wearing a particular brand of clothing. With such simple greetings as, "How is your Porsche driving this morning?" or "That is a beautiful handbag", the staff is communicating to a guest that they are specifically "noticing" that particular guest and noticing the "little things" that matter to them. In a sense, the guest feels the staff is "watching out for them". Other good examples are showing specific consideration for guests when certain unexpected changes will be occurring to a guest's regular routine, which may have unusually high emotional reactions if the change is a surprise. For example, when a Four Seasons hotel changed their valet parking policy for its health spa members, the staff made sure that they communicated this change with a simple personal note in each of the guest's lockers well in advance of the change. They followed up with a face-to-face discussion to ensure there were no issues brought about by the change.

An important part of a business showing that they know the customer is the ability to track each customer's previous service issues so the business can be extra-sensitive to those issues and avoid any possibility of future reoccurrence. Four Seasons have a "glitch" system that tracks in a database when things go wrong with customers. This information then gets sent out to the appropriate people at Four Seasons over their e-mail system. They can then watch for trends when "glitches" start to form patterns beyond simple customer service anomalies. They also use traditional comment cards that are rolled into a report published every quarter for each department. Employees have "pre-shift" exercises that essentially review all of the "glitches" that the other shifts experienced. Glitch lists are printed out regarding customers with any recurring problems for each employee so they can refer to this information throughout the day.

Learn in the process of acknowledging you know them

The process of fulfilling customer needs should always be undertaken with the awareness that there is the possibility to learn. In other words, by the very act of serving a customer, the business is simultaneously learning about the customer. Four Seasons refer to this service philosophy as their "cycle of service", which states that from the minute the guest walks in the door, the staff may have three hours with potential guest interaction in which to serve and learn about them. Not only does this entail simple smiles, recognition by name, when possible, and pointing them in the right direction but also assessing what their current level of comfort is and how to make improvements for their greater fulfillment.

Ritz-Carlton train each employee to be responsible for identifying and recording individual guest preferences. This directive is included in their "three steps of service", which is a guide for employee behavior. Their "three steps of service" are:

1   A warm and sincere greeting. Use the guest name, if and when possible.

2   Anticipation and compliance with guest needs.

3   Fond farewell. Give them a warm goodbye and use their names, if and when possible.

Ritz-Carlton also created their Customer Loyalty Anticipation Satisfaction System (CLASS) which is described in detail in Chapter 9, "Implementing technology to humanize (not dehumanize)". CLASS is a guest-recognition database that anticipates repeat customers' preferences and requirements. Beyond individual guest preferences, Ritz-Carlton management can glance at customer satisfaction results and employee surveys in any city in the world from Chicago to Shanghai. These customer and employee surveys are supported by detailed information on financials and accurate sales forecasts. In a prior age, Horst Schulze, the founder, could have only hoped that his hotel in Chicago or Shanghai was doing well, now he knows.

> *A major challenge faced by The Ritz-Carlton is to remember each of its 800 000-plus customers. In response, a special organization exists in each of our hotels called Guest Recognition. This special function uses the CLASS database to remember returning guests and generate essential preference and schedule information to all concerned. In this way, the Ladies and Gentlemen of The Ritz-Carlton and our suppliers understand what is "new or different" about each individual customer or event.*
>
> (from the 1999 Malcolm Baldrige Award Application)

Acknowledge impact of societal events on needs

Acknowledge the changes that societal cycles and events have on customer needs and emotions. Apply macro-emotional changes of societal cycles to understanding cyclical customer sensitivities –

understand that customers' emotional sensitivities are often influenced by the changing cycles of society.

Learning which emotions customers want to avoid is just as compelling as observing which emotions they want to feel. There is a much more dramatic reaction for human beings in avoiding negative emotions than seeking more positive emotions. Fear is the most powerful human emotion. Likewise, if a human being feels that something is being lost in their life, they will prioritize filling that emotion prior to seeking to fill a more positive emotion.

In the telecommunications industry, the events of September 11th caused a tremendous spike in the sale of wireless handsets. Hearing the horrible stories of airline passengers calling their loved ones to tell them goodbye for the last time created a tremendous human value to wireless handsets. They became the only way a person could reach out and communicate to loved ones in their final minutes. Customers now view cell phones as a means to alleviate fear and loss – there is human comfort in that.

Because of September 11th the entertainment industry experienced a profound shift in the kind of entertainment customers chose to view. Comedy videos were constantly checked out of video stores, whereas the more violent action pictures remained on the shelves. At the same time, many action films that were in the process of being made were put on hold because the industry realized the emotional appetite for such films was almost nonexistent after September 11th.

Dr Ravi Batra (*Regular Economic Cycles*, New York: Palgrave Macmillan, 1989) studies the effects of circular motions of society and significant societal events. He believes that certain cyclical motions of society heighten specific human needs that correspond to the human need for survival. He characterizes these societal cycles as the Builder, the Renaissance, the Destroyer, and the Reconstructor. These societal cycles parallel the seasons of nature; spring, summer, fall, and winter. He believes that we are currently in the Destroyer cycle of society, i.e. barbaric, broken-down, destroyed, unrest, conflict. Society then moves into the Reconstructor cycle, i.e. wanting peace, wanting serenity. The Builder cycle then moves society forward to construct, develop and improve; and from there into the full flowering of the Renaissance cycle. These cycles constantly repeat themselves over time.

It is important to consider these societal phases as human emotional needs ebb and flow along with them. A society that is at a point of high stress, high conflict, and high turmoil creates a higher need in customers to validate themselves on a human emotional level. The firm must understand current sensitivities and approach branding and interactions with similar sensitivities and need fulfillment. It is not simply what a single customer personally experiences but what society as a whole is experiencing.

Acknowledge Their Feelings

Customers want to feel like they are being heard and that their feelings are valid.

In order to understand what customers feel, a firm must survey customers on specific points. Asking questions in this manner, i.e. do you "feel" ... is key to obtaining useful information to assess whether the series of multiple interaction channels most companies utilize are effective in delivering these two key elements of human perception.

When you are there in person, it is best to start every interaction with a welcome and friendly but businesslike greeting; recognize the customer personally when possible; look into their eyes when you can, i.e. say "I care". Then address the customer's needs by complying with what they want. Finally, thank them for letting you serve them and wish them well.

The science behind customer acknowledgement

While acknowledging customers can be an intuitive act, which should be encouraged on an individual basis, creating consistency and unanimity requires that these acts of acknowledgement be standardized to the greatest extent possible. All interactions are emotional exchanges with an optimum sequence. Therefore, it is important to standardize problem-solving techniques for handling the exchange of emotions during any interaction while still addressing the vital needs of respect, acknowledgement, and trust. A standardized process by which the employee can interact with a customer to best satisfy the customer's emotional needs is important because any interaction has an emotional discharge and exchange whose outcome will be greatly influenced by the sequence of how the emotions are addressed during the interaction. In a very simple example, a customer communicates that: "I'm angry", and the employee responds by first communicating: "I'm sympathetic". Human beings often prefer a certain order of emotional exchange during an interaction with another human being. Most of the customer's needs from a problem or concern are emotional, not product feature oriented.

An excellent method for a business to satisfy all three types of needs for acknowledgement (their existence, you know them, being heard and feelings validated) is the following sequence of steps designed for handling customer complaints and problem solving.

This interaction sequence should be done in separate distinct steps in order to help the customer cognitively and emotionally process each step as the customer service rep sequences through the interaction, e.g. complaint, problem-solving.

In the following sequence (source: Wendy Eggleton), the human aspects are addressed in the beginning and the end of the interaction with the business elements being addressed between the two.

Step #1: Thank them for their effort

In the first step, the business must thank the customer for their effort to communicate the problem. This step also allows the company to retrieve the customer's interaction history, which can be used to send a message to the customer that "you know them" by reviewing recent pertinent interactions, if appropriate. Saying "thank you" not only sends a message of respect but also acknowledges the customer's existence and dignity as a human being. The sequence of interaction is best started by the employee's immediate recognition of the customer's concern and possible stress. It is critical that the employee show a high degree of interest in solving the customer's problem. Typical words for this first phase would be:

"Thank you for telling me about it", thanking the customer for bringing the problem to the firm's attention. It is also critical in this first step that the employee communicate an explicit recognition of the customer's efforts to communicate the problem and the emotional effort it took to face the trepidation of the initial contact. This trepidation could emanate from the customer's perception that their efforts will only yield, a further hassle, a solution with little or no usefulness, further wasted time out of a busy schedule, a potential contentious argument, or just plain apathy, i.e. why bother? Another important reason to start with a "thank you" is that this is the best method of gaining and retaining the fullest attention from the customer, as the first process of human memory is attention, i.e. the choice as to what a human focuses on. This occurs because there is far more information in the customer's environment than they can process at any one time. Therefore, they need to make choices, either consciously or unconsciously, as to where they will focus their attention. A human's ability to recall items is typically limited to seven.

Step #2: Apologize for the emotional cost

In the second step, a genuine apology acknowledges the customer's emotion and communicates that their reaction is a valid one. An apologetic acknowledgement works well to begin dissipating negative emotions. This acknowledgement can be as simple as "I'm sorry" and why. The "why" should be centered on the emotional cost to the customer? Otherwise, the "I'm sorry" could be taken as an inappropriate admission of guilt. It serves the customer's underlying emotional need to have their emotions validated. This emotional cost or "fallout" can take the form of frustration, anxiety, anger, and humiliation as well as added effort or work.

Step #3: Listen carefully

In the first two steps, the focus was on acknowledging and addressing the customer's emotional needs. Now the interaction can move to an efficient exchange of information (the business steps). The process of collecting facts and data with careful listening and questioning is critical to truly understanding the events that created the negative emotions for the customer. It also serves to increase the "you know me" information for future interactions. It is also critical that the customer contact person not jump to conclusions about facts surrounding the problem. It is often the case that the problem the customer is communicating is not the true source of the negative emotions. For example, a customer may call a financial institution complaining about a service charge when the root of the irritation actually comes from a chronic misspelling of their first name on written communications. More importantly, customers do not necessarily want a problem fixed; they just want to be heard.

Step #4: Fix it or agree on how

Fix the problem immediately (if possible) or create a mutual agreement for a follow-up remedy. Fixing a problem as quickly as possible minimizes the negative emotional impact on a customer. If the problem cannot be remedied at the time of the call, it is important that the customer call representative come to an agreement with the customer as to specific steps that will be taken to remedy the problem.

Step #5: Engage the customer in problem solving

It is important to engage the customer emotionally in the problem solving process because this helps achieve an emotional buy-in to the agreed-upon solution. Suggested wordings are as follows: "How could we avoid this problem in the future?", "What sort of resolution will most please you as our valued customer?", and "What suggestions do you have to help us avoid this problem in the future?"

Step #6: Record it

It is important to make a record of the problem, the process, and the agreement to better enable the company to systematically fix the problem. This is clearly an administrative step. Superior technology is invaluable here in tracking and analyzing customer complaint patterns. The Web is an excellent medium to enable this function. Once the problems are recorded in a database, patterns of repeat problems can be discovered, and then addressed for long-term, systematic solutions. The ability to determine which complaints are repetitive in nature is helpful in addressing such issues as fraud, e.g. a customer attempting to get multiple credits on a merchandise return. The technical systems supporting this administrative step should also enable an employee to fix the customer's problem without having to go through processes or systems that require input by other divisions of the company unconnected to the customer service representative who is attempting to efficiently and effectively solve the customer's problem. A system that has the complaint log ability and reimbursement capability in one and the same system adds tremendous speed to solving the customer's problem. This speed translates into much higher levels of satisfaction due to reduction of the emotional cost to the customer. These technical systems should also be able to report complaint trends at frequent intervals for the best possible chance of solving a problem before it spreads to additional customers. The power of today's databases allows almost any permutation of these complaints, e.g. customer service representative level, business unit level, category of complaint, and subcategory of complaint. From an emotional perspective, if the customer is present or involved in the recording of his complaint, this reinforces for him that the company "feels" his complaint is valid.

Step #7: Ensure closure

Following up with a customer is critical in order to make sure that the customer perceives that there is emotional closure to the problem. It also acknowledges that many times a business may be satisfied with the interaction as being closed but the customer may emotionally not have closure. This step can take place at the end of the initial conversation or can be done as a follow-up contact several days later. Not only is the follow-up effective as a procedural step, but also as a "reminder" that the company cares enough to make sure the customer is happy. While the customer may remember the explicit demonstration of "caring" from the first conversation, human memory capabilities are limited. Follow-up also validates that the previous problem resolution process is important enough not to forget about as soon as the customer hangs up from the call-center or leaves the retail outlet, i.e. it was not an "out of sight, out of mind" exercise.

Approach shopping as therapy

To facilitate the acknowledgement of customer feelings, it is helpful for businesses to be proactive in understanding what potential feelings the customer may have in any given interaction or situation. In the retail environment, 75% of shoppers shop to consciously or subconsciously lift their spirits or moods. An informal store opinion poll taken of a portion of the 5000 weekday customers who visit Wal-Mart each day and a portion of the 8000 weekend shoppers who visit the store each weekend day revealed that roughly 75% of shoppers are not in the "best of spirits" when they first decide to go shopping. In fact, most of these 75% are shopping because they want to feel better. It is this statistic that reveals that the shoppers are not in the best of spirits when they enter stores. Therefore, businesses should approach shoppers with the understanding that they are shopping to create some level of emotional healing, i.e. to "feel" better or less bad, not necessarily to consume. They realize that shopping is an emotional release. A human customer's decision to shop is prompted by a conscious or unconscious awareness that shopping or spending money fulfills a need within them, provides a release of anxiety, or makes them happier or less unhappy human beings. For one customer, shopping may "blow off steam" from work, whereas another customer may have had a fight with their spouse and need to relieve tension with the distraction of shopping. Another scenario could be a tired mother who just needs a short break from being in the house all day with her children or a commuter who is angry from the traffic congestion and shops to relieve stress. In most of these scenarios, the purchases are not driven out of a need for physical consumption but a need for emotional fulfillment. This is particularly true for customers who enter the store in the evening hours. This is why Wal-Mart have their strategy to "turn their frown upside-down", hence the smiley face. The majority of customers who are not in the best of moods are easily identified if associates take the time to observe their customer's facial expressions and body language.

Acknowledging customers as people fulfills a central need within them as human beings. In the most basic sense, customers want business to acknowledge their existence and importance. They want to feel appreciated, not only as customers who have trusted the business enough to give them their hard-earned money but also as individuals – individuals who are uniquely different with unique human needs. They want the business to balance knowing enough about them as an individual to understand their personal characteristics and interaction history with allowing them to feel their privacy has not been compromised. Another significant aspect of "knowing them" is to understand and acknowledge the validity of their feelings. A business can only accomplish this when it understands those feelings and the sequence by which feelings need to be addressed and acknowledged. Acknowledgement will always be one of the determining factors of where a customer buys and continues to buy their products and services.

4

Treating Customers with Respect

HUMAN BEINGS HAVE A STRONG NEED TO FEEL RESPECTED. AS IMportant as showing respect to a customer, is the need for business to avoid showing disrespect. Whether disrespect is intentional or unintentional does not change the impact of disrespectful behavior on customers.

Show Respect by Putting Yourself in "Their Shoes" – Be the Customer

One of the simplest ways for a business to check itself as to whether a particular action or behavior shows respect for a customer is to apply the "do unto others" rule, i.e. putting yourself in "their shoes". A common activity for top human businesses is to regularly place themselves in the customer's situation and actively view their business's experience through the customer's eyes.

The good example of this is how Jane Manfre of Tudor Day Spa approaches putting herself in her customers' shoes. Each time she enters/walks through/departs her business she "becomes" her customers. She opens herself to all five human senses. In addition, she asks the same of her staff – "If you were a customer, would you like to be sitting here smelling this? Would you like to be walking through here looking at this? Would you like to be touching this?" Jane observes that, while her competitors may have soothing music playing or other "standard" methods to create atmosphere, they have really not taken the time to observe all the negative sensory touches most human beings find consciously or unconsciously disturbing. One of the indicators that this is an effective approach is that 60–70% of Jane's clients are "regulars", i.e. long-term. Jane grew up in Nottingham, England, where she had a great deal of experience with beauty salons. When Jane finally reached the point in her career where she could have her own business, she had discovered what she did not want to do. She did not want her business environment to feel impersonal because she is a "people person". When she started her own business in the United States it was with an emphasis on the personal touch. To Jane, this means using all of her human senses every day, viz. sight, smell, sound, touch and taste. Each day as she physically moves within the environment of her business, she places herself in her customers' human sensory position so that she understands what they feel and absorb when they are there. For any particular action or activity, a business can hypothetically place themselves in the customer's position and ask such questions as: Is this activity worth the customer's time and effort? Is this new service charge fair? Does this process show respect for the customer?

Common Courtesies Are King

The easiest and quickest ways for a company to start showing more respect and less disrespect to customers is to revitalize their employees' understanding of the impact of common courtesies on customers as human beings.

From the research, it is clear that there is a tremendous need for this revitalization. Nearly four in ten (39%) who work outside the home say they have colleagues who are rude or disrespectful; three in ten (31%) say their workplace has supervisors who behave in this way.

Nearly half (47%) believe a major reason for disrespectful behavior in our society is that "life is so hectic and people are so busy and pressed for time that they forget to be polite".

Six in ten (61%) admit, "sometimes I am so busy and pressed for time that I am not as polite as I should be".

Nearly seven in ten (69%) say, "I am less likely to be nice when I have to deal with someone who is very rude and impolite".

(Source: *Aggravating Circumstances*, 2002 Public Agenda.)

There is a popular misconception that common courtesies are about social manners, which have only ancillary meaning in a business situation. The essence of common courtesies runs much deeper when they are viewed from a behavioral and social science perspective on how they impact the customer.

Two out of the three most important human needs for a customer's buying behavior are respect and acknowledgement. These are the central messages communicated by the use of common courtesies. As a result, whichever business is best at showing respect and the least likely to show disrespect has the highest probability of earning the customer's business.

> *The heart of courtesy is respect for persons; it has less to do with manners than with a manner of relating, a manner that acknowledges the worth of human beings.*
>
> (*Say Please, Say Thank You: The Respect We Owe One Another*, by Donald W. McCullough, New York: G.P. Putnam's Sons, 1998)

The rationale for treating every customer with respect is not just because when the businesses treat a customer with respect they increase the probability of a favorable buying decision but also:

Customers who feel respected by a company are more likely to:

1   Be loyal (buy more and different products).

2   Recommend the company (propagate a favorable brand image).

It could be said that any form of "bad service" communicates disrespect to customers. A recent study was completed that revealed what percentage of moderate-income customers walked away from companies with bad service – see Figure 4.1.

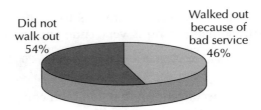

Figure 4.1   Moderate-income customers walking away from bad service
(data from *Aggravating Circumstances*, 2002 Public Agenda, used with kind permission)

The same study also revealed what percentage of high-income customers walked away from companies with bad service – see Figure 4.2.

How many of these customers would not have walked out if they had been shown simple common courtesies?

If more businesses understood the immense impact of these small messages of thoughtfulness to customers, more businesses would immerse themselves in the unanimous and consistent delivery of simple common courtesies.

One of the hidden benefits of showing common courtesies is that not only does it enhance the likelihood of a favorable buying decision from a customer but it also enhances personal employee fulfillment by the very act of showing respect to another human being.

If an employee treats a customer with disrespect, it is highly likely that the customer will in turn treat the employee with disrespect. This vicious cycle will quickly spiral downward, leaving both employee and customer further dehumanized. In most cases, people

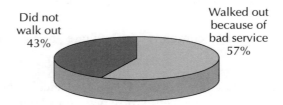

Figure 4.2   High-income customers walking away from bad service
(data from *Aggravating Circumstances*, 2002 Public Agenda, used with kind permission)

who later come in contact with this particular employee or customer will also receive some negative repercussions in a totally unrelated event.

In addition to common courtesies delivering favorable messages to customers, they also serve as a guideline to business etiquette when employee emotions may have deteriorated because of other stresses from employment or personal issues. Because etiquette is concerned with a standard of behavior, not personal feelings, it may be used to even out some of the negative emotional extremes that sometimes occur between employee and customer, i.e. people are more able to control their actions than their feelings.

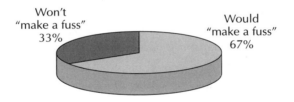

Figure 4.3   Would make a fuss to overcome bad service
(data from *Aggravating Circumstances*, 2002 Public Agenda, used with kind permission)

Not only does bad service drive customers away from businesses but it also creates extra work for the businesses as 67% of people will "make a fuss" if they experience bad service – see Figure 4.3.

Say the two words with the most impact to customers often – "Please" and "Thank-you".

Say Please

One of the most underestimated methods of giving the customer the perception that they have control is saying "Please". By saying please, the business is acknowledging to the customer that they have a choice in the matter. It gives them control. It acknowledges their rights as a human being. It is showing respect for the freedom and ability to choose. Recognizing this personal freedom is part of acknowledging the dignity of the customer's humanness.

Personal freedom is part of the dignity of being human and should always be acknowledged in our relationships.

(*Say Please, Say Thank You: The Respect We Owe One Another,* by Donald W. McCullough, New York: G.P. Putnam's Sons, 1998)

During customer interactions, when please should be used and it is not, its absence will permeate every other aspect of the conversation.

If the businesses can't afford the extra time set aside to utter the word "please" to the customer, does the business really deserve the customer's business?

Each bit of discourteous behavior flows down a line until we are all infected. Treat another with lack of respect, and that lack of respect will spread, not only back to you but toward others. The opposite is also true.

(*Say Please, Say Thank You: The Respect We Owe One Another,* by Donald W. McCullough, New York, G.P. Putnam's Sons, 1998)

Say Thank-you

Saying "Thank-you" sends a direct message to the customer about how important they are. The business depends on them for its very existence and survival.

Another idea is to start each meeting with "Thank-you". "Thank-you" is a universal phrase that helps almost any meeting get off to a good start. Don Evans, President and Chief Executive Officer of OMI, believes that his employees should start every meeting with clients with a genuine "Thank you for letting us serve you".

Nothing we do, have or achieve is done on our own – we are always dependent on others for help and support. Not acknowledging this with a simple "thank you" fatally inflates our own self-importance and denies the contributions of others in our lives.

(*Say Please, Say Thank You: The Respect We Owe One Another,* by Donald W. McCullough, New York: G.P. Putnam's Sons, 1998)

If a thank-you is appropriate and absent from the conversation, its absence will also permeate every other aspect of a conversation.

Below is a list of other common courtesies and observations that can enhance customer fulfillment:

+ Always be mindful of other people, remembering their feelings and sensibilities.

+ Every action ought to be done with some sign of respect to all those present.

+ Never belittle another person.

+ Never embarrass someone who needs your help.

+ Never forget to thank one who helps you.

+ Good behavior is a better teacher than any amount of lecture.

+ Insincere warmth toward a customer will alienate most customers.

+ Always treat any person accompanying a customer as an honored advisor – bring a chair, invite an opinion, engage in conversation.

+ The little things are important and the only honest place to begin.

+ Write thank-you notes.

 (*Rules of Civility*, by George Washington, edited by Richard Brookhiser, New York: Free Press, 1997; *Miss Manner's Guide for the Turn-of-the-Millennium*, by Judith Martin, New York: Pharos Books, 1989; *Say Please, Say Thank You: The Respect We Owe One Another*, by Donald W. McCullough, New York: G.P. Putnam's Sons, 1998; "Vanishing Etiquette" info from *Letitia Baldridge* by Meredith Moss in the *Dayton Daily News*)

The simple courtesy of responding to customers in a timely fashion is one of the business basics of respect. Los Alamos National Bank (LANB), a Malcolm Baldrige National Quality Award winning company, made the commitment that a human being will always answer the phone. In addition, e-mail and voicemail will be returned twice a day. For example, if an e-mail is received in the morning it is returned by noontime. If an e-mail or voicemail is received in the afternoon, it will be returned before the employee leaves for the day. LANB believe that this is simple "garden variety" courtesy. Further, LANB believe that if a business cannot meet this "garden variety" level of courtesy, how can they ever aspire to more sophisticated levels of customer service? They also give their direct numbers out to customers. LANB believe the sincerest form of courtesy is being humble enough to ask the customers: "What do you expect us to do in order for us to deliver on our promise?", i.e. what do you need? What do you want?

Respect Your Customers' Time

Time is one of the most cherished commodities that customers covet today. When a business goes out of its way to show respect for this precious commodity, the customers deeply appreciate it because they feel the business has truly demonstrated respect for them. Unfortunately, most businesses prioritize their time and scheduling requirements over the customers' time, which sends a clear message of disrespect to customers.

Set Back the Customers' Clocks

Give "time" back to your customers at every opportunity to show respect as well as reduce stress and anxiety. Over the years, people's available free time has significantly decreased and their need to free up available time has increased equally.

Norman Mayne of Dorothy Lane Market has witnessed this phenomenon over several decades of customer's available time decreasing. Norman characterizes these human need and lifestyle changes with the phrase: "Ozzie and Harriet don't live here anymore". Ozzie and Harriet were the co-stars of an old American television program called *The Adventures of Ozzie and Harriet*, which aired on television from 1952 to 1966, epitomizing the traditional American family during that time period. The structure of the traditional American family as it existed back in the 1950s has all but disappeared. At that time in history, it was the norm for the husband to work a full-time job and the wife to stay home full-time to care for the children. In today's world, the norm is for both parents to work full-time jobs. Norman continues the analogy by saying, "Ozzie and Harriet both come home from work and Harriet looks at Ozzie and says, 'I love you Ozzie and am crazy about you but I'm not going to cook dinner tonight'". This represents the present-day scenario that "Harriet" may have got up earlier and worked harder, may have earned more money than Ozzie, and wants someone else to cook the evening meal. This dramatic shift in available time and income for double-income households has prompted families to spend increasingly more money in restaurants and in prepared foods from supermarkets. With regard to restaurants in particular, customers also have added emotional needs fulfilled, such as feeling pampered, self-important and cared for. At the peak of the popularity of the Ozzie and Harriet show, only 15–20% of a family's food budget was spent in restaurants with the balance being spent in supermarkets. Currently, families spend over 50% of their food budget in restaurants and that percentage is increasing each year. These changing family dynamics prompted Dorothy Lane to offer an increased selection of prepared food. Dorothy Lane employ many chefs dedicated solely to cooking prepared foods in DLM's many restaurant kitchens to serve their customer's new lifestyle. In the "Ozzie and Harriet days", DLM's prepared food business represented roughly 1% of their overall business. Today, DLM's prepared food business is 7% of total sales. As a result, not only have customers' human needs changed but also who the leading competitors are. Norman now views restaurants as his biggest competitor. As a result, Norman believes that he should do everything in his power to offer restaurant-quality foods with the added benefit of time convenience that a restaurant cannot offer. In addition, DLM have instituted a home delivery service as an added convenience to their customers. Norman comments, "It takes time to pull into the local grocery store parking lot, park your car, walk into the grocery store, push a 30–40-lb shopping cart around a grocery store searching for items, and then wait in a checkout lane. Home delivery is something that Dorothy Lane have been doing for 20 years simply as a human kindness to their customers at no charge". Norman explains, "A lot of those customers who we do home delivery for are eighty to ninety years old and have shopped at Dorothy Lane since the 1950s, and we owe it to them". As Norman looks to the future, he would be satisfied if DLM could have 5% of their business as home delivery and do it profitably. To that end, he has instituted a new home delivery program called

"DLM in a Dash". "DLM in a Dash" offers customers the convenience of 24-hour online grocery shopping via a secure Internet
ordering system with a convenient pick-up service at their store of
choice. DLM charge a small minimum fee regardless of the order
size that is waived for the first order. The customer views the value
of this minimum delivery charge as "buying back" several hours of
personal time or additional business time, which can be used to earn
incrementally more money.

By losing present time, we lose all time.   W. GURNEY BENHAM

Promptness Reduces Anxiety, Which Communicates Respect

In almost every instance, if a firm can reduce the amount of time a
customer spends interacting with a business, the customer feels less
stressed and perceives the business has truly shown respect for the
emotional consequences of coping with a time-pressured life. In
addition, when a firm is prompt, not only does the customer win
but the firm increases its productivity and many times reduces its
costs as well. For example, Wal-Mart strive to be prompt with
customer service in the checkout area as well as helping their customers carry larger items out to their car. Every retailer struggles
with helping their customers check out quickly. One of the unique
ways this retailer addresses the promptness issue, which it refers to
as its "check out quickly" objective, is by using a program they
refer to as their "line buster" program. The checkout associates
monitor checkout lines to determine whether they are acceptable.
If any of the lines become longer than necessary, a roaming associate will approach a customer who is waiting in line and scan their
items with a hand-held scanner and give them a "line buster"
printout card. The customer hands the "line buster" card to the
cashier once they reach the checkout and it is scanned by the cashier
to immediately bring up all the scanned items from the hand-held
scanner. If there are any items that could not be scanned by the
hand-held scanner, the cashier enters the items at that time. The
cashier then accepts payment and the customer is promptly on their
way. An added benefit of this program is that if this particular
cashier is fairly new and not yet up to speed, the line buster card
created by the "line buster" associate transforms a potentially slow

cashier into a faster cashier. In addition, the "line buster" associate will many times pre-bag the customer's items while the customer is standing in line.

Men talk of killing time, while time quietly kills them.
DION BOUCICAULT

One of the worst industry offenders is the medical community. The medical industry has consistently shown that they have little regard for a patient's time. Industry average waiting time for doctors is 49 minutes in the reception area and 20 minutes in the treatment room. While wait times vary considerably between medical establishments, CDC studies have shown that patients wait an average of 49 minutes to see a doctor. Once the patient has waited in the waiting room and the examination room, the doctor must interact with a patient who is not only sick but also further agitated and frustrated by the long wait for care. One particular specialty doctor (Dr Levitt) has broken away from the standard medical practice of insisting that patients wait to be seen. He has set up his schedule so that there is little wait for patients. Dr Levitt's objective is that the patient will be shown to the examination room within five minutes of arriving at his office and from there will be seen by a physician within several minutes. Dr Levitt views waiting time as important because he has a high volume of patients under continuous treatment for chronic skin conditions. Not only has Dr Levitt virtually eliminated waiting, he also strives to create a warm and caring environment from the moment the patient walks in the reception area. For the few minutes that the patient does have to wait in the waiting room, there is an up-to-date supply of interesting magazines to read. Simple human touches such as having current magazines in the reception area make a strong statement that the patients are important. Conversely, when waiting rooms have old, worn magazines it is a subtle message that the doctor is apathetic about the patient's care. The underlying premise is that the doctor focuses equally on the convenience of the patient relative to the convenience of the practice. Creating this balanced focus on convenience does not occur without added effort from the doctor and staff. Dr Levitt is awake at 4 a.m. and sees his first patient at 5 a.m. every day, except Sunday. Not only do the extra hours reduce waiting time for patients but they also accommodate the work and school schedules that most people have. This is especially true for hourly workers who, because of the typical waiting time for a doctor, must take a half-day off of work and lose a half-day's wages. This scenario is not far removed from the hours kept by the milkmen of a bygone era. The milkman of 50 years ago would get up at 4 a.m. in the morning and start delivering by 5 a.m. because the needs of his customers dictated his delivery schedule. An added benefit to Dr Levitt's official scheduling comes from the fact that the insurance industry has ratcheted down the percentage of dollars that a doctor can earn from each treatment. Dr Levitt's hours have not only created more content customers but also enabled Dr Levitt to maintain a higher level of income.

Another good example of time consideration is Tudor Day Spa. The owner fine-tunes the appointment schedule to get the client where they need to be on time, not to suit her business appointment schedule. This focus on being considerate of the customer's time not only shows courtesy and respect but also promotes business efficiency. When Jane and her clients are focused on a scenario where both benefit from effective scheduling, both can operate more efficiently. For certain "hard to get" time slots, Jane encourages her clients to schedule three to four weeks in advance, providing better planning for both Jane and her clientele.

Respect Them as Equals, not Parent or Child

Create "equal partnership" type caring; avoid parental-type. It is important to always institute the right type of caring for customers. In some cases, firms will mistakenly institute almost "parental" type of caring for customers, which in many cases only serves to create a sense of disempowerment for the customer, i.e. I'm caring for you … because you are unable to take care of yourself". It is much more healthy to institute an "equal partnership" type of caring which is more advisory in nature than parental. This equal partnership type of caring recognizes a customers' individuality as well as their competence as adults (source: Wendy Eggleton).

Respect Cultural Differences

Understand cultural sensitivities – a customer's human sensitivities vary from culture to culture and country to country. These variations are important, particularly when these sensitivities can dramatically impact customer perception. For example, a leading North American financial institution was receiving a significant number of complaints having to do with a particular fee that had recently been levied on certain customer segments. Upon further investigation, the financial institution found that the customers who were complaining were not complaining because they felt unfairly treated themselves. They were complaining because they were concerned that other less financially fortunate customers were being burdened with these fees.

Respect Their Personal Space

Respecting the customer's personal space while being proactive in acknowledging them and offering them help is a critical skill for almost any business situation. An excellent example of this is how the world's largest retailer addresses the subject of its customers' personal space. Wal-Mart establish a personal, human connection with its customers by using a customer's physical space as the criteria for when to offer them personal assistance. Wal-Mart call this their "ten foot rule". Wal-Mart also refer to this "ten foot rule" as the "10-foot attitude", handed down from Sam Walton, Wal-Mart's founder. During store visits, Sam frequently encouraged associates to take the following pledge: "I want you to promise that whenever you come within 10 feet of a customer, you will look the customer in the eye, greet the customer and ask the customer if you can help him or if there is anything you can help him find". If the customer responds, "No thank you, I'm fine", the associate responds with, "Thank you for shopping Wal-Mart". If the customer responds with, "Yes, I'm looking for a particular item", the associate is responsible for personally and physically guiding the customer to where the item is located on the shelf as opposed to just giving a series of directions as to where the item may be located. In certain instances, this personal escorting of the customer by the Wal-Mart associate may lead to helping the customer with their entire shopping list. While some retailers feel that guiding the customer through their entire shopping list may take treating a customer like a human being to excess, Wal-Mart encourage their associates to rise to this customer humanizing opportunity. It is the opportunity to serve the customer in such a personal way that Wal-Mart place above all other store directives. This pledge was actually something that Sam had practiced since his childhood.

Balance Need for Personal Space with a Message of Caring

Balance the human need for "space" with the human need for acknowledgement. The need for space is an important facet of interacting with any customer and should be balanced with the parallel human need for recognition and attention.

John Higgins trains his salespeople to balance this fine line when customers enter the dealership. There is a fine line between giving customers the freedom to browse around the dealership and the need for acknowledgment or assistance from a salesperson. This "fine line" is even more delicate because of the legacy of heavy-handed sales tactics that dealerships have created over the years. When the salesperson initially approaches a customer on the dealership lot, it is simply the common courtesy of welcoming the customer and letting them know that someone is available to answer questions. In other words, the salesperson is communicating, "We acknowledge you're here and are at your service when you are ready". John realizes that customers don't want to be sold cars; they simply want to be assisted in making a good decision about buying a car. He employs a friendly and warm receptionist in his new car showroom who briefly explains that the customers will be given complete freedom until they desire attendance from one of the sales staff. It has been John's experience that after being given their freedom for 4–5 minutes, the customer will approach his receptionist to ask her if someone could assist them. Customers are also offered the simple hospitality of complimentary beverages, e.g. coffee, soft drink or water. This type of human freedom alleviates the legacy response by many consumers who fear they will be "attacked" once they enter what is perceived as an aggressive sales environment. This legacy response of being defensive and protective has been created over the years by over-aggressive dealerships. This is the worst possible emotion a dealership can elicit because helping customers buy luxury automobiles is about communicating in an emotionally neutral, non-threatening environment. Statistically, the average Lexus customer will visit a Lexus dealership four times before the customer purchases the automobile. If a customer feels attacked or threatened on the first visit, it is highly unlikely that they will feel comfortable returning to the same "threatening" buying environment. Most importantly, the customer will inevitably be "shopping around" other dealerships and will remember how they "felt" about their interaction rather than specific product attributes.

Respect Your Customer's Castle

There are few situations in which a customer's need for respect is more heightened than when they are in their home and are being visited by a business. Most face-to-face customer interactions are done on a business's premises where interactions follow fairly prescribed, traditional patterns. When a business's service rep or salesperson enters the sanctity of the customer's home, the rules change. The home visit experience by a business can be divided into two parts. The first part is with the person who schedules the home visit and the second part is with the person who actually makes the visit. This second and last part of the interaction usually has the greatest impact. A great scheduling experience can be shot down by a poor on-site experience.

Both parts may or may not be the same person. If it is a different person, the quality of the scheduling interaction will affect how the customer perceives the person who actually visits their home, either in a sales or service capacity. If the scheduling experience (with, for instance, a call-center rep) is an average experience but the experience with the person visiting the home is exceptional, the customer will still perceive the entire experience as an excellent experience. An excellent experience with a service rep will also positively influence how the customer perceives the call-center rep did with their scheduling job. An important part of making this scheduling call is to ensure that customers are transferred as few times as possible and that during this process, enough information has been gathered so that when the customer reaches the correct call representative, the customer can be helped without repeating their "story" for the second and third time. If the customer leaves a voicemail message for return call, how fast a business responds is critical to the customer's perception of service quality.

The call-center rep should be courteous and respectful, and most importantly should listen carefully to the customer without rushing them as if they are looking at a stopwatch and racing for a call volume goal. A critical component of being courteous and respectful is being able to narrow down the window in which the service technician arrives at the home. Usually creating a two-hour window for customers is a workable timeframe for them to coordinate their busy day and also allow the technician a big enough window to increase the probability that they can arrive at the agreed-upon time. The call-center rep's focus should be: "What do I need to do to remedy the customer's situation as quickly as possible?"

When the sales/service representative actually visits the customer's home, the customer's sensitivity and expectations of the interaction are heightened significantly. As with any visitor, the homeowner will be carefully assessing what type of person they are about to allow into the sanctity of their home. This makes having a neat and well-kempt appearance while maintaining a professional demeanor critical for any business guest. An important aspect in the customer's mind is how "respectful" the "business guest" acts toward their home. There are "little" signals of respect, such as offering to remove their shoes or place plastic over their shoes. Asking permission before entering different areas of the house is also a sign of respect. All of these "little touches" have a tremendous impact on whether the customer perceives the business visitor as "excellent" in whatever activity they have come to the home to accomplish. If the business guest is a service repairperson, it is important that they explain their activities or discoveries in simple terms with the homeowner. A simple but clear explanation of what the problem is and how it will be repaired is important. It is very helpful to physically show a homeowner the repair area itself as well as the damaged or malfunctioning parts. Repairs will often be made and the bill presented with little or no explanation about the repair. If any repair is not done right the first time the customer will perceive not only any additional visits but also the original visit as unnecessary intrusions. It will dramatically affect the customer's perception of the business's product and service. Correct and complete information must be gathered at the very beginning of the interaction so that, on arrival at the customer's home, the technician is not only prepared by knowing the nature of the repair but also has been dispatched with the correct parts.

When making a service call to repair a nonfunctioning item such as a dishwasher or garage door, by far the greatest impact a repair person will make on the customer's perception of the company is to fix this bad situation. However, there are additional points to be made by simply improving an average experience. Knowledge of the fact that most customers do not like to read instruction manuals offers a great opportunity to improve the customer's expereience by educating the customer. As a general rule, most customers do not like to read instruction manuals. This fact offers a great opportunity for the service technician to educate the customer about the functionality of the product, which increases their enjoyment of the product further, e.g. "Oh, by the way, if you press that button, it will make it easier on you and it will also function better ...". This is an unexpected courtesy that the customer will remember long after the sales or service rep departs. Another powerful human courtesy is for the service rep to offer information or advice on additional items in the customer's home. For instance, though he may be there to repair a refrigerator, he could offer helpful information about the microwave or dishwasher.

Once the sales or service representative has departed, a follow-up call can have significant impact on the customer's perception of the visit. Follow-up calls do not have to be made in every instance but should be done at least on a representative basis.

Show Respect by Trusting Customers' Integrity

Customers aren't criminals but in some situations a business may treat them as such. It is a common mistake to regard too many customers with suspicion. This occurs most frequently in activities such as returns to retail stores or other businesses. Little things such as forgetting a receipt when returning an item will cause many employees to cast a disbelieving eye on their customers, which can embarrass, frustrate, and even humiliate the customer.

It is usually better to treat customers as if they are honest (because they are) and not give them a "hard time" during such activities as returning items. A good example of this principle in action is Wal-Mart. Wal-Mart train their staff to give their customers the benefit of the doubt when returning items. As a result, customers don't get treated "as criminals" but simply human beings.

Respect Men and Women Equally and Their Differences

Businesses need to consider subtle gender differences when communicating respect. At his Lexus dealership John Higgins has observed that women are more comfortable being approached earlier than men because there has been a history of women not being treated as seriously as men in terms of being a legitimate buyer of automobiles. John has learned that it is best to give men slightly longer to browse because men value the space to investigate and evaluate information about automobiles on their own. There are numerous "faux pas" stories from other dealerships in which a woman will enter a dealership to purchase an automobile and the salesperson will ask when her husband will be in to make the final decision. There are countless stories of women who immediately left dealerships when they were ready to buy but didn't because of such disrespect.

> *The true republic: men, their rights and nothing more; women, their rights and nothing less.*   SUSAN B. ANTHONY
> (1820–1906; American suffragist)

> *Man's love is of man's life a part; it is a woman's whole existence.*   LORD BYRON

Show Respect Regardless of Social Status

This type of disrespect occurs most often when there are a wide range of differences in socioeconomic levels between customers and the people who interface with those customers. One of the most well-known examples of this, of course, is the medical industry. It is not uncommon for doctors to take on an air of superiority when interacting with patients. The "I'm better than you" attitude of some doctors is degrading to patients, particularly when these patients are feeling vulnerable and physically unwell. Dr Levitt makes every effort to be approachable, rather than superior, to his patients. Dr Levitt is a dermatologist and treats many adolescents where the potential for a large communication gap exists. As a result, he has developed several interaction styles to present himself as more approachable and to allow them to feel comfortable. Dr Levitt will sometimes break the ice with an adolescent by using language that disarms the aura of being an "almighty doctor", with greetings such as "How the 'f . . .' are you today?" or other collo-quialisms such as "Ssss . . . up?" (What's up?). This invariably relaxes the adolescent patient and they think, "Okay, this guy is cool". Another challenge for Dr Levitt is treating diseases that cause the patient to feel embarrassed or ashamed, such as sexually transmitted diseases. The sensitive nature of doctor/patient discus-sion requires exceptional sensitivity. Dr Levitt always seeks to find a common ground on which to disarm the patient's sensitivity in order to effectively communicate with the patient on any sensitive subject.

Trace Disrespect to Its Root Cause

In many situations, when customers feel that there is a lack of respect for their time or energies, the problem can be traced to an operational or "root" cause. An excellent example of this scenario occurred when Los Alamos National Bank (LANB) used their quality programs to increase customer satisfaction on their ATM network. Not long ago, LANB began receiving numerous customer complaints about their new ATM cards not working. Customers spent excessive, valuable time trying to use their new cards but could never complete a transaction. Thirty ATM customers found that their new cards would not function with the ATM. LANB had mailed out several hundred new ATM cards in this same batch. From their quality work, they knew that every cus-tomer complaint arises from a "root cause". They began by first investigating the actual mechanics of their ATM's, as well as any technology problems from the network itself. The quality team could find nothing initially. Ultimately, they did find the root cause in the physical card itself. Their supplier of ATM cards had inadvertently mailed out several hundred ATM cards with incorrect PIN numbers. Their quality process allowed them to avoid inconvenience and dissatisfaction for the remaining customers who had not yet used their ATM cards.

Create the Ultimate Respect – Hand Them the Controls

Focusing on increasing a customer's control, not decreasing it, shows the ultimate respect. Human beings as a species have an innate desire to control their environment. Many firms make the mistake of instituting procedures or policies of interaction that reduce a customer's control and as a result have a profound impact on their feeling of well-being and security. Therefore, it is always important for a firm to ask: "Are we enabling or taking away control from our customers by instituting this procedure or process?"

A firm can use problem scenarios to increase a customer's control over their environment. Human customers feel a loss of control when there is a problem in their interactions with a firm. The best way for a firm to return the sense of control to a customer in a problem scenario is to approach the customer only when the firm has a choice of potential solutions from which the customer can choose. This is an effective way for the firm to enable the customer to feel empowered to solve a problem by choosing a solution to the problem. Ultimately, helping the customer feel empowered and knowledgeable about potential solutions to problems will give them a sense of well-being because they have controlled their own destiny. Many firms approach problem solving with a dictatorial attitude – "Here's a problem and here's what we will do about it". This has a far less positive impact on the customer's sense of control and ultimate satisfaction with the firm's solution to the problem. The far more effective approach is – "Here is the problem, and here is the list of potential solutions. Which one would you feel most comfortable with?" Another powerful approach to increasing a customer's control is to create "rituals" or routines to guide the customer's interaction with the firm. The underlying emotional premise is that most people feel that routine gives them a sense of control and when the routine changes, they lose control.

Enable Control through Choice

Customers have an emotional need for respect. Businesses who enable customers to have control over interactions communicate respect for customers. Enabling customer control is created through choice. When businesses proactively create choices for customers, they actually increase their control at the same time as increasing the customer's control or "choice" in the interaction.

1   Customers need respect.

2   Giving control communicates respect.

3   Choice enables control.

Choices show respect for the customer's freedom and ability to choose. Recognizing this personal freedom and ability is acknowledging their dignity as human beings.

Build Commitment through Choice – People Having a Sense that They Are Involved in the Control of Their Lives

One of the most primordial instincts of human beings is to be in control. This goes to the essence of their instinct for survival. Giving a customer the perception of control indicates respect while alleviating negative emotions such as anxiety and fear. The desire for control in humans generates one of the eight primary emotions – fear. Fear creates anxiety and anxiety lessens trust. Trust is required before customers will purchase products. The more a business can give the customer the perception that they are in control of the interaction and its outcome, the more the customer will feel in control and therefore experience less fear and anxiety.

Businesses need to proactively create choices for customers prior to interactions. The choice could be a product feature, a service option, or to address the specific customer service problem. For example, if a business has scheduled a customer for a particular appointment, the business should always make a concerted effort to notify the customer immediately if there is a problem (appointment times are running late) to give them the choice to "go run an errand" or simply rebook at their convenience.

Provide Choice through "Can Do's", not "Can't Do's"

Customers find little or no value in being told what a business "can't do" for them. They are primarily interested in what the business "can do" for them. This is a common mistake for firms to fail to train employees to communicate in a "can do" mode rather than the "can't do" mode. Part of the Los Alamos National Bank's (LANB) "experience" is that customers are never told "no" without being offered a reasonable solution as to what can be done for them.

Show Respect for Extraordinary Life Events

Businesses need to create special provisions for those extraordinary life events that deserve extraordinary respect. These are situations in which customers are experiencing either a life crisis or celebration – both can be emotionally charged negatively or positively. Most businesses lose the tremendous opportunity to show enduring respect for life celebrations such as the birth of a child, marriage, or a new home purchase. Recognizing the importance of these events and offering special discounts can easily create a long-lasting, positive emotional reaction in the customer.

The biggest impact from not adequately showing respect is the damage from the lack of preparedness in reacting to a life crisis. It is often best to make a significant departure from normal procedures to avoid long-lasting and sometimes permanent scarring of the individual and the company's reputation/brand. Most of the time when there is an emotionally charged event between the customer and a firm, both end up losing, either emotionally or finan-cially. The customer loses faith in the company as well as having to endure further emotional pain beyond the root cause of their crisis. Employees can experience emotional damage from having to "fight" with the customer and there can be additional negative fallout, such as lost product and service patronage as well as ex-tensive negative word-of-mouth damage to brand. Complete dis-loyalty can be created if the company does damage to the extent that the customer decides – "I will never do business with that company again".

In most cases, the root causes of long-lasting damage in high crisis, emotional events are simple: a failure in technology or information, poor training, or just a bad day for a customer call representative. Damage to all concerned (the company, the customer, and the employee) can be avoided through excellent information systems, training and enabling customer-facing employees to react with extra compassion and leniency, and crisis process provisions. The cost of such activities is minimal compared to the potential damage created by poor handling of highly charged emotional situations.

The Cost of Disrespect

The following is a brief story of how information systems and policy provisions could have avoided major damage to a previously profit-able and loyal customer. For anonymity, I will refer to the customer as Pastor Rick. Pastor Rick's retired father died unexpectedly in the late 1990s. Prior to this time, all of Pastor Rick's family had been devout customers of their long-distance carrier for two generations. When Pastor Rick's father died, he became executor for the first time of his father's estate. One of his responsibilities was handling any outstanding bills that his father owed at the time of his death. As in many estates, certain assets were frozen and certain payments, such as social security, were stopped at the time of death. Pastor Rick traveled to his father's hometown in order to administer the estate locally. One of the first companies he approached was his father's local phone service provider, as his father owed them roughly $200. Pastor Rick provided the local carrier with his per-sonal address for all correspondence to be forwarded. They did express sympathy for his father's death and upon leaving Pastor Rick felt that the local carrier would handle this delicate situation in a humane way. After their return, Pastor Rick and his wife planned a short weekend trip away to rejuvenate themselves emotionally from the death. They decided to leave their daughter at home. It was her first time being left alone in charge of things at home. They lived in a fairly rural area, which meant that in order to make almost any phone call, they needed to use the services of their long-distance provider. It was extremely important that she be able to use their long-distance service in case of emergency. When they returned, they discovered their long-distance provider had cut off their phone service without warning. Upon investigation, Pastor Rick found that his father's local carrier had generated a list of customers who were delinquent on their bills and had transferred the list to the long-distance carrier. Pastor Rick's phone service had been cut off because he had provided his address in order to deal with his father's estate and the computer categorized him as being a delinquent customer. This happened despite the fact that Pastor Rick had informed the local carrier of the fact that his father had died and that the estate was in probate, and despite the fact that Pastor Rick had been a loyal customer for 25 years and in that time had never been late with a payment. This unannounced, and probably illegal, action by the long-distance carrier affected Pastor Rick on many emotional levels. One of his feelings was that the long-distance carrier had needlessly endangered their daughter after they had left her alone for the first time during that weekend. He also felt tremendous humiliation to have his phone service cut off without warning. Pastor Rick's attempts to contact the long-distance provider led him through a very long and complex process. As part of the process, Pastor Rick insisted that he be able to talk to a senior executive. He did manage to talk to senior executive's secretary and was assured that he would receive a formal letter of apology. No such letter ever arrived to ease the damage of their insensitive act. During this same time period of emotional stress, the local phone company contacted Pastor Rick by phone several times to "talk to his father about his father's outstanding phone bill". This was done after he had notified them in writing that his father had passed away. As a result, Pastor Rick decided to sever his relationship with a long-distance provider after 25 years of loyal patronage. Equally passionate decisions were made by all of Pastor Rick's three siblings and their families. All four of the siblings make it a

point to communicate this "heartless act" of both telecommunica-
tion companies to whoever is about to make a choice on telecom-
munication services. As with Pastor Rick, these stories get told in
both their personal lives and professional lives. Pastor Rick also
issued an edict at his 750-member church that no telecommunica-
tion services (local, long-distance, Internet, e-mail, cable) of any
kind would be purchased from this carrier or its business partners
regardless of the reason. The pervasiveness of this damage is
apparent when examination is made of the siblings careers –
Pastor Rick is a pastor of a large church; his brother is a researcher
at a major university; another brother is a salesperson for a national
firm, and his sister is employed at a major insurance company. Not
only did Pastor Rick adamantly refuse to ever use this long-distance
carrier but also made it one of his missions to communicate this
inhumane act to as many people as possible both professionally and
personally. Since then, Pastor Rick has been solicited numerous
times by the same long-distance carrier both personally and
professionally. Each time this long-distance carrier attempts a
solicitation, it only conjures up an image of an immoral and un-
ethical company which he, his family, and his church will never
patronize again. Call-center people who call Pastor Rick must
bear the emotional burden of his indignant diatribes to them
about their employer. The claims of superior price advantages
and excellent service fall on "deaf ears" as almost nothing would
ever erase the actions by the long-distance carrier during their time
of overwhelming grief and sadness from his father's unexpected
death. Ultimately, his father's estate was held in insurances,
which cannot legally be used for probate, i.e. to pay outstanding
bills after one's death. As a result, both the long-distance carrier
and local carrier did not recoup any outstanding bills. Pastor Rick
felt this was one of their "paybacks" for being so insensitive. While
Pastor Rick realizes that this release of anger (convincing potential
customers of this telecommunications company not to become a
customer, verbalizing his anger with unsuspecting phone
company solicitors) may be somewhat unfair, he still feels justified
in doing so because any company who has allowed itself, its employees, its systems to enable the perpetration of such insensitive acts is
deserving of it. A conservative estimate of the potential costs over a
ten-year period of Pastor Rick, his family, and his relatives not
patronizing these long-distance and local carriers as well as spread-
ing damaging "word-of-mouth" discouragement is $147 490 as a

result of his deceased father's $200 phone bill. This estimate is based on the following facts and assumptions over a 10-year period. If the cost is divided by the original $200 phone bill, the ratio is over 700 : 1.

Annual personal phone bill	Amount	No. of years	Total
Pastor Rick's	$1 200	10	$12 000
Pastor Rick's Church	$2 749	10	$27 490
Sibling 1	$1 200	10	$12 000
Sibling 2	$1 200	10	$12 000
Sibling 3	$1 200	10	$12 000
20 affected people	$14 400	5	$72 000
Total			$147 490

Note. The 20 affected people is the assumption that the negative word-of-mouth affected people such as business associates, other relatives, and grown children with an average annual phone bill of $720, who would not have patronized these phone companies for 5 of the 10 years in this calculation.

Respect Every Customer; Please Most of Them

Set the objective of making "most" of your customers feel like fulfilled human beings. It is important to acknowledge that not all customers will react in a positive way, no matter what efforts a business makes to please them. Certain human beings can be un-reasonable and all customers are human beings. In some cases, customers will be purposefully dishonest.

A recent research study revealed that 76% of people too often have seen customers being rude or disrespectful to sales or service people.

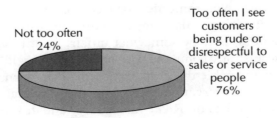

Figure 4.4   Customers can be rude and disrespectful

(data from *Aggravating Circumstances*, 2002 Public Agenda, used with kind permission)

Enjoy the Reasonable Customers;
Be Polite to the Rest

Most customers have reasonable requests and these customers should be the focus of a business. Unreasonable customers are either reacting to a previous emotional episode or are simply unreasonable people. Nevertheless, they still deserve a certain level of respect. Don Evans of OMI asks his employees to focus on customers who are reasonable. His philosophy is that each employee should focus on the positive aspects of a person or job. It is the tendency for people to become preoccupied with negative issues. Don has observed that if he asks his children what five negative events happened that day at school, they can almost immediately recount them. If he then asks for five positive events that happened that day, they have difficulty coming up with five events. When the five negative events are examined, they are not events that dominate the children's day yet they seem to be higher in their consciousness.

The owner of a leading Lexus Dealership, John Higgins, recalls several occasions in which customers have unfairly manipulated John's impeccable service practices. John recalls one incident where a customer brought in an older car for a $39 oil change with the main objective of using one of John's luxury service loaners for a six-day vacation. This person accumulated 2500 miles on the car over a six-day period. This scenario is very much the exception rather than the rule and is part of the relatively small price that being a human-oriented dealership creates. Even with a high-quality automobile such as a Lexus, some customers are impossible to completely satisfy. John recalls a customer who bought a previously owned Lexus and had driven it for four and a half months. He had left the car for service many times complaining of a mysterious odor which none of his service technicians could detect after multiple service sessions. Ultimately, John told the customer that he would return the customer's money for the automobile and other expenses such as insurance. John made clear to the customer that the check he had given him could be applied to buy another car from him or any other dealership in town. John's honesty and show of goodwill was retold by this particular customer to countless people. John also recalls dealing with a customer where he lost $4000 on a transaction but found that the positive public relations benefits in future business far outweighed the cash outlay. The other important cost advantage is that John has not litigated an automobile problem in his dealership in over ten years, i.e. doing the right thing for the customer is cost-effective. John realizes that the time, money, and bad public relations damage done to his dealership could not be recouped after litigating an automobile problem with a customer. In another scenario, John provided a customer's son with a twin turbo sports car as his 18th birthday present. The son got into an accident and the car ended up in John's dealership for repair. John's dealership couldn't adequately fix the car so John ended up returning the customer's money. All of these seemingly costly expenditures have paid dividends in customer loyalty far beyond their initial short-term cost outlay. Ultimately, John believes that 95% of his customers do not have unreasonable requests or expectations. They simply want to be treated with the respect every human being deserves and to receive value for their hard-earned money.

Address Customer Issues as Anxieties

Many times, it is far more effective for a business to approach business issues for what they really are – manifestations of human anxieties. A client's concerns (anxieties) are fundamentally a reflection of their management's concerns (anxieties) driven from their respective business objectives. The three primary anxieties facing most clients are Price, Time, and Quality (PTQs) of the project/service. New clients have high PTQ anxieties because there is a lack of history with a supplier, and therefore lack of trust. Longtime customers have low PTQ anxieties because there is a track record of performance in all three areas and therefore a foundation of trust. Most new clients will have high anxiety about the cost of a project and whether or not the deadline will be met. Clients are often fearful that management will criticize the output if it is lacking certain quality attributes. If the project is filled with robust features that cost more money, management may criticize the amount of money spent. Recognizing these three "concerns" as anxieties rather than demands is helpful in addressing them realistically and humanly for what they truly are – anxieties existing because of a lack of trust. It is always best to address this human anxiety head-on with human understanding, with honesty, and possibly with some humor. These PTQs will need to be addressed both in the negotiation process and throughout the project. An old humorous business adage, which is helpful in addressing these anxieties, is "you want cheap, you want fast, you want good ... take any two ...". In most situations, it is difficult to provide all three of these project attributes at the same time. There is no harm in telling the client that your business will attempt to achieve all three project attributes with the realization that achieving two out of three is still the most realistic scenario. This type of healthy attitude requires constant communication between client and supplier in order to give the client decision points at each stage of the project that will enable the client to change priorities or focus on any one of the three attributes. This fluid approach is effective because many clients only start off with a rough idea about any project. The more projects accomplished by the supplier and client, the lower the PTQ anxieties and the more efficiencies both for supplier and client are realized, i.e. less dwelling on added constraints and stipulations because of lack of trust and more focus on creating fundamental value.

The heart of treating customers with respect is to recognize their dignity as human beings. Respect begins with common courtesies such as please and thank you. Unlike other customer treatments in which certain customers may be afforded more attention and focus, respect should be awarded equally to all people regardless of how important they currently appear to the business. Respect must not be rationed based on how they behave, their similarities or differences, or position in the social scheme of society. Consistently showing respect means recognizing a person's dignity, time, differences, freedom, privacy and personal space. Showing disrespect is to dishonor any one of these areas. For business to show respect to all people is not only dignifying another human being but also keeping the door open to all business opportunities. Every effort applied to treating all people with respect will ultimately be fully rewarded over the lifetime of the business.

The word courtesy comes from the word court. To be courteous is to adopt the manners of the court, to treat one another like royalty. All day long we are, in some degree, helping each other to a better or worse self. We should conduct all our dealings with a view to the possibilities – there are no ordinary people. The little things, like please and thank you, are important and the only honest place to begin. Our lives are built one small brick at a time. With each little expression of thoughtfulness we create something of immense significance – character, both our own and that of others. Small acts of courtesy can have a big role in creating a more humane humanity.

(*Say Please, Say Thank You: The Respect We Owe One Another,*
by Donald W. McCullough, New York: G.P. Putnam's Sons, 1998)

5

Building Trust with Customers

BUILDING TRUST IS AT THE VERY FOUNDATION OF EVERY PURCHASE made by every customer. A customer will not purchase without trust. The customer must believe that the company will conveniently deliver the best product for them at a fair price, and treat them humanly. When businesses use the term "customer loyalty", they are actually referring to extended "trust" from a behavioral and social science perspective. When a customer says, "I am loyal to that company's products and services", they are really saying, "I trust you will consistently deliver the best value to me over time".

Trust helps forgive occasional performance issues. The trust built between business and business or business and customer fosters tolerance for intermittent operational issues.

> *Everything in the world may be endured, except continual prosperity.*   GOETHE

Jo Ann Brumit of Karlee found that if she had a more human relationship with the customer or vendor, the existence of that relationship would help through both the good and more difficult times of any economy or market. Jo Ann has witnessed specific instances in which Karlee are equally matched with their competitors' product delivery capabilities but, because of Jo Ann's more human relationship, the client has chosen to stay with her company.

A very simple way of testing whether an action will build trust or damage trust is to spot check yourself as a reference, e.g. "How

would I honestly react to those new service charges from my bank?"
If an employee in a business is distrustful of them, why would the
customer react any differently?

Trust is the customer's belief that the company will deliver on three
promises:

1   I will conveniently deliver the best product for you.

2   I will deliver it at a fair price.

3   I will interact with you as a human being.

Customers Don't Buy Until They Trust

Provide a sufficient amount of knowledge to employees about both
the customer and the products so that the customer begins to
develop sufficient trust to make a buying decision. This is very
important because every customer is continually assessing a firm
and its employees as to whether or not they are knowledgeable
enough to be trusted with the customer's business. The follow-on
to this is being honest enough to say, "I don't know", but being
willing and able to get the facts. Another aspect of this "trust"
dynamic is to be able to convey the facts clearly.

Focus on activities that build trust and avoid creating distrust.

Customers are continually judging firms as to whether to condition-
ally trust them. From the human perspective, any time a customer
decides to give a firm their money in exchange for a product or
service they are essentially "trusting" them to deliver something
of value. In the period after they have paid for the product or
service and before they have actually used the product or service,
they have made themselves vulnerable to the firm they chose to
patronize. Therefore, it is their vulnerability that the customer is
actually deciding to entrust to the firm, not specifically their money.
This alliance is in the form of conditional trust until such time as
the relationship experiences some form of trauma. When a traumatic situation occurs, the firm's reaction to this trauma causes
the customer to decide the degree of their trust.

It is not until trust has been tested that the customer is able to validate their initial trust of the firm. If the firm's reactions support an added sense of a customer's self-survival, the customer feels:

1   I was right to depend on this company.

2   I did the right thing by placing initial trust in them.

3   My trust in them will be less conditional moving forward.

If the firm's reactions reduce the sense of a customer's self-survival, the customer feels:

1   I was wrong to depend on this firm.

2   I did the wrong thing by placing initial trust in them.

3   It is a good thing I did not place any more trust in them than I did initially.

4   My trust in the future will be more conditional.

5   Their reaction tells me exactly how little importance I hold in the eyes of this firm.

Trust (and therefore loyalty) is created during trust "proof points" which can range from atypical interaction to handling a major customer crisis. The more significant the trust proof point is, the greater the trust that is built, and therefore, the greater the loyalty.

How loyalty is created is also evident in personal lives where life-threatening events unlocked lifelong loyalty to another human being. In most cases, casual friendships will remain as such until there have been one or more events that evolve this casual acquaintance into a true, long-lasting friendship. This degree of trust and loyalty remains dormant until it has been tested. Similar to personal relationships, a customer's relationship to a business will generally "coast along" with minimal degrees of trust and loyalty until some event happens to threaten a human being's sense of emotional security. When a business begins to consistently respond to problems in an exemplary way, the casual customer/business relationship will typically evolve into a higher degree of trust and loyalty.

One particular financial institution witnessed this pattern of trust and loyalty increase beyond normal levels following problem-solving events when they began segmenting customers who felt their problem was handled with excellence versus those who felt it was merely adequate. The firm's measurements indicated that the customer trust and loyalty of those customers who had experienced a problem was actually higher than that of those customers who had not experienced a problem. Until the customer experiences a problem, their trust is conceptual only, i.e. the customer only hopes, not believe, the business can be relied upon.

A firm can accomplish this trust building by surveying customers specifically on how their trust is affected by what the firm does during their interactions.

Do What's Right, Do It Right, Do It Right the First Time

Doing the "three rights" is a useful strategy for building trust. One of the many useful ideas that came from the Malcolm Baldrige Quality Award process is the "three rights", i.e. do what's right, do it right, do it right the first time. Doing what is right lays the foundation for customer fulfillment. Doing it right is a more rewarding and satisfying way to work than doing the wrong thing, doing it incorrectly, or procrastinating.

Doing it right the first time saves time, as the task doesn't have to be redone later.

Work without a Net – the Efficiencies of Trust

One of the most damaging business attributes on operational efficiency in today's business environment is lack of trust.

In the video production business, it's common for most businesses to strive to receive the largest deposit possible "up front". As soon as the "shoot" is completed, the client is required to pay for the shoot (progress payments). When the editing is completed, all monies must be paid before the client gets the final product. One video company, Kern Video, have taken a different approach by applying a trust-based approach based on honesty and a good working relationship with their clients. Kern Video's policy is no deposit, contract, or progress payments required. The initiation of the invoice only occurs when both business and client agree that the project is completed. On the surface, this approach appears to be high risk compared to traditional video business procedures. In practice, Kern Video have found this approach has less risk, more efficiency, generates more business and achieves an impeccable payment history. In order to operate in this trust-based business model, a business must deliver a little more than expected and the client must be basically honest. Kern Video has found that even if the client's payment history is inconsistent, a client is more apt to first pay the supplier who has delivered the best value. Kern Video save tremendous accounting and administrative time by not drawing up contracts and not collecting deposits and progress payments, plus there are tremendous savings from the legal expenses of drawing up and enforcing legal contracts and payments. They have also acquired business from competitors who require hefty deposits at a time when the client does not have the capacity to pay a large deposit. This policy keeps his business/client relationship from starting with a legalistic framework rather than with a highly human and personal relationship. If business is handled with the traditional "lack of trust", all of these additional costs will probably exist; but the potential added expenses of the "trust" approach rarely manifest themselves. Kern Video apply these savings toward revenue-generation activities. They also create a "human" environment far beyond their competitors, who operate with strict contractual guidelines. As a result, the "working without a net" approach also increases work enjoyment for both Kern Video and their clients. Starting a relationship by discussing detailed legal contracts is an explicit communication to clients that the business does not trust them. Most contracts are initially designed to give the upper hand to whoever writes the contract. Conversely, when the business "works without a net" and knows that the client will not be paying until they are satisfied, it is a compelling reason for the business to do the very best job it can. In addition, the client probably would give a more favorable "word-of-mouth" advertise-ment for a business that totally satisfied them without a contract compared with a business that shackled them to a rigid contract and whose satisfaction was marginal. In many situations, a supplier may have legally satisfied the provisions of the contract and be able to force payment, despite the fact that the client was not satisfied, but legally bound to pay by the terms of the contract. The likelihood of this customer engaging in a long-term profitable relationship is minimal.

One of the small "trust" items for Jane Manfre of Tudor Day Spa is the manner in which she processes customer payments. For regular clients, Jane keeps credit card numbers on file so it is painless for the client to receive a service and pay for that service with little or no effort. This can only be done because Tudor Day's clients im-plicitly trust Jane with their financial details. Trust breeds trust.

Honesty Increases the Customer's Ability to Forgive

It is more important to focus on how honestly a business commun-icates performance issues such as service delays rather than focusing on covering up the delay. John Higgins comments, "When the cus-tomer is notified, they're notified why (the problem occurred); that's all they want to know, they just want to be informed; they're not mad at you when it happens; they just want to know; they don't want to make a trip out (to the dealership) to find that out; you just have to have a dialogue with the customers". For example, if a parts availability issue arises for a car that is promised at 5.00 p.m., the customer will be notified of the delay two or three hours prior to the promised time. In most cases the customers are very comfortable with any delay because of the common courtesy shown to them in communicating the problem. Also, because they have been given a brand new Lexus loaner car, they are "feeling" quite special as it is, i.e. "that's no problem, I'm driving a brand-new Lexus with a full tank of gas". John maintains a strong fleet of 33 brand-new service loaners exclusively for his customer's convenience. Maintaining this fleet of service loaners costs him, operationally, $8000 per month in terms of interest, gas, and insurance. He believes that the repeat business and long-term loyalty gained from this $8000 expenditure has returned exponential financial rewards. This is not to say that operational effectiveness and efficiency is a second priority. In fact, excellence is the top priority in every aspect of the underlying operational effectiveness to deliver on promises to customers. John estimates that 95% of their service commitments are kept. This percentage of service commitments is kept both for new and for previously owned automobiles. Keeping service commitments is far easier with a high-quality automobile such as a Lexus. John previously sold other manufacturers' automobiles that had continual problems, multiplying the difficulty of delivering on such a high percentage of service commitments. The very nature of a complex mechanical product makes it a reality that repairs will sometimes need to be reworked. In addition, the increasing sophistication of the automobile's mechanics and electronics has created many service problems that are intermittent and extremely elusive. This increases the importance of admitting the human challenges of attempting to repair sophisticated and elusive service problems. Allowing employees to be "human" with customers frees them from the awkward and compromising position of having to "bend the truth" regarding certain human errors. The real tragedy is not the mistake itself but the awkward way employees are forced to handle the mistake.

When Contemplating Ethics, Picture Your Next Decision in Tomorrow's Headlines

Test the ethics of a contemplated action by asking the question, "Would I want to see it in the headlines tomorrow morning?"
LITTLE YELLOW BOOK

Be Proud and Bold about High Ethical Standards

Be Bold and Mighty forces will come to your aid. GOETHE

Most highly ethical businesses find that the more outspoken and proud they are about their ethics, the more support they garner for their business. Jo Ann Brumit is often asked whether Karlee's public stand on their business's humanizing Christian values offends other businesses and customers. Jo Ann has found that their business relationships are not offended by their stand on humanizing Christian values but, in fact, it creates a rallying effect of support.

Be Proud and Bold about Where and How the Business Makes Its Profit

There are few secrets about how most businesses make a profit, yet many businesses continue to create the "shell game" in attempting to hide their pricing strategy. The abundance of information available to customers today over the Internet makes such efforts futile in almost every industry. It is the best strategy to be honest with the customer in order to gain their trust. It is only through trust that any customer buys any product. This is particularly important in industries where trust has historically suffered. Honest communication will also add the unexpected benefit of a self-segmenting market. John Higgins's Lexus Dealership is very upfront with his customers about his pricing strategy. He communicates that he will be competitive on car prices but it will not be "the cheapest price in town" because in order to deliver the level of impeccable service that he consistently delivers, a portion of the service funding comes from car sales. John is very clear that his dealership is in business to make money and reveals its profit margins openly to its customers. He realizes that over 60% of his customers have already price shopped the Internet to research exactly what John's costs are for any particular car model prior to walking into his dealership. His clientele consists of physicians, attorneys, and corporate executives who appreciate his honesty about profit margins and do not begrudge him reasonable margins (6–7% gross margin on new cars). If his customers believe there is value in his level of service and human integrity, a reasonable profit margin is acceptable. An extremely well-managed, profitable automobile dealership generates roughly 4% profit margin on total sales. A large, domestic US automobile manufacturer dealership will make roughly $1\frac{1}{2}$% profit on total sales in comparison. At this level of sales volume, it is more challenging to be "warm and fuzzy" with the customer. In the case of these large domestic automobile dealerships, if they made $1 million in profit, they would have had to sell approximately

$100 million dollars in automobiles and service. These margins are similar to that of the grocery industry.

John's philosophy is that his dealership will still be very competitive on price without having to court customers who are only interested in the cheapest price and do not place a high value on service excellence and the human touch. John Higgins has observed that most customers forget within 30 days exactly what price they paid for their automobile. On the other hand, the customer will always remember if the first time they brought their luxury automobile back for service they felt abused or dehumanized. Ultimately, customers fundamentally don't want their purchase free of charge. They do want to be informed about what they paid for, what that "something" was, and what the reasoning was. They also want to feel that the business is pleased they have been chosen, and that the business is thankful for their patronage. The typical customer does not want to be overly fondled and doted on. They just want basic acknowledgement and recognition of their human existence.

Without passion man is a mere latent force and possibility, like the flint which awaits the shock of the iron before it can give forth its spark.   HENRI-FREDERIC AMIEL

Life is either a daring adventure, or nothing. Security does not exist in nature, nor do the children of men as a whole, experience it. Avoiding danger is no safer in the long run than exposure.
HELEN ADAMS KELLER (1880–1968)

Promise to Keep Your Promises

The best way to keep your business's promises is not to make promises the business can't keep. Unfulfilled promises will cause tremendous damage to trust. In some business environments, employees make promises they never intend to keep. This is a recipe for disaster. Don Evans of OMI, clearly instructs his employees not to make a promise to begin with. He states that if an employee makes a promise for OMI, OMI will keep it.

Earn Loyalty, Don't Buy It

Make decisions on how much loyalty the business really wants and what lengths the business is willing to go for it. Avoid creating loyalty through incentive-based loyalty programs as these type of programs create "empty" loyalty with little or no trust created in the process. Companies who use incentive-based loyalty programs soon find that these programs only create loyalty to the incentives, e.g. money, coupons, points, upgrades, and deals. Loyalty disappears as quickly as the incentives disappear. Either the incentives are no longer offered, or a competitor offers a better one.

Build Trust through Building Customer's Knowledge and Behavior

Customers only buy when they have created some level of trust with a business. Trust is created through knowledge. Therefore, a business must be able to educate their customers both through their employees and through automated systems.

At John Higgins's leading Lexus Dealership, it is critical that his salespeople know as much as possible about a very technical product – the luxury automobile. John's efforts to educate his salespeople are supported by the extensive education the Lexus manufacturer provides. Lexus have also created a luxury car comparative tool called Lexus labs. This automated tool is designed to assist in comparing Lexus automobiles with other comparable luxury cars on an attribute-by-attribute basis, e.g. Jaguar, BMW, and Mercedes-Benz. The Lexus labs system will output competitive comparisons for almost any product attribute (engine size, interior size, stereo wattage, etc.). While the Lexus labs system provides this detailed information at the salesperson's fingertips, most of John's salespeople already know this level of detail without referring to the system.

Build Trust by Cultivating Business Relationships with Similar Ethics

Building trust between two businesses has a much higher probability of occurring if both businesses have similar ethics. Therefore, it is important to use ethics as one of the criteria for any future business relationship. Jo Ann Brumit of the Malcolm Baldrige National Quality Award winning company, Karlee, states that she would not do business with companies whose ethical standards are not on the same level as Karlee's standards. There would not be enough trust for the relationship to function effectively.

Build Trust to Create Loyalty

Trust is the primary prerequisite for loyalty. Trust equates to "I'll believe in you". It is the primary prerequisite for loyalty, which equates to "I'll be there for you". Complete trust is unconditional. If a business truly desires to establish long-term loyalty, they must understand the underlying code of trust. Achieving degrees of trust and loyalty has its costs and should be reserved for those customers who a business feels justify the cost of creating the respective degree of trust and loyalty desired.

Build Trust through Operational Excellence

Operational excellence is one of the foundations of trust for customers. Without delivering on the basics, e.g. product quality, price, and availability, other efforts to build trust with customers will be academic.

Wal-Mart are a good example of the business that strives for operational excellence as one of their three basic beliefs.

1   Service your customers.

2   Striving for excellence.

3   Respect for the individual.

In regard to servicing your customers, associates are taught and believe that customers always come first. Customers' needs come above and beyond any project that is going on in the store at the time.

In regard to striving for excellence, associates are always asking operational questions such as:

+ Are we in stock for our customers?

+ Do we have the right products in stock or did they have to wait?

+ Are we priced correctly?

+ Do customers believe we're getting them through checkout quickly?

+ Is our store clean?

Wal-Mart measure the execution of these beliefs by conducting simple monthly surveys. They call 12 Wal-Mart customers within the store's local community each month to track their success. This is all part of the Wal-Mart report card that each store receives.

Wal-Mart expand their operational excellence with specific follow-up processes. Consistent and caring follow-up not only serves to ensure that the necessary customer activities have been completed but also creates a feeling of importance in the customer. Wal-Mart has made customer follow-up an important aspect of customer strategy to ensure that customers do not "fall by the wayside" because of the fast-paced days retailers often have. They log every customer call into a store manager's logbook with a designated follow-up process called "Letter to the President". This record of each customer's need or complaint is then entered into a computer log. A manager or associate returns each call to discuss the customer's needs with annotations made in the computer log as to:

1 The identity of the customer.

2   The result of the conversation.

3   When the customer's complaint was resolved.

This log is then printed out and physically placed in the store manager's "Letter to the President" logbook. The logbook is then systematically sent to Wal-Mart's President for review.

Build Trust by Sending Customers to Your Competitors (based on an idea of Norm Kern)

Having the courage and honesty to send customers to a competitor who is better suited to the customer's needs, will ultimately serve the recommending business's long-term objectives. In many cases, competitors have some relationship with each other. If that relationship is built on an appreciation for each other's strengths and weaknesses, each can direct customers to the other when it serves the customer best. In this type of cooperative environment, the referring company will get additional respect and trust just from the simple fact that they had the courage and honesty to put the customer's needs first. Most businesses have experienced that referred customers will almost always either return to the referring company for additional projects or create very positive word-of-mouth advertising. When they accept a project from a client for which they are less suited than their competitor, not only will the business have to expend an inordinate amount of resources to compensate for its relative lack of competency, but also they end up falling short of the client's expectations. Further damages to the company occur when the client ultimately finds out they would have been better served by going to a competitor in the first place and they will lower their opinion of the business that accepted their project. The client may not express explicit resentment toward the business for being "quiet" about their lack of expertise but they will have lost out on a unique opportunity to create an indelible impression of honesty and integrity. Good impressions are priceless and almost always reward a business with future activity. In many cases, just the show of intent of having the clients' interests at heart will cause the client to respond, "I don't care, I want you to do it". In this scenario, the business has lost absolutely nothing and has actually gained an invaluable attribute of integrity and trust. What makes this impression so long-lasting is that the client knows that such an unselfish recommendation is not in the short-term best interest of the referring business. A business that is only honest when it serves their best interests to be honest will almost always fail to gain the customer's full trust. A business having a reputation for integrity and honesty will find decisions involving referrals biased in their favor. A business, knowing that a client was referred by a competitor, will not only go to great lengths to satisfy this client but also will feel comfortable making reciprocal referrals. An unexpected benefit of this seemingly altruistic approach is that it provides an unquestionable competitive sanity check. If a business finds itself increasingly sending clients to other businesses, it is an indication that the business may need to reassess its core competencies. This could entail either changing the business's core activities or seeking ways to improve its core business activities. The chain of being honest with your customers as well as being honest with yourself keeps the customers fulfilled and the business focused on what it does best. Sending customers to your competitors was captured in Valentine Davies's 1947 novel and movie, *Miracle on 34th Street*, where arch-rivals Macy's and Gimble's department stores sent customers to each other if either store didn't have what the customer really needed. Their new benevolent policy was created after they witnessed the tremendous upswell of loyalty and added business when Macy's "real" Santa Claus genuinely began the practice. *Miracle on 34th Street* continues to draw its appeal from audiences around the world by reaffirming ideas of faith in a modern, often-cynical world. This movie explores, philosophically, the always-timely seasonal issues of faith and trust as the basis of real-life miracles.

Knowledge Builds Trust

A significant aspect of creating trust is educating the customer. Educating the customer requires information to create customer knowledge. The customer knowledge is applied to a decision about whether to trust the company (buy or not buy). This knowledge transfer can take the form of such activities as sales calls, service calls, marketing and advertising.

As referenced in Chapter 6, "Communicating humanly with customers", Wal-Mart use knowledge to build trust for its promise of "always low prices, always Wal-Mart" branding statement by:

+ Knowledgeable and friendly greeters.

+ Paging announcements.

+ Display flyers.

+ "Was" cards.

+ "Starburst" price signs.

+ "Competitive cart rail" display.

+ "Dare to compare".

Educate Your Employees to Educate Your Customers

A business cannot build trust unless it can effectively transfer knowledge to customers. One of the central ways of transferring knowledge to customers is through employees.

Wal-Mart use a computer-based learning program (CBL) to educate their associates. Every associate must go through the CBL training course before they spend time on the sales floor. Their CBL transfers product knowledge to the associates for the departments in which they will be working or, as they refer to it, "living" (more humanization). The associates start with a one-hour CBL session, and then are put on the sales floor for a two-hour period to put into practice what they have just learned in the CBL training session. Each associate has a store "sponsor" who is part of the sponsorship committee that is set up to ensure that associates have the best mentor possible. These sponsors are experienced store associates who are mentors to the newer associates during their training. Knowledge transfer is best undertaken when new associates have a mentor to help them understand how to apply it in the place where they "live", i.e. work. In addition, they conduct update meetings for all three of their shifts. These update meetings consist of the introduction of new products and their promotions, associate policy changes, community events, and safety. In addition there are bulletin boards posted for associates.

The owner of Tudor Day Spa begins building trust in customers by making sure employees are up-to-date on all the latest techniques and product advancements. She regularly holds education sessions with her staff, both off-site and on-site. Jane herself is a certified instructor and holds open discussion meetings monthly with her staff to discuss products, clients, and any factors that add or detract from their ability to treat customers like human beings. These staff meetings include role-playing activities to enhance interactions with clients and keep the stylists informed of the latest trends and styles, plus break room bulletin boards are regularly updated with information. Jane also pays a portion of her stylists' state certification education, which requires that each stylist have eight hours of education for license renewal every two years. Jane also ensures that customers can acquire knowledge themselves through the "launch pad", an unobtrusive area in the entryway detailing the beauty products, trends, and styles in which customers are interested. Another approach for helping customers gain knowledge is allowing them to educate themselves in the privacy of their own home. Any stylist who sells a customer beauty products will offer detailed instructions about to how to use those products. Jane has created a special instructional format called a "prescription pad" to be used as a roadmap for applying the beauty products at home. Without these detailed instructions only 10–20% of clients could achieve the same results at home that the salon achieves.

Build Trust by Taking Ownership When Rightful Ownership is Unclear

A company's willingness to initially own a problem regardless of the contractual "fine print" goes a long way in building integrity, trust, and loyalty. This proves a business works toward the "always there for you" scenario that is based on long-term trust. Businesses who seek to look for gray areas in their customers', suppliers', or business partners' contract may avoid certain short-term expense items but will ultimately pay the price in trust and further business. Jo Ann Brumit of Karlee has found that taking ownership of a problem when rightful ownership is unclear will be repaid in future loyalty and further business.

Build Trust by Keeping Promises

For every one promise that is broken, regardless of how small, it will take six continuous promises kept to erase the legacy of distrust created from the original broken promise.

When Promises Fail, Compensate the Customer

All businesses are human and make mistakes. As such, all businesses make promises that sometimes cannot be kept. When a business makes a promise to a customer that cannot be kept, the business should compensate the customer in a satisfactory manner. This compensation oftentimes will help erase a negative impression and restore lost trust. It is extremely important to keep your promise to the customer because the consistency of promises kept directly affects the customer's trust, as well as the customer's level of anxiety. This trust must be intact for any follow-on purchases. Many times, keeping promises to customers comes down to simple product availability. Product availability typically has three dimensions that must be satisfied to keep customer trust:

1   Price.

2   Location.

3   Time.

An additional burden in terms of promises kept is being subject to a local vendor's delivery schedules. For many large retailers, local vendors play an important part in supplying products to their stores and are usually not directly routed through a major retailer's main logistical system. Wal-Mart's food department is comprised of roughly 25% of products delivered directly by local vendors. Their electronics department has 10% of the products delivered by local vendors. The main way to control poor delivery practices is simply to monitor and then take action to replace vendors who are consistently "disappointing" customers. Another approach is to have a plan in place to compensate customers for the promises that were broken. Empowering store managers and associates to authorize additional discounts, e.g. 10% off the purchase or a $10 gift certificate, can accomplish this. Special plans should also be in place for higher compensation depending on how much emotional fallout occurred when the promise was broken. In these cases, an additional percentage or larger gift certificate maybe appropriate.

Create Trust Based on Unquestionable Integrity

Land Rover have instituted a special program promising customers that the price offered for their used car will remain valid whether they purchase a Land Rover or another automobile. This program sends a strong message of integrity to customers. It is referred to as Land Rover's "bid to buy" promise. In this program, the Land Rover Center will offer a prospective customer a better than market price for their used car when they are considering purchasing a new Land Rover. After making the commitment to buy the customer's used vehicle, Land Rover will still follow through with its promise even if the customer buys a different car from another dealership. This "bid to buy" program speaks a clear message about Land Rover's integrity.

Because of the potential loss of trust from customers, a Land Rover dealership have chosen not to take advantage of a state legal loophole allowing them to increase their profit margins by adding a 10% incremental service charge to a customer's service bill. This dealership's state law allows automobile service providers a 10% variation between the repair estimate and the actual repair. Even though the law allows this variation, the emotional repercussions for the customer who receives any discrepancy between the estimate and the actual repair is significant. This scenario quickly damages customer trust in the dealership. This dealership have decided to take the road of integrity and therefore build trust.

Regain Trust from a Legacy of Distrust by Differentiating Behavior

Creating a legacy of trust to dismantle historical distrust based upon the industry, a predecessor, a partner, or through a supply chain is a difficult but necessary goal if your business is prey to historical trust issues. The automotive industry is one that suffers from a legacy of distrust. When prospective customers walk into a dealership, they fear that while they may be able to negotiate a "great" deal on the car, the dealership will attempt to make up the foregone margin on follow-up service and maintenance activities. The distrust in the automobile industry of dealerships and the fear that dealerships will "rip them off" with unreasonable and unfair service expenses is a disadvantage. John Higgins's Lexus Dealership has had success in fighting this uphill battle to prove his dealership's fairness and integrity in all their dealings. John has witnessed that this distrust is most effectively alleviated simply through "word-of-mouth" about the integrity of his service department. In terms of the supply chain, the Lexus manufacturer has created a "trust lineage" with their dealerships that is the exception rather than the norm in the automobile industry. Most Lexus dealerships view the Lexus manufacturer as a true partner and not an adversary. This level of human trust permeates every aspect of their relationship and those subtleties can be felt right through to the retail customers themselves. John has found that whenever his dealership has approached their manufacturer with questions about systems or standards, the manufacturer has listened with an open mind for change and improvement. John estimates that over the past 10 years, 90% of the dealership/manufacturer interactions have led to positive improvements in handling customers. Ultimately, this trusting relationship has better prepared them for the future. There are other well-known automobile manufacturers with large dealership networks whose relationship is characterized by an adversarial and distrusting relationship. Another strategy that John takes to defuse the historical distrust in the automobile industry is specifically avoiding the clichés that surround the negotiation process of car buying. He has instituted a process whereby customers will not have to be engaged in the proverbial "running back and forth to the sales manager's office for a better price". This type of "haggling" promotes the perception that the automobile buying process consists of "a winner and a loser", i.e. dealership wins, customer loses or customer wins, dealership loses. John is also very public about his "fairness in pricing" policy where what one customer pays compared to another customer on any given day will only fluctuate by several hundred dollars. On certain occasions there is a larger price spread between customers because of the trade-in factor. This fair pricing policy is specifically aimed at defusing the distrust created by certain automobile dealerships. The irony of the situation is that automobile dealerships are often held accountable for honest dealings but the customer is not. Much of this has to do with the public perception that it is OK to "pull a fast one" on a dealership by sneaking a car with a hidden problem for a trade-in. Certain customers justify this by thinking the dealership would try and do the same thing to them if they had the chance. In this unfortunate situation the dealership has virtually no recourse for being "tricked" by a dishonest customer whereas the customer has several recourse options against a dishonest dealership. This places an added burden on defusing a legacy of distrust and creating a new legacy of trust with Customers as People. John recalls a customer who was sure that his new automobile emitted some strange gas from the heater system causing him to pass out while he was driving. John personally took the customer's car 1300 miles and his service manager drove it 800 miles with no sign of any such gas. John ultimately gave this customer a brand-new car and sold this customer's car to his brother. John's brother subsequently never had a problem with the car and the customer's new car never had any such problem.

Do the "Right Thing" for the Customer

Always doing the right thing for customers will build long-term trust. Norman Mayne of innovative Dorothy Lane Market realizes that many of his competitors set up their stores to optimize sales and not necessarily cater to the convenience and human needs of the customers. Many retailers place the commonly purchased items, e.g. milk, eggs, coffee in the furthest corner of the store hoping for impulse buying as they force customers to walk past all the other items in the store. This self-serving tactic casts a shadow of distrust over the entire store as to whose best interests they are serving. This distrust causes the customer to wonder, "This store is inconveniencing me by making me walk all the way across the store just to buy milk just so they can coerce me into buying more. I wonder what else they are doing to prioritize their interests over mine?" In contrast, DLM place their coffee at the very front of the store where customers can conveniently purchase their cup of designer coffee. This allows them to quickly get in and out of the store if all they are interested in at that time is their morning coffee. DLM also place their homemade bakery shop next to their coffee shop not only for convenience but to enhance the feeling that DLM is more like a "home" rather than an institutional grocery store. As Norman is fond of saying, "Whatever direction our competitors go, we go in the opposite direction".

In another example, Norman proved to his customers that they could trust him to take care of them in competitor price wars. Several years ago, Norman was faced with a "milk war" between local grocery stores. Milk prices had been slashed to 99 cents per gallon when it had previously been selling for $1.99. The grocer's cost for a gallon of milk remained at $1.75. DLM continued to sell milk for $1.99 despite its competitors selling the same gallon of milk for 99 cents. In order to do the right thing for its best milk customers, DLM analyzed who its best milk customers were and mailed them each a coupon offering a gallon of milk for 49 cents with a limit of five gallons per week. Norman believed that it was possible to still do the right thing for his customers without losing as much money as his competitors were during this frenzied milk war. Norman's logic was, why should DLM lose 75 cents on every gallon of milk at a weekly volume of 10000 gallons, i.e. $400000 potential annual loss when it could do the right things for its best milk customers with minimum losses. They also realized that if DLM had participated in the milk war, many more transient "cherry picking" customers would have taken advantage of the low pricing and increased DLM's potential annual loss. Norman's actions clearly showed that any business can show customers acknowledgment, respect, and trust even in the most cut-throat of business environments without having to imprudently slash profits caused by impulsive reactions to protect customer patronage.

The time is always right to do what is right.
MARTIN LUTHER KING, JR

To implement the human touch in a business with the certainty, conviction, and depth of a passionately courteous individual, a business will need strong leadership and the rigors of process management to evolve the intuitive art of the human touch into a repeatable and reliable discipline. Through the strong leadership of Horst Schulze, Ritz-Carlton were able to make important strides in proving that genuine caring can be successfully implemented as a process and the most important driver of long-term profitability. Ritz-Carlton have proven that what many had previously thought was a soft and indefinable art is definable, measurable, and an improvable science. Ritz-Carlton's path has been well structured by applying the Malcolm Baldrige Quality Award criteria as a means to an end. They have approached their genuine caring as a continuously improvable process and the lack of it as a "defect" with specific root causes. At the foundation of their genuine caring is the careful selection of a truly caring staff that are trained by the best, respected by all, and fully empowered. From their three steps of service that includes a warm and sincere greeting, anticipating and complying with guest needs, and a fond farewell to the declaration that "We Are Ladies and Gentlemen Serving Ladies and Gentlemen", Ritz-Carlton have shown that when both staff and guests are treated with acknowledgement, respect, and trust, extraordinary levels of service can be achieved and sustained.

6

Communicating Humanly with Customers

The greatest compliment that was ever paid me was when one asked me what I thought, and attended to my answer.
HENRY DAVID THOREAU

I T IS CRITICAL FOR EVERY BUSINESS TO FIRST UNDERSTAND WHICH human needs (if satisfied) will most likely create the greatest feeling of humanness. Secondly, they must understand what type of behaviors and their respective messages have the highest probability of fulfilling these specific human needs during a customer interaction. And third, they must also understand what behaviors facilitate the communication of humanness between business and customer. It is actually the ability to listen or receive messages from customers that is the most important communication skill and the one that is most often absent.

In order to accomplish this, business must understand the process by which human messages are sent and received during customer interactions. Business must learn how to be both a good listener (receiver) and a good communicator (sender) of messages that foster emotional well-being. While customers have a complex array of emotions and needs that create feelings of humanness, it appears, from the results experienced by early practitioners and through research, that there are three primary human needs that cause customers to feel most human before, during, and after buying decisions. These human needs are acknowledgement, respect, and trust. After business develops a basic understanding of these needs, they can communicate messages specifically targeted to satisfy these needs.

It is also important that these messages are perceived as genuine and not "put on" to elicit a desired response from the customer. Messages of acknowledgement, respect, and trust building perceived in this manner actually damage interactions. In many cases, it may have more impact to initially focus on erasing "negatives" rather than enhancing or adding the "positives", i.e. initially alleviate disrespect or distrust rather than enhance respect or trust.

Figure 6.1 offers a framework for understanding the process of how a business communicates humanness as well as how the customer interprets the messages of humanness from a business.

Leaders represent the needs of themselves and their shareholders. They communicate these needs through behaviors that create messages, which are interpreted by employees. There is up to 80% correlation between how "human" leaders treat employees and how fulfilled employees feel about their work. The employees' behavior, based on their own personal needs plus the communicated business needs, sends messages to customers for their interpretation. There is up to a 70% correlation between how fulfilled employees feel and how fulfilled customers feel. If the firm has targeted their customers effectively, the employees' humanizing behavior will drive profitable behavior by customers. This

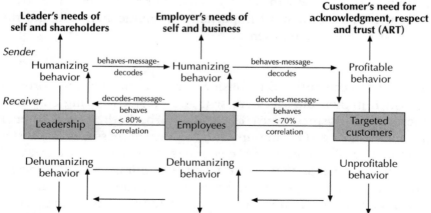

Figure 6.1   Process of how a business communicates humanness
(data from *Looking Out, Looking In*, by R. B. Adler and Neil Towne,
used with kind permission)

humanizing behavior should be focused on messages that create acknowledgement, respect, and trust with the targeted customers. The employees' behavior is a combination of face-to-face behavior with customers and behaviors that build supporting infrastructure, processes, interfaces, and systems which either enhance acknowledgement, respect, and trust or decrease the fulfillment of these central needs in customers.

In order to achieve this positive result, business must first become a good listener. This is probably the weakest point of most businesses in communicating the message of acknowledgement, respect, and trust. Given below are some key insights into the art of listening.

Business as the Listener (Receiver)

Businesses are constantly being sent messages by customers as well as themselves soliciting messages (information). It is the ability to learn from these messages that is at the core of understanding how to interact in a human way with the customer. The following represents several strategies that have proven helpful to many companies.

Listen first

It is always important to be a good listener first. Only when an employee listens well can they be a good communicator or conversationalist. The employee who listens well the first time can further the conversation and relationship in the following interactions.

Listen to fulfill the desire just to be heard

The very act of listening without judgment leaves an impression of genuine caring and compassion. Listening carefully and with genuine concern can solve the significant emotional issues involved with many customer problems. The fact that this reaction is the result of simple listening comes from a human being's emotional desire to be "heard" and validated by another human being.

Positions which require constant empathetic listening need relief

Achieving the goal of being compassionate and empathetic with every customer each day is reliant on an employee's ability to maintain these high human attributes. Employees deal with personal emotional issues as well as the emotional issues of their customers and human beings can only handle a limited amount of pressure. This is why it is important to create a human environment and the option of ongoing "emotional releases" for the employee.

Ritz-Carlton came to grips with this problem when they found that the highly empathetic people at the front desk were being overtaxed emotionally simply by virtue of their highly empathetic nature. This Ritz-Carlton approach is detailed in Chapter 8, "Human touch as a process". This resulted in a higher turnover rate for front desk staff, prompting Ritz-Carlton to increase the frequency of rotation from these positions into other less emotionally taxing positions. This need to rotate front desk personnel more frequently, as well as the increased level of turnover, is a calculated cost of fulfilling the objective of truly delivering to Ritz-Carlton's guests a sense of caring and well-being.

Balance listening techniques for convenience and caring

The technique a business uses to listen to their customers should be balanced: a message of genuine caring with the customer's need for convenience.

Caring is best face-to-face

If the message of caring is the top priority, communication should be done face-to-face. It is the method that shows the most acknowledgement, effort, and respect. The following is a list of methods in decreasing order of genuine caring messages.

1   Face-to-face.

2   Phone call.

3   Personal letter.

4   E-mail.

Listening without judgment

Business must listen to the customer's perception of a situation without judgment. The goal should be to take a compassionate and empathetic view of each customer's problem, through the eyes of the customer. The validity of the customer's perspective should not be questioned in the initial interaction. It is the customer's perception of the problem that should define the nature of the interaction, not the employee's perception. The customer might wait in a line that they perceive to be unacceptably long. The employees believe that the time the customers are required to wait in line is relatively short compared to other similar lines, e.g. five to ten minutes. Therefore, they believe the customers are unreasonable. Upon further study, the business finds that the lines that don't sufficiently move "appear" to take longer than lines that have movement to them. The resolution is to create movement in the lines, increasing the perception of a shorter wait for the customer. Ultimately, the employee's initial perception of the problem was irrelevant.

Communicate your humanness; don't be the quiet hero

The best managers handle bad surprises by informing the customers and then managing the surprise with honesty and efficiency. A common downfall for managers is to try to be "heroes" and save the day with little or no communication. Their thinking is that if a bad surprise can be kept secret for as long as possible, a clandestine fix can be applied before the customer "finds out".

Let them tell you how to tell them

There are two equally important questions that should be answered before communicating with a customer:

✦   How does the customer want the business to relate to them?

✦   How do they not want the business to relate to them?

Most often, customers are willing to teach business how they want to be communicated with. It is a business's failure not to teach their employees how to recognize customer's subtle and not-so-subtle signals revealing how they want to be communicated with. Customers have specific preferences in communication just as they have specific human needs. Therefore, a business should be constantly sensitive to subtle signals from customers revealing the degree and manner of communication desired.

Encourage your employees to recognize signals from the customer that reveal how much they want to "chat" and the level of familiarity with which they are comfortable. Some clients value a good deal of verbal interaction while others want to spend their time in solace and quiet reflection. Also, gauging a customer's personal borders will help create an appropriate and pleasing interaction for the customer. This is connected to how "personal" the product or service is to the customer's sense of esteem and well-being. Particularly, in industries such as health and beauty, the nature of products and services are usually close to a customer's sense of themselves. This issue of sensitivity becomes even more complex when employees are of a more artistic nature and tend to also be more sensitive human beings. Combining the sensitivities of both the employee and the customer, interactions have the potential of being highly charged emotional events. This situation calls for emotionally aware leadership and managerial skills throughout the day. In many cases, simply listening well and legitimizing each person's emotions works well.

Train employees to both observe and complete tasks

"Customer radar" must be kept on high alert in order to ascertain customer behavioral patterns. It is important to encourage employees to engage their "customer radar" to actively observe each customer's unique behavioral patterns. Even when employees are focused on a particular task, e.g. administrative, operational, or conversing with another employee, they should always have a part of their senses tuned in for customers. It is only in this way that communications can be initiated, either with eye contact or verbally (genuine welcome, by name if possible) as guests approach. This "customer radar" should also observe a customer's body language, activity patterns, and behavioral idiosyncrasies, e.g. returning to the hotel for a nap, an early breakfast, what the daughter orders for breakfast. The employee should also be developing a "feel" for what the customer likes or dislikes. Accomplishing this deeper understanding and knowledge of a customer is dependent on the nature and frequency of customer exposure, e.g. same housekeeper, server at breakfast, front desk person. It is equally important to acquire the ability to assess whether the customer wants to be approached or helped and to be aware of when a customer is "leaving" the premises. Saying "goodbye" creates a feeling of acknowledgement. In some business situations, the logistics of saying goodbye can be more difficult than greeting a customer. This typically has to do with controlled entrances for entrance fees and free flow exits.

Ask them what role they perceive you play in their life

Most businesses are more focused on what role the business wants to play in their customer's life as opposed to listening to what the customer wants from them. This is a central issue when it comes to truly understanding what value the business can offer the customer, as well as how to communicate and deliver that value.

Listening to the customer will reveal what the customer actually values relative to the activities of the firm. It is critical to constantly gauge what a customer values because it will change based on specific actions taken by the firm. A business must first create an infrastructure to measure how the customer perceives the firm starting with everyday, normal interactions, then moving on to more sophisticated compliments and complaints interaction. Then, customer markets should be segmented in terms of customer need groups and profitability in order to measure their activities. A further level of sophistication in ranking customers is to prioritize customer needs based on where the customer wants the firm to excel in adding value to their lives. Once the firm understand what role the customer wants the firm to play in their lives, they must decide where to focus their marketing communications in order to target the precise interests of the customer. This knowledge is then used to create normative scripting as a guide to engage the customer. Normative scripting essentially is "using the words the customer wants to hear". This can only be done when a business knows what interaction the customer wants to be created by the business and how the customer wants to experience that interaction. One important detail answers the question: what process does the customer prefer to use to contact or communicate with our company?

Prepare employees for effective responses after listening

One critical component of listening well is the ability to respond after listening. One way to ensure that employees can respond to customers' questions after careful listening is to track frequently asked questions and then to create an FAQ (frequently asked questions) list to train employees. These FAQs should go beyond simply informational content but should also be designed to address the emotional content of questions. Creating a more completely functional FAQ list should also consist of information on "how" to respond with the appropriate body language. Also important is ensuring that the employee completely answers the question because incomplete answers to questions will almost surely prompt the customer to ask another employee. This type of "rework" creates does unmeasured damage to productivity and the perception of professionalism.

Listen to customer issues and then communicate them quickly and widely

In Mead's packaging division, their 16 different business units in different countries around the world found that responsiveness was one of the major drivers of customer satisfaction. As a result, Mead established a complaint system in the United States that enters every customer complaint called in into a separate database, which then automatically triggers an e-mail to that customer's account representative. Mead also track the time period in which the complaint is addressed. This allows Mead to measure their complaint resolution time for each customer complaint.

Listening and learning in a natural social setting

A business can garner important behavioral learning from listening to customers in less formal social settings to supplement formal research. The field of study utilizing this approach is referred to as "ethnography". Ethnographers can help business by observing how human beings interact during the act of consumption of a product or service and the patterns that underlie them. Ethnographers describe how these communications occur and attempt to understand communication patterns (e.g. the opening of a telephone conversation, roles, ethnic groups, rules of etiquette and social class, behaviors deemed appropriate and competent). Ethnography uses direct contact with the human beings they study. The central benefit of ethnography is that it studies the interactions as they occur naturally in an active social setting, e.g. retail store, bank branch, service call. Ethnographers believe that how human beings interact is influenced primarily by how they interpret themselves, the person they are interacting with, and the situation they are currently in. This approach contrasts with behavioralists who look for universal laws which govern human behavior. To understand interactions and their underlying patterns, ethnographers can apply either an external (etic) or internal (emic) approach, or both. The external (etic) approach focuses on observing the interaction phenomenon of such things as cultural and environmental forces. Using interviews, the internal (emic) approach searches for a pattern that will reveal how human beings think about their interaction and what categories, assumptions, or rules guide the person's behavior. The ethnographers do not attempt to prove a hypothesis but simply collect and analyze information that they themselves have gathered. Because they are the ones collecting the information, they must be very careful not to impose their own biases on their observations. Some businesses will use their own employees plus behavioral professionals to observe their customers interacting with "people and products" at company-sponsored events that are more socially oriented, such as automotive shows and motorcycle rallies, product-sponsored sporting events, and product-oriented selling parties. The best activities to observe customers interacting with products are unencumbered social activities reflecting the lifestyle connected with the product. The benefit of having employees observe the lifestyles and interactions is that it is efficient because they are in place and understand the product. The drawbacks are that the customers may bias their social interaction because they are aware the employee works for the business. The benefits of the ethnographers are that they are trained behavioral professionals and being unconnected to the company they are totally inconspicuous observers.

Listen for what motivates people to buy ... emotionally

Most businesses have only a minimal understanding of what underlying emotional motivators compel customers to buy their products. One helpful method of understanding and segmenting emotional motivators is called cultural archetypes. This is a method pioneered by the psychologist, Clotaire Rapaille. His work has been used to create marketing campaigns for Procter & Gamble and General Motors, to structure quality initiatives for AT&T and American Society for Quality Control, and to identify attributes in customer loyalty, teamwork, and leadership initiatives for Ritz-Carlton. Rapaille suggests that people are motivated at three levels: the reptilian, the limbic, and the cerebral level. At the cerebral level, people deal with the "intellectual alibi" for why people do what they do. Rapaille gives the example of someone living in New York City who justifies buying a large SUV by arguing that parking in snow is very difficult. People are drawn to purchase SUVs not because they plan to regularly drive off-road but simply to feel a deeper sense of security from being in a larger automobile as well as being seated much higher than most conventional automobiles. This is directly linked to a person's "self survival" directive. Still another group of people buy SUVs for the allure that an SUV will be their vehicle to "commune with nature" as they dream of taking off-road excursions through the virgin countryside. Statistics reveal that 97% of all SUVs never leave the pavement for off-road excursions. At the limbic level, people act and react based on their earliest experiences. Rapaille states that people's imprinted, learned patterns are created as a conditioned response stemming from our earliest positive and negative experiences. The earliest experiences are very strong because they are "learned" in the context of the emotion of the experience. For instance, Procter & Gamble asked Rapaille to determine the American cultural archetype for why people buy coffee. Rapaille determined that Americans are not emotionally drawn to the taste of coffee. Americans' early positive associations with coffee are emotional memories of "home" and "smell". These memories come from experiences as young children who remember the warmth of their home as their parents drank coffee by the fire in the family room. From this research, Folger's created a successful ad campaign built around images of home and aroma, not taste. Finally, on the reptilian level, people react based on their instinctive need to survive. Convincing others that the products offered would influence their survival can produce powerful levels of commitment and performance. Rapaille's method for discovering cultural archetypes involves gathering representative groups to engage in a series of interviews. Each group is asked to describe what they think about the product, service, or topic. This reveals the cerebral response. The group is then asked to tell a story about it. This reveals images and emotions. Using relaxation techniques, the group is asked to write down their own earliest experiences with that subject. The results are analyzed both at a content and a semantic level. From what the groups think about the topic, Rapaille constructs a synthesis of their cerebral responses. Focusing on the verbs used by the interviewees in their stories and recollections, he constructs a structure with both positive and negative images of their limbic responses. Rapaille's theory is that business needs to understand as much as possible about people's limbic response mechanisms in order to position products and services which compel them to buy. If a business can affect a person's limbic response, which resonates with emotionally charged reactions, the probability for customer commitment is high. If business can influence people at the reptilian level, the chance of achieving complete commitment is higher. Tapping into a person's reptilian level is generally not possible in most business settings. Appealing to people on a cerebral level with a logical argument makes only a minimal impact because it is not emotionally based.

(Source: Karen Bemowski's article "Quality, American Style", *Quality Progress*, Vol. 26, No. 2 (February, 1993), pp. 65–68 reproduced by permission of the Center for Quality of Management, Inc.)

Business as the Communicator (Sender)

Once a business has become a good listener, it can move on to becoming a good communicator (sender of messages). The following are strategies that will make businesses more human in their customer interactions.

Go ugly early

One of the most effective ways to create trust is to freely admit your own mistakes. Admitting your own mistakes openly and in good humor shows character, strength, and honesty, and most everyone can relate to mistakes because everyone makes them – no exceptions.

It is common sense to take a method and try it. If it fails, admit it frankly and try another. But above all, try something.
FRANKLIN D. ROOSEVELT

If indeed you must be candid, be candid beautifully.
KHALIL GIBRAN

Truth never hurts the teller.   ROBERT BROWNING

Truth is always exciting. Speak it, then. Life is boring without it.   PEARL S. BUCK

When you blame others, you give up your power to change.
DR ROBERT ANTHONY

Be the bearer of bad news

Communicate dehumanizers quickly and broadly for proactive and systemic resolutions. Tracking regular customer issues and their resolution does little good unless the issues are widely and quickly communicated. This is the beginning phase of creating a systemic solution to reoccurring issues. In the case of negative customer feedback, information should include both the customer issue and also the actions the employee took to overcome the issue. Both solicited surveys and unsolicited guest comments from customers should be taken with equal seriousness. In addition, both positive and negative comments should be taken with equal importance. Customer feedback should be used to educate everyone as to how customers are reacting to a business experience. If these issues are not communicated quickly, the employee who experienced the problem resolution may have ended their workday without sharing the problem, thus creating an opportunity for the same problem to reoccur during the next shift.

Don't "blow your horn" unless you've got the wind

Advertising and branding are too often a dream; without operational competencies to make it real, the confusion between the dream and reality never goes unpunished.

For a successful technology, reality must take precedence over public relations, for nature cannot be fooled.   RICHARD FEYNMAN

Do not advertise or brand "human kindness" deliverables prematurely. While it is tempting for a company to advertise that they truly care about customers, premature advertising of this operational competency will do significant damage if the expectations of an improved ability to interact with caring and empathy are not met. In addition, each advertisement or branding statement is seen as a "test of trust" in the eyes of the customer. It is how a company performs against this test that either validates whether this firm can be trusted and relied on or not. In fact, the further the expectations are away from actual operationally deliverable human interactions, the more damage that is done. In many studies, it has been shown that a customer's perception of how humane a firm is can be closely linked to the firm's preceding image and reputation. A substantial piece of this reputation comes from word-of-mouth from both customer and employee opinions of the firm. Many firms discount the significance of the word-of-mouth impact from their own employees whose perception is based on how humanely they themselves are treated by the company.

Determine whether it needs "fix'n'" or "sell'n'" Determine whether the problem needs to be fixed or whether the customer simply didn't notice the value or benefit because there was insufficient communication (marketing or selling) of the benefit, i.e. operational or expectation-oriented issue. Expectation levels largely determine human emotional fulfillment. A business should determine early on whether a dissatisfied customer is an operational problem that needs to be fixed, i.e. improve performance, or whether it's a communication issue related to setting appropriate levels of expectation for business performance. A business is best served by targeting the measurement of perceptions that are the determinant of customer behavior. The business can then decide whether resources are best spent to "fix" problems or simply "communicate" more effectively. The "fix" is typically more expensive then the "sell". The "fix" is improving performance, whereas the "sell" is communicating the facts to enhance the perception. After deciding whether to "fix" or "sell", the business must "leverage" the "fix" or "sell" in order to take advantage of key strengths or improvements. The business must decide what is the easiest action with the least costs to create the best improvement/opportunities. For example, if a business receives a very low score on product innovation, particularly in its marketing efforts, the business needs to increase their investment in product innovation. Measuring these perceptions can cause reactions of disbelief from the business units involved. For example, a business unit may defensively disagree with a customer survey, believing it doesn't accurately reflect its performance. These defensive reactions typically arise from two situations. The first is that the business unit may not be accustomed to accepting rigorous customer survey results. The second situation is that it may not have effectively communicated its "value" appropriately, i.e. setting appropriate expectations for performance levels in the business relationship. In this latter case, the business will need to invest resources in setting these expectations appropriately. The most common mistake businesses make is assuming customers automatically create the appropriate level of performance expectation based on historical methods of communication. Further problems arise when a business makes quality improvements to either products or services but does not effectively merchandise those improvements to its customer, i.e. communicate the facts to enhance the perception. An unusual but vital part of this communication is actually using the survey process itself to cycle back to the customers their own responses. This opens a healthy dialogue between business and its customers as to both operational and expectation-oriented issues. Just creating this dialogue can have a noticeable improvement in customer perception, but it also adds a sense of honesty and builds trust because the business is willing to share its "warts" as well as its victories. The dialogue also creates an opportunity to address survey issues as well as issues unrelated to the survey. Finally, a business needs to explicitly leverage its key strengths, i.e. take advantage of the key strengths revealed by top scores on a survey. Not only must a business understand whether to fix it, sell it, or leverage it, there is also a ripple effect to deal with when a business "fixes" a problem. The fix must then be sold, i.e. communicated to the customer.

Show them accessibility – communicate approachability

It is extremely important that a business be able to communicate that it is "there for" the customer when the customer needs it. When accessibility stops, the relationship stops. One of Wal-Mart's key competencies is letting the customer know that they are important and will readily find help in the store. The difference between Wal-Mart and their competitors in both the accessibility and approachability of associates is two of the most immediate observations customers make. There are powerful emotional con-sequences when customers are either unable to find an associate or find one who appears unapproachable. In both cases, the emotional reaction of the customer is similar, i.e. I can't find anyone to help me so I must be unimportant, or that associate doesn't look like they want to be bothered, so I must be unimportant and I suspect they are incompetent anyway. Accessibility is related to associate scheduling and store layout. The approachability attributes of an associate are related to their personality traits augmented by their training. Given the fact that most customers shop in multiple com-peting stores, they quickly form an opinion as to which stores give them a feeling of importance as human beings. The best way to ensure associate accessibility is to schedule at least one associate in each department. This goal is not always attainable due to un-avoidable circumstances, such as illnesses. However, just having an associate physically in each department does little to help the cus-tomer feel recognized as a human being. The associate must also take the initiative to greet and communicate with customers who are nearby. It is easy to test for these accessibility and approachability attributes by walking into any competing retailer and observing whether there are more friendly greetings, a sense of being recognized as an individual, and being communicated with in a verbal or nonverbal human way by the store's associates. A good example of this is the story of a manager for a major retailer who would perform competitive price shopping or "comp shopping" in a local competitor's store while wearing her company work vest. In most cases, the competitors' associates never approached her because there was a lack of staffing and genuine interest. In addition, she appeared so much more approachable and "human" that as a result, the competitor's customers would approach her for assistance.

One of the lesser-known benefits of this accessibility and approachability is that when customers find a particular retail store that gives them a feeling of importance, they learn to rely on this retailer. Therefore, the customers become more dependent on shopping at a particular retailer when they know the retailer will "be there" for them when they need them.

Teach common courtesies to create approachability

Common courtesies, such as a genuine welcome and farewell, are at the heart of such civilities. One retail store boosted their same store sales by 10% by simply prioritizing common courtesies to create a more human and approachable store environment. Abercrombie & Fitch Co. are a leading specialty retailer dealing in high-quality merchandise for the casual classic American lifestyle. Abercrombie's powerful lifestyle brand of clothing is sold in hundreds of stores across the United States. Their powerful retail brand and a healthy retail economy keep their customer service levels at parity with competitors. As with many other retailers, a downturn in the retail economy prompted Abercrombie & Fitch to refocus on their customer service efforts to gain any competitive advantage in a tightening economy. A more competitive retail environment also causes customers to expect additional acknowledgement and appreciation for where they do choose to shop. Prior to this effort to refocus on customer service, one of their top retail stores in the United States was run by a manager who was more merchandise-oriented than customer-oriented. This particular manager instructed his employees to execute the following store directives:

1   Keep the store neat and clean.

2   Make sure that the right shirts or pants are on display.

3   Under no circumstances talk to customers without having the customer speak to the employee first.

These directives had multiple negative impacts on customers. First, the employees focused their efforts on the store and merchandise rather than customer interactions. Suddenly, their interactions with customers were very limited because they had to wait until the customer initiated communication. The directive against initiating communication with customers created the perception among customers that the employees were rude, lazy, and aloof. Customers also described the employees as being "stuck on themselves" or "too good" to talk to the customers. The employees also ended up spending more time just talking with each other rather than helping customers. This continuous "employee chat" only added to the affront customers felt about entering the store and not feeling they would receive assistance. As customers began to expect this behavior, employees became worse by living up to expectations. There were several occasions when employees would refuse to look for items in the back of the store if those items were not already on display. The manager's non-communication directives created behaviors that became a culture. On busy days when there could be as many as 60 customers in the store and only six employees to assist them, this problem only compounded itself. A new manager was brought in to take over this poorly performing store, though it was still one of the company's top stores in the country. He immediately recognized how dysfunctional customer interactions were. The reason customers shop at an Abercrombie & Fitch store to begin with is the powerful brand image that invokes feelings of esteem and strong self-image for the customers. Once inside the store, the employee's behavior canceled out the positive brand images that initially drew people to the store. The new manager started by instructing employees to proactively greet every customer with a simple "Hi" or "Hello". He guided the employees to always attempt to convey warmth and welcome in their greetings. This new approach transformed the customer's perception of the employees as being "rude" to the perception of employees as actually working and being receptive to communication. This new approach also caused the customers to perceive the store as more physically attractive, as well as being a "fun" work environment. He also encouraged employees to answer all questions from customers completely and quickly. A warm, simple greeting broke down the communication barrier. Receiving this warm greeting, the customer is more apt to feel comfortable enough to ask such things as, "Do you have this shirt in a small size in the back of the store?" Otherwise, customers who have not found what they are looking for will often leave the store without purchasing any merchandise. Simple courtesies and approachability improvements propelled this store to increase its sales volume by 10% without any other significant changes, e.g. aggressive sales techniques, advertising, discounting.

Adapt communications for left brain/right brain customers

Apply left–right brain behavioral dynamics for focused customer fulfillment. The first international recognition of the importance of understanding left brain/right brain dynamics occurred in 1981 when Dr Roger Sperry won the Nobel Prize for discovering that each hemisphere of the brain "thinks" in a different way. This behavior theory holds one of the key determinants of customer behavior – whether the customer is predominantly right-brained or left-brained, i.e. hemispheric dominance. First, there is no human being who is totally left-brained or totally right-brained. This follows the same logic that every human being has a dominant hand, dominant eye, and dominant foot, but the person is not completely reliant on their dominant feature. Customers who are left-brain dominant are more adept at verbally oriented interactions, i.e. processing words. Customers who are right-brain dominant are more adept at processing pictures. Although the right and left hemispheres work together, each side of the brain has a different function and processes information differently. Most human beings seem to have a dominant side. One of the primary responsibilities of the left side of the brain is to process written and spoken information. One of the primary responsibilities of the right side of the brain is to interpret information visually, creatively, and emotionally. It is therefore important to understand the type of customers who are attracted to your products and then interact with your customers based on their propensity to be right- or left- (hemisphere) -brained. For example, customers who purchase products that enliven many physical senses, e.g. motorboats or motorcycles tend to be geared toward more "right-brain" activities, i.e. visual, creative, and emotional. It is therefore important to cater sales, marketing, and service (interactions) toward those emotional biases. Other products are connected with the "left brain" which is more analytical in nature, e.g. food basics or toiletry basics – products or services with little emotion tied to them. In catering to the "right-brain" customers, it is not the product itself but the "feeling" when experiencing the product, the lifestyle associated with the product, and the interaction the customer has with the business supplying the product. Harley-Davidson are an excellent example of a business with an incredibly loyal customer base that tracks predominantly "right-brained" people. This is evident on their website as the simple introduction contains the following descriptive words: Freedom, Adventure, Pavement, Leather, Orange, Black, Passion, Self-determination, Proud, Mile Markers, Parties, Tattoos, Anniversary Rides, Chaps, Chrome, Apehangers, Flames, MDA (Muscular Dystrophy Association), Saddlebags, Eagles, Iron, Bugs, Sturgis (City S. Dakota), Daytona Beach, and Fat Boy. These descriptive words capture the thoughts, feelings, and experiences their loyal customers embrace. An ad Harley-Davidson ran several years ago depicted a Harley-Davidson owner wearing a T-shirt with one sleeve rolled up exposing a Harley-Davidson tattoo. The ad simply read: "When was the last time you felt this strongly about anything?" Harley-Davidson has one of the strongest customer loyalty bases of any manufacturer. For them, it is equally as important to nurture the "feelings" surrounding the brand as it is to create new and improved products. In an era where customers are surrounded by "new and improved" products, Harley-Davidson remain the oldest, continuously operating motorcycle company with 100-plus years' history. This type of "self-survivor" mentality coupled with the air of mystique and authenticity may also add to the "feel" of owning a "Harley", i.e. almost every motorcycle manufacturer has created a Harley "look-alike" but there is still only one true "Harley". Their competitors have made one fundamental error – they have focused on re-creating a product, not the incredible human aura of all that is "Harley".

Communicate your relative value

Without the customer understanding the businesses relative value, the customer will not have sufficient trust to make a buying decision. Therefore, supplying the customer with sufficient knowledge in order to create that trust is one of the main prerequisites for a buying decision. Informed customers buy products, uninformed customers do not. The following are several strategies to ensure that customers have the highest degree of trust created by the effective communication of your relative value.

There are four fatal mistakes businesses make in communicating their value:

1   Sending value messages using business jargon, not everyday words.

2   Sending value messages and assuming they have been effectively communicated.

3   Sending value messages that are not relative to competitors.

4   Sending value messages which aren't easily differentiated from competitors'.

1. Sending value messages using business jargon, not everyday words. One common mistake businesses often make in their efforts to communicate with customers is to use words from their everyday business vocabulary instead of using words people use in their everyday lives. Using business terminology in customer communications is a fairly easy mistake to make because most businesspeople work and develop their creative ideas within the atmosphere of their business in conjunction with other businesspeople, not with customers. Any customer communications should always be tested by gauging customer reactions outside the business context. Unfortunately, customer communications are rarely tested for their understandability and use of common, everyday language. Processes should be set up to 'tune' communications using interactive feedback from customers in order to confirm that the emotional response from the customer is actually the same response that the business intended to elicit. For example, Suncorp (highlighted in Chapter 7: 'Human Touch as a Series of Interactions') experimented with both wordings and intonations to hone the specific emotional response it desired in its customer communications. The absence of this experimentation relegates communication with customers to 'rolling the dice' as to whether or not the desired emotional effects will be achieved.

2. Sending value messages and assuming they have been effectively communicated. Suncorp, a major financial and insurance institution in Australia, found that even though they had gone through the steps of communicating their value, it was unsuccessful. The story begins when Suncorp initially investigated the emotional dimensions in a typical customer's insurance claim. They discovered that most customers were under growing time constraints in their normal lives. For these customers, any event or activity placing increased potential pressure – imagined or real – on this time constraint caused a significant increase in their anxiety level. Due to this early information, Suncorp began focusing on the cycle time of the end-to-end insurance claim process. As they investigated further into the emotional aspects of the customer's perception of the overall experience, they found that there was a series of activities, or lack of activities, beyond the time issue that left customers with "nagging" doubts as to whether they were truly being taken care of by Suncorp. This customer anxiety was rooted in years of negative word-of-mouth about banks and insurance companies, and their impersonal and dehumanizing manners. The result was an ambient background noise or legacy of customer distrust, which functioned as a fertile breeding ground for suspicion and fears of somehow being tricked. It was common to have a customer's lack of trust breed thoughts such as, "There must be some tiny loophole that they are going to use to cheat me". This legacy of distrust, along with the customers' time constraints, led Suncorp to focus not only on providing a quick turnaround for the customers' auto claims but also on leaving the customer in no doubt that their car would be properly repaired with high-quality parts and craftsmanship. An important lesson for Suncorp to learn was that, even though they had operationally already addressed this legacy of distrust by providing a lifetime guarantee on the repairs, they had failed to adequately communicate this to the customers, so that many customers did not realize that this guarantee applied. A promise inadequately communicated to the customer doesn't exist in the minds of the customer. Suncorp discovered this communications issue after it applied high-level statistical analysis to its surveys. It analyzed several of the statistical patterns and delved into the statistical suggestions of this problem with additional focus groups. They also investigated how to best communicate this guarantee to the customer so that they would be most likely to emotionally accept it and understand it. Suncorp found that until they effectively communicated this quality of work guarantee, the customer continued to have doubts as to whether their insurer would really stand behind the repair work.

Another area in which they failed to adequately communicate their value was their accident claims area. An important human need which emerged from additional qualitative work around accident claims was the fact that customers just wanted Suncorp to handle all the "hassles" from the minute the accident happened to when they picked up the car. An auto accident can be a traumatic event. Any entity that can lessen some of the burden arising from that event will garner favor with the customer. As with the lifetime guarantee of quality work, they had already operationally set up processes to handle all the "hassles" of the claims process for the customer. But, again, they had not adequately communicated this competency and its value to customers and to the overall marketplace. This prompted Suncorp to be more explicit in communicating how they handle "all the little details" of the claim process and how that benefits the customer emotionally, i.e. "Yes, you will get your car back in seven days, and yes, your repairs will be guaranteed for life, and yes – the actual process is hassle-free because all you do is drop your car off at one of our assessment centers and everything else is taken care of by us – you don't have to even think about it until you get your car back".

> *If you have an important point to make, don't try to be subtle or clever. Use a piledriver. Hit the point once. Then come back and hit it again. Then hit it a third time – a tremendous whack.*
>
> WINSTON CHURCHILL

3. *Sending value messages that are not relative to competitors.* Customers only buy when they trust. Trust comes from interactions and knowledge of relative value. At Wal-Mart, the strategy to regularly "teach" customers about products occurs both before they enter the store and during the actual shopping experience. They issue paging announcements to their customers every 15 minutes and also display flyers at different locations in the store for cus-

tomers to read. There are flyers on the marquee in front of the store for added knowledge transfer to customers. For products that require more information than is printed on the packaging, they will post additional information on the display surrounding the product. Their strategy to teach customers the "best value" of a price or service is usually some form of relative comparison, either a price change or the price relative to competitors. Wal-Mart accomplish this by using a "was" card, which is displayed on their featured items. This card displays what the price "was", and then displays the new price. A similar technique is displaying the new price with a "Starburst" price sign showing prices that have been rolled back, i.e. reduced. Another important aspect of teaching value is communicating the value relative to competitors. To regularly "shop the competition" then show a competitor's prices on the display without actually naming the specific competitor teaches customers the difference. Withholding the competitor's name is part of a commitment to support ethical business practices by the local business in their communities. Wal-Mart refer to this as their "competitive cart rail" display. This display is intended to show at least a 5% differential between their prices and their competitor's price. Another name for this competitive price comparison is "dare to compare". For example, if a competitor is running a special on Pringles for $1.04 per can and Wal-Mart's regular price is 94 cents per can, this price differential would be suitable for a "dare to compare" display. By keeping the customers informed in this way, they show proof to their customers that they are truly getting the best value for their money when they shop at Wal-Mart.

4. Sending value messages which aren't easily differentiated from competitors'. Another important issue in communicating Suncorp's value to customers and the marketplace was striving to differentiate their very specific market offerings from their competitors' offerings, which could easily sound very similar. Suncorp found that a powerful way to achieve this was to use a certain level of specificity clearly delineating their quantifiable service offering from their competitors' "feel good" promises. By being "up front" and specific, and quoting a numeric measure that customers can easily relate to, they could achieve measurable differentiation in the mind of the customer, e.g. seven-day turnaround, 60-second response time.

Say "I'm here and I care" without words

Businesses need to be proactive in communicating that they are available, approachable, and affable using all available avenues of communication, e.g. words, smile, eyes, voice intonation, and body language. This will create the perception in the customer's mind that businesses are both physically accessible and emotionally approachable.

Harvard Business Review published an article stating that:

+   55% of what humans sense is not verbal or vocal.

    —Body language.

+   38% vocal intonations and inflections.

    —"Thank you" can be said as an insult or as genuine gratitude.

+   7–8% is the actual words.

Train employees for effective nonverbal communication skills

Nonverbal messages are especially important when trying to create a high degree of humanness in an interaction because it is the nonverbal communications that typically express attitudes and feelings, e.g. genuine caring, empathy, compassion. It is the verbal messages that tend to best express ideas. Most employees need some specific training to effectively use their nonverbal communication skills. Used effectively, nonverbal communications can repeat, substitute for, complement, accent, and regulate verbal messages. Used ineffectively, nonverbal communications can completely contradict verbal messages. These nonverbal communications can take the form of body orientation, posture, gestures, facial expression and eyes, voice, touch, physical attractiveness, clothing, proxemics (personal space), territoriality, physical environment, and time (see Ronald B. Adler and Neil Towne, *Looking Out, Looking In*, Orlando, FL, Harcourt Brace and Co., 1999).

The employee needs to communicate through body language that he or she is approachable. This can be achieved effectively with as simple a gesture as a genuine smile or a short verbal greeting. A smile can also be with just the eyes. As long as it is genuine, most friendly facial gestures are effective. Another important aspect of body language is the angle of the employee's body relative to the customer. In most cases, the employee's body should be facing the customer rather than angled away. There are many books focused entirely on body language and its implications in basic communication. Not only do these "approachability" signals help employees become more approachable, they also help customers become more comfortable with being approached. This also creates the perception that there are actually more employees. This is called the "employee multiplier" effect. Another "employee multiplier" effect is training non-customer-facing employees to exhibit the same level of approachability through basic training on how to assist a customer.

Teach employees the importance of a smile

The smile is one of the most universally understood and simplest nonverbal communications to send to customers. Every company could be served better by smiling more. The following are some observations about the simple and powerful value of a smile.

+ "It takes 43 muscles to frown, but only 17 muscles to smile. That makes it 2.5 times easier to smile."

+ "A smile is an inexpensive way to improve your looks."

+ "A smile costs nothing, but gives much. It enriches those who receive, without making poorer those who give. It takes but a moment, but the memory of it sometimes lasts forever. None is so rich or mighty that he can get along without it, and none is so poor but that he cannot be made rich by it. A smile creates happiness in the home, fosters good will in business, and is the countersign of friendship. It brings rest to the weary, cheer to the discouraged, sunshine to the sad, and is nature's best antidote for trouble. Yet it cannot be bought, begged, borrowed, or stolen, for it is something that is of no value to anyone until it is given away. Some people are too tired to give you a smile.

Give them one of yours, as none needs a smile so much as he who has no more to give."

Make employees physically identifiable

Another important part of communicating that you are there for the customer is making it obvious to them "who" is there for them. Jane Manfre of Tudor Day Spa has her staff wear black and white uniforms especially to allow customers to quickly identify "who is and is not" staff. In doing this, the customers always know who they can turn to for help or assistance. Jane also believes that it helps in leveling any class distinction; this is a result of her upbringing in the UK. Each month the employees choose a different uniform color to be worn every Thursday of that particular month.

Communicate with touch

Physical touch during business interactions when done in the appropriate context adds a dimension of humanness that few other communication methods can match. The universality of the simple handshake is one of the most accepted and effective methods of nonverbal communication using physical touching for a person in a business context. A firm handshake coupled with good eye contact and a genuine smile can get most customer interactions off toward a good "human" start. For most business interactions, physical contact beyond the handshake or a hand on the back moves into territory that can typically be considered as potentially inappropriate. However, it is worth the effort to explore companies whose business it is to physically touch their customers (and have the legal right to do so), e.g. medical, dental, health and beauty. Taking the time to consider what they have learned may offer insight into subtle ways to which other "non-touch" industries can apply the same principles in appropriate and acceptable ways. The smallest physical touch can communicate a humanness and warmth while breaking down barriers that few other nonverbal communication practices can replicate.

The owner of a fashionable health spa (Jane Manfre of Tudor Day Spa) trains her receptionists to greet customers by physically "touching" them. For example, when a client walks in the door and the receptionist offers to hang up their coat, they are trained to lay a hand on the customer's arm. Jane refers to this initial touching as "breaking the barriers". Jane's people do this for both male and female customers. Breaking this initial "human barrier" is just the first in a series of physical human touches that offer a gentle transition into further human touches in activities such as massages, facials, and pedicures. Jane emphasizes that businesses need to break the customer's barrier at the first opportunity for physical human contact. She says, "You only have one shot". If you don't break that physical human barrier down at your first opportunity, you have sent a subtle signal to the customer that this experience will be distant and impersonal. A second opportunity to touch the customer's hand occurs when they are handed a drink. After seven years of observing how these simple physical human touches affect her customers, Jane has learned that after one or two physical touches the customers will almost immediately exhibit external signs of physical and mental relaxation and began talking and having fun. In addition, she has observed that both men and women are equally relaxed in her spa, in part because of a physical touch. A completely gender-neutral environment is a difficult environment to create. But it is extremely important because over 30% of her clients are male. Jane commented that her male clients are, in some ways, even more receptive to the physical touch than her female clients during such activities as shampoos or basic hairstyling. She observed that once a stylist starts giving a man a head massage, which is standard with every shampoo and styling, "they melt". One of the reasons that this type of physical touch is so powerful and well received by customers is that, increasingly, the world's businesses are filleting out, consciously or unconsciously, the humanness of interaction between customer and business. The increasingly impersonal and sterile nature of our society in such industry standard practices as drive-through fast foods, electronic banking, and online prescriptions is increasing the speed of our lives but cutting back on human interaction in the normal course of consuming. In addition, society, often over-reacting to behavioral aberrations of human touch in our society, provides strict rules against inappropriate areas of human touch. While these sanctions protect a minority of cases of inappropriate and dysfunctional human touch, they cast a larger, dehumanizing net of fear over the vast majority of society who are in desperate need of physical human touch. Some examples, which have legitimate roots, have led to a climate of fear in touching: children are told that, "if your uncle touches you, you should go to school and tell the teacher"; or employers can be sued if they touch an employee in ways such as placing their hand on the employee's shoulder. Our world is increasingly becoming a non-touch, non-affectionate place for people to live. As a matter of law, health spas are one of the few businesses that have a license to touch people. Other industries that can legally "touch" people are the medical and dental professions. That physical touch is very powerful. Ironically, the massage/spa professionals focus on the warmth and personal nature of the physical touch, whereas the medical and dental professional's touches are often cold, clinical, and sterile. The luxury that Jane has to be able to welcome a client into her place of business and then sit down with that new client, place a hand on her client's shoulder and start a warm conversation is relatively unique. Jane recently did a survey with her clients asking what was most important to them. The response was the atmosphere of being treated like a human being, not just another customer, was what they remember the most about their experience.

Communicate only valued information and in the manner they want

It is becoming increasingly important to understand what messages (information) are valuable to customers, as well as understanding the manner in which those messages should be communicated. This is due to the overwhelming amount of valueless information currently being "dumped on" the consuming public.

When the marketing efforts of the major credit card companies are analyzed as to what they are communicating to their perspective customers, the message they are sending could be interpreted as them making a purposeful decision to send 97% of the over 3 billion potential customers an offer with no value to the receiver. From a behavioral perspective, most of these potential customers interpret their message as:

1   You don't respect me.

2   You don't know me.

Contrary to popular belief, mailings such as these are not neutral acts of communication but dehumanize customers, creating negative brand equity.

The same is true for telemarketing calls, which at a minimum dehumanize and typically create stronger emotions such as anger and frustration. Seventy-seven percent of people view intrusions of telemarketing as "rude and pushy". From a behavioral perspective, most potential customers react with the same negative feelings as those who received mailed solicitations; feeling unknown and disrespected.

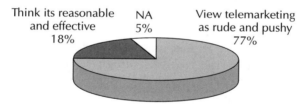

Figure 6.2   View telemarketing as rude and pushy
(data from *Aggravating Circumstances*, 2002 Public Agenda, used with kind permission)

Before communicating, it is important for a business to understand what information is valuable to the customer and in what manner does the customer want us to communicate? Knowing the value of information to customers is just as important as knowing the manner in which they desire to communicate, e.g. mail, telephone, e-mail, fax. The value of information to customers should be seen as something beyond just keeping them informed so they do not become anxious. Technology can automate the processes by which a firm manages communication type and informational preference for each individual customer. Ideally, customers should be able to select the types of information and methods of communication in which they are interested. The technology should then be modeled on the customer's choice. This should be a proactive

activity of the firm and not one that is driven by customer complaints of being sent needless information by undesirable communication methods.

Communicating humanness with people-friendly spaces

Many businesses underestimate the impact of physical surround-
ings on a customer's emotions, e.g. decision to buy, impression of
service. Business interiors and exteriors are powerful tools for creating positive emotions and abate negative emotions with customers.

Create environments to create emotion

Creating an environment in which the desired human feelings can
be easily fostered is an important strategy. One leading Land Rover
"Center" (the No. 1 Land Rover Dealership in the US for CSI
(Customer Satisfaction Index) and SSI (Sales and Service Index))
have extended the Land Rover strategy by creating a distinctly
different "feel" in their centers. The idea behind these specialized
centers is that they are constructed to be as different from traditional automobile dealerships as possible. The main reason behind
this differentiation is that traditional automobile dealerships carry
the legacy of evoking feelings of distrust, apprehension and emotional sterility. This center's manager likened a visit to an automobile dealership by some customers to that of visiting a dentist
to have a tooth pulled. The centers are constructed in such a way to
explicitly promote the "Land Rover Way", i.e. emotionally charged
principles surrounding Land Rover ownership. These principles
are: individualism, authenticity, freedom, adventure, guts, and
supremacy. Another emotionally charged word that is often used
to capture the essence of the Land Rover brand is "courage".
Because most potential customers who first enter the Land Rover
center know little or nothing about Land Rovers, the visual cues are
an accelerated way to educate the feelings of their customers before
any conventional knowledge transfer takes place. As customers walk
in, their first impression is: "I have never seen anything like this in
my life". To create this unique environment, the center's manager

and owner began searching for artifacts depicting wilderness hunting and safari scenes that would convey the desired emotions of the Land Rover Way. The management team made numerous excursions to various antique shops to collect hunting artifacts, adding warmth and comfort to the hunting and safari scenes. At the perimeter of the upper level display areas are six distinct scenes representing hunting, fishing, safari, and camping. Even the carpeting was hand chosen with designs of Bengal tiger and leopard skins. The center also exhibits a huge leather rhinoceros (Land Rover's symbol). To give the Land Rover center a feeling of local community connection, they also display various paraphernalia representing local colleges and universities, sports teams, and celebrities. They have purposefully injected a sense of humor by adding some "disarming" artifacts, such as the figure of a dog lifting its leg on one of a Land Rover's tires. While the management team followed Land Rover's guidelines, they also wanted to place their own unique branding on their center. When customers enter the center, they enter a pressure-less atmosphere with an open, airy feel like that of a remote hunting lodge. Each employee is dressed in khaki Land Rover shorts and shirt and hiking boots as if they were working at an exclusive safari lodge. This dress further supports the message that this is not a "typical" car dealership and that no one will be "attacked" by the proverbial high-pressure car salesman. Not only does it disarm the legacy of dealership salespeople but it also injects a sense of fun into the human interaction. Wearing this Land Rover apparel also creates an irresistible "mood" that helps employees "feel" what the brand is attempting to say to customers. If the service or salespeople know the customer, they will be referred to by name. This unique, relaxed atmosphere immediately puts customers at ease, with the typical customer reaction being: "Wow, I have never been in a store like this, especially a car dealership". To add a sense of exceptional warmth and comfort, a separate area in the center features hot coffee, satellite TV, and a mechanical massage chair for the ultimate in customer comfort. It is common for a service customer, while waiting for their vehicle, to indulge in a cup of coffee and lounge in the massage chair watching their favorite movie. This creates a powerful contrast in the customer's mind to what is thought of as a traditional automobile service lounge. Most people would rather be in their homes than waiting in the service department. Land Rover's strategy effectively blurs these lines.

Customer colors

Colors can create physical reactions (red has been shown to raise blood pressure). Colors evoke different reactions depending on the culture in which they are applied. In the United States, white is accepted for weddings, whereas, in some Eastern cultures, white is the color for mourning and funerals. Colors can also be associated with trends and time periods. Avocado (a shade of green) can be synonymous with the 1960s and 1970s for many people.

Certain categories of colors can be somewhat predictable in the emotional responses they elicit, e.g. cool, warm, mixed, neutral colors.

+ Cool colors (calming): blue, green (and white).

+ Warm colors (exciting): red, yellow, orange (and black).

+ Mixed cool/warm colors: Purple.

+ Neutral colors (good for backgrounds): brown, tan, beige, gray, silver, black, and white.

(Source: It's a Colorful, Colorful World – Symbolism of Colors, by Jacci Howard Bear, see the Desktop Publishing website)

Transform any space into a human place

Jane Manfre's Tudor Day Spa is a testament to the fact that any physical structure can be transformed into a place of human warmth and comfort. Jane's building was first built as a gas station, and then transformed into a fish market full of, as she says "wet, smelly, fish". As Jane transformed this building into a place for people to enjoy being human, she had the outside of the building constructed to feel business-like but not stuffy. The physical building beckons customers to "come on in and ask me a question". In the summertime, Jane plants many flowers outside her building. She's careful not to make the outside "too perfect" because perfection is not human. When visiting a house with a perfectly manicured lawn and garden and perfect decorating, it is a normal human reaction for people to believe that somehow they "won't measure up". Small details on the outside of her building, such as the metal cover to her

American Color Associations

(modified version of the 'Modern American Color Associations' table from *Color Psychology and Color Theory*, by the world-renowned Faber Birren)

Color	General Appearance	Mental Associations	Direct Associations	Objective Associations	Subjective Impressions
Red	brilliant intense opaque dry	hot fire heat blood	danger Christmas 4th of July Valentine's Day	passionate exciting active	intensity rage fierceness
Orange	bright luminous glowing	warm metallic autumnal	Halloween Thanksgiving	jovial lively energetic forceful	hilarity exuberance satiety
Yellow	sunny incandescent radiant	sunlight	caution	cheerful inspiring vital celestial	high spirit health
Green	clear moist	cool nature water	clear St Patrick's Day	quieting refreshing peaceful	ghastliness disease terror guilt
Blue	transparent wet	cold sky water ice	service flag	subduing melancholy contemplative sober	gloom fearfulness furtiveness
Purple	deep soft atmospheric	cool mist darkness shadow	mourning Easter	dignified pompous mournful mystic	loneliness desperation
White	spatial – light	cool snow	cleanliness Mother's Day flag	pure clean frank youthful	brightness of spirit normality
Black	spatial – dark	neutral night emptiness	mourning	funeral ominous deadly depressing	negotiation of spirit death

plumbing access, are left unpainted because it adds to the casual quaintness of her business. As the customer walks through the wooden doorway, there is a cozy visual sense of home and tradition stimulated by a beautiful personal space warmed by oriental rugs and hand-painted china plates displayed in antique armoires. The air is scented with neutral, earthy fragrances with no particular scent being distinguishable from another. An "aroma of the month" is an integral part of Jane's humanizing spa concept. All the senses are carefully blended in a potpourri of gentle humanness with no one sense being overloaded at the expense of another. Advertising of any particular beauty products is subtle and blended into the environment. The "feeling" of the main entry room has no gender bias but is equally appealing for both men and women. Jane holds a "men only night" with cigars and port to make sure her male clients feel as welcome as her female clients. Jane has even taken great care to make the rest rooms feel "like home" yet still retain a professional air about them. A small, intimate book collection is shelved in a venerable antique bookshelf allowing customers to borrow books at their pleasure. To borrow a book, the customer puts a dollar in a small jar next to the bookshelf as a donation for a local charity. Jane has emphasized the humanness of her business and, therefore, her customers make a connection in their minds between warm, human feelings and her business. Jane is a stickler for cleanliness in her shop. Neatness is a priority as well, but not the highest priority because, in a busy shop such as hers, it is difficult to maintain a neat appearance consistently. More importantly, Jane feels that striving for perfect neatness creates a less human environment. Jane's creation of a "home away from home" atmosphere is so well done that customers will "drop in for coffee" to enjoy the humanness and warmth of the environment. An important part of creating a "human" space is allowing each customer enough room to feel comfortable and special. Jane is careful not to place her clients too close together when receiving treatments. Her competitors tend to place clients close together to increase revenue per square foot but lose the feeling of being special that Jane creates and thus lose long-term customer loyalty. Jane believes that focusing first on the clients' needs ultimately will allow her business to outperform her competitors' focus on short-term revenue gains. The challenge is to look beyond the tempting calculations of space productivity toward the focal point of fulfilling customers as people for the long term.

The art of placement

Feng shui has been called the art of placement. It is a Chinese philosophy based on experience of over a thousand years about how to create or select an environment that enhances a person's well-being, with the laws of nature. Feng shui is an ancient Chinese discipline dating back at least 3000 years, although its philosophy can be traced back to the teachings of the *I Ching*, from 6000 years ago. Despite these origins, however, its core truths are central to human awareness and experience. When it is stripped of culture and ritual, and synthesized with other bodies of knowledge to meet the specific requirements of culture, geography, climate, and human uniqueness, the essence of feng shui can be applied to any space and time.

Feng shui means "wind and water" – the two most powerful forces of nature, and the fundamentals of life. The underlying principle of feng shui is to live in harmony with your environment so that the energy surrounding you works for you rather than against you. Feng shui is a complex art involving many disciplines from site planning to psychology, based on the Chinese understanding of the dynamic flow of energy throughout the universe. Feng shui explains how the environment in which people live affects their lives. Beyond this, it is the art of using the environment to influence the quality of a person's life. Ultimately, feng shui is a sound and sensible way of living with a conscious connection between our outside environment and our inner world.

The integration of the external world and our internal environment is a cornerstone of most traditional philosophies. Indigenous people all over the world have long understood that we are not separate from our planet, our homes, or one another.

In the West we have lost this connectedness with our earth and our environment and this lack of balance is a cause of much physical, mental, emotional, and spiritual disease. Feng shui offers a means to reconnect and regain our balance, our health, and our good fortune.

The Chinese have always considered that success in life is dependent upon five influences: (1) fate, destiny or karma; (2) lucky and unlucky auras; (3) feng shui; (4) virtue; (5) personal factors such as our background, inheritance, and family, and our actions, education, and experience, and so on.

Whether you concur with this Chinese belief or not, it does make an important point. The first two of these influences – fate and luck – are beyond our control, as are many of the personal factors. Therefore, feng shui is only one of the few influences on our lives that can be controlled.

(Source: The Feng Shui Society)

Communication is the vehicle and competency through which all customers' impressions are created. It is a business's ability to communicate effectively both as a listener and a communicator that will determine what the customer remembers about the business. The ability to listen is important, not only for acquiring customer knowledge and understanding, but also to acknowledge and show respect for the human need to be heard. Listening sympathetically with all the human senses is a good beginning to effective listening. Effective listening will enable a business to determine what and when to communicate with customers. Once this is understood, carefully selected and understandable messages should be delivered in a caring and human manner. Effective communication also requires the development of both verbal and nonverbal skills. Verbal skills range from knowing what words to say to voice intonation. Nonverbal skills range from simple things such as a welcoming smile to body positioning. A business also communicates powerful messages through humanly designed physical spaces and machine interfaces. All of these factors directly affect, either positively or negatively, a customer's decision to buy.

7

Human Touch as a Series of Interactions

FROM THE MOMENT A PERSON BEGINS BUYING OR A BUSINESS begins selling, there will usually not be one but a series of interactions that will occur between them over the course of product ownership and repeat buying. Interactions may cascade in a recognizable sequence, such as marketing – sales – installation – service – repair – billing, or take on a more random interaction pattern. Regardless of this, businesses must strive for a consistently human interaction every time because how the customer feels about the business is made up of all of these interactions.

This chapter presents a time-proven approach for consistently accomplishing human interactions based on the ongoing work of Ray Kordupleski. The foundations of this approach began with AT&T's customer satisfaction group headed by Ray Kordupleski and a group of doctoral statisticians at Bell Labs. Their team analyzed tens of thousands of customer surveys in an attempt to find response patterns that explained when and why customers felt the highest degree of fulfillment from a business. The research revealed that how a customer perceived a business had more to do with the fact that the customer is a human being with specific emotional needs than with just the functional usefulness the customer gained from the consumption of specific product and service features. Despite this fact, most businesses focus a majority of their resources on the delivery of high-quality products and service features without sufficiently resourcing the predominant determinants of a customer's perception – the humanness of customer interactions.

The research also revealed that a majority of a customer's perception of a business was linked to a distinct set of human interaction attributes. This set of human interaction attributes has been frequently tested by several firms around the world since this early research and it has been found that the initial findings remain valid and consistent with adjustments being made only to the weighting of the core human interaction attributes. These weightings are dependent on the nature of the particular industry or market. Therefore, it is important for every business to embed these human interaction attributes consistently into each interaction and throughout the entire series of interactions.

There are three aspects of a customer's buying decision:

1   What they get, i.e. product and service features.

2   How they get it and how they are treated after they get it, i.e. interaction humanness.

3   How much they pay, i.e. price.

In most cases, the customer's perception of "How they get it" will be determined predominately by how "humanly" the business interacts with the customer using different channels of interaction, e.g. face-to-face, web, call-center, kiosk. All of these human perception factors must always be thought of as relative to a competitor's ability to provide them. Otherwise, the factors are meaningless, unless the business is a monopoly.

Once all three of these factors are understood, the business can begin to understand and manage how the customer perceives the value of the business's products and services. Given that a business's products and price are reasonably competitive, 70% of what determines a customer's perception of value is the degree of humanness in their interactions.

"The Best Value Wins" (CVA)

In order to understand how these three factors work together, an approach referred to as customer value added or CVA can be applied to understand, measure, and manage this perception of value. Customer value added is similar to economic value added (EVA) in which a business strives to provide a return to shareholders beyond the average they could expect from investments in companies of similar risk. The CVA approach is based on providing products and services to customers that are a greater value than they could expect from purchases from competitive companies in similar markets.

Was It "Worth What I Paid for It"?

The central concept used to help define the measurement of a customer's perception of relative value is called "worth what paid for" (WWPF), i.e. "Is it worth what I paid for the product or service relative to my other choices?" The answer to this question is a strong loyalty indicator. If the business receives an excellent score on the overall customer value measurement, i.e. the degree to which the customer perceives that the product or service was "worth what they paid for it" relative to the competitor's product or service, there will be a very high probability for strong customer loyalty. This customer loyalty is indicated by measurements that track the responses to questions such as:

1 I'll buy again.

2 I'll tell my friends.

3 I'll buy more from you.

An example of the "I'll buy more from you" would be "I'll buy not just your washing machine but your dishwasher too". In order to receive consistently high responses for these loyalty indicators, the business must receive at least a 5 on an overall 5-point scale, or a 9 or 10 on an overall 10-point scale, of an overall customer value measurement. In order to get an excellent score on these overall scores, there are distinct human interaction attributes that a business must embody in each one of their interactions.

The equation view of the CVA approach is as follows:

$$CVA = \frac{\text{Perceived worth of a business's offer}}{\text{Perceived worth of a competitive offer}}$$

The concept of "worth what paid for" focuses on the three aspects mentioned above which create the perceived worth of a business's offer relative to competitors. In addition, a business must ensure that the price of their product or service as well as any of the customer's lifecycle product costs, which affect the perception of cost of the product, create a good relative competitive price for the customer. This will allow the business to create the best relative value for their product or service, which in turn creates the best market share. If the business does this, while at the same time not "giving the product away" and also ensuring efficient processes in the delivery of the product or service, the probability for success is high. The concept of "the best value wins" for the customer value side of the equation is as certain as the concepts of profit equals revenue minus costs, and whenever a business can make the best profit over time, the shareholders win.

From a strategic perspective, the CVA approach helps a business understand and manage the three necessary components of business success:

1   Choosing the right value proposition for products and services to be delivered.

2   Managing the delivery of that value better than the competitors.

3   Successfully communicating that value because customers need to know.

The most surprising downfall to most firms is that they failed to communicate the value they created to their customers. They dedicate so much of their resources to choosing and delivering value, they end up under-resourcing the step that communicates value. As a result, they fall short of actually communicating that value to their customer. In this scenario, the value to the customer doesn't exist.

CVA measurements can also be a good leading indicator of the fluctuations in market share. The amount of lag time between changes in a business's CVA score and the market share fluctuation varies with the speed of the marketplace. Some highly dynamic

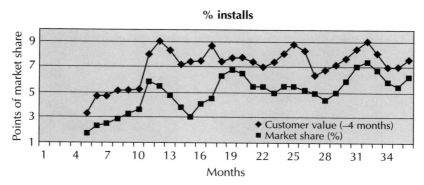

Figure 7.1   Market share and CVA scores
(reproduced by permission of Ray Kordupleski)

industries, such as delivery services, can experience fluctuations within 48 hours of fluctuations in their internal CVA measurements. Other industries with slower purchasing cycles can produce lags of several months. Industries with highly reactive market shares are typically industries having a small number of explicit and simple customer promises, e.g. on-time delivery, packages not lost or damaged. (See Figure 7.1.)

CVA measurements can also be a good indicator of share of wallet predictions. If a business receives a relative customer value score of 10% less than its competitors, statistically it will receive 0% wallet share. If a business receives a relative customer value score of 5% less than its competitors, it will statistically only receive 20% of the customer's wallet share. If the business receives the same relative value score as its competitor, it will statistically receive 50% of a customer's wallet share. It is not until the business receives the relative customer value score of 30% higher than its competitors that it will statistically receive 100% of the customer's wallet share. (See Figure 7.2.)

The CVA journey

In order to implement the CVA approach effectively, businesses must first clarify their vision and mission. They must then endeavor to understand themselves and their market by not only collecting good data but also teaching themselves how to use the data. This

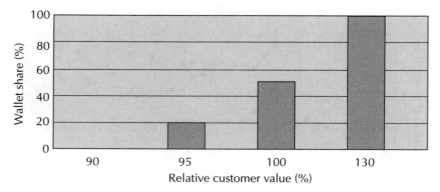

Figure 7.2   Share of wallet vs. relative customer value
(reproduced by permission of Ray Kordupleski)

data must drive the changes in business priorities. As priorities change, efforts must focus as much on "what not to do" as on "what to do". From these priorities, new process changes and their respective measures must be put in place in a process-oriented culture for systemic change.

This entails first analyzing what the customers want. This is accomplished through applying market research and statistics. The next step is to understand how well the business is doing relative to its competitors. Once this is done, economic models can be created to prioritize the business's focus. Then, quality improvement teams can be created and taught quality process improvement skills by quality experts. The business will then need to be taught how to understand and accept the data as meaningful to the business objectives. Once this is accomplished, the measurements can be turned into actions through quality improvement programs.

+   Analyze what customers want.

+   Apply market research and statistics.

+   Compare the business's success with that of its competitors.

+   Create economic models to prioritize focus.

+   Create quality improvement teams and teach quality process improvement skills.

+   Teach the business how to understand and accept data.

+ Turn measurements into actions through quality improvement programs.

Balancing the science and art

Balancing the science and art of a CVA project requires understanding the art and science of the project and their dynamics. The science is the mechanics of the project and the art is the human factors that will cause those mechanics to actually occur. Most of the art occurs at the beginning and the end of the project where human elements need to be managed carefully. The beginning art is expressed in such activities as project design, architecture, meaning, purpose, creating a vision, and the hope for the future, and getting the right "players" in place. This mix of players should be able to create the right "art and science" for the project. Most of the science or mechanics occurs in the middle phases of the project. The initial questions of science are:

+ How does the business capture the information?

+ How do they organize it?

+ How do they analyze it?

The science aspects of the project define such questions as:

+ What are the most important markets?

+ Who are the most important customers?

+ Who are the toughest competitors (currently and in the future)?

+ How many customers do we survey (sample size)?

+ How do we get the telephone numbers/e-mail IDs?

+ How do we conduct the survey (phone, face-to-face, Internet, mail)?

+ Which statistical technique do we use, e.g. multilinear probit, probability, multivariant regression?

The continual learning with regard to the subtleties in different competitive situations of applying the art and science of the CVA fundamentals is never-ending.

The science

The science aspects start with basic fact-finding regarding the "hard" questions. If a business blindly moves forward without answering these critical questions, the chances of succeeding are minimal. The following is a sample set of questions that drive the more important science aspects:

+ Which markets and customers create the highest value for the company?

+ What is the relative importance of those markets?

+ Where should the business start to understand the customer value proposition?

+ Who and what do the most important customers think the business is?

+ What are the products and services?

+ What are the combinations of products and services?

+ What are the key geographical, product, and customer markets?

+ Who are the business's main customers?

+ What are the business's services?

+ Who are the competitors?

+ Who are the toughest competitors?

+ Who are the specific individuals the business needs to talk to?

+ What is the business going to talk to them about?

+ What are the revenue generators that the company has to critically focus on?

+ What are the critical new markets that will sustain growth in the future?

Once these questions are answered, the following provides an approximate sequence of steps that should take place for accomplishing the CVA process:

✦ Business units inject their perception of their value proposition.

✦ Validate this value proposition perception with selective customers.

✦ Design, test, validate the survey, i.e. decide which questions to ask.

✦ Administer the survey and collect the data.

✦ Analyze the data to create trees and value maps with profiles and interaction waterfalls.

✦ Link the trees and value maps to specific business processes.

✦ Collect internal business process measures and link them to the customer perceptions.

✦ Place output in report format so that people can understand it and use it.

The art

Most of the art comes into play toward the later stages of the project as the data becomes available. The art needs to answer such questions as:

✦ How does the business get their business units to understand the value of the data?

✦ How does the business communicate internally?

✦ How does the business get its business units to accept the data?

✦ How does the business get the business units to act on it?

Once the data is available, the art is "capturing the attention" of the business as to what the data means and what the data can do for achieving business objectives. Ultimately the business wants its business units to have the following reaction: "Yes, this is good for me and I can, should, and want to do this." Once this critical acceptance occurs, the data can be improved upon with further refinements and sophistication of human interactions. Running through the entire process is the art of role modeling. The executive champion is the snow ski instructor applauding the first of his five students for skiing down a difficult slope, with the other four students looking on and wondering, "Why is he getting all this attention?" And then the other four say to themselves, "I can do that too!"

The value tree ... the art and science

The art and the science of the CVA process begin with building a value tree. This first step focuses on a particular customer group or segment by creating a value proposition or "value tree". The value tree will depict what creates value for the customer. Once the business decides on its value, the tree branches into the two or three major components:

1   Products and services, i.e. what they get.

2   Humanness of interactions or business relationship, i.e. how they get it.

3   Cost to the customer of doing business with them, i.e. the price.

This "tree" is continually branched into its sub-branches to understand what it is that creates value for that customer. A value tree can be created across an entire industry supply chain that will link the entire value of the industry. For example, Texas Instruments could study their customer satisfaction with their digital signal processing products (integrated circuitry that enables a cellular phone to work, i.e. the heart of a cell phone). One of Texas Instruments' biggest customers is Nokia. Texas Instruments could be helped by studying Nokia's customers' satisfaction with their digital signal processors, e.g. product quality, how the customer gets the product, the technical services, technical training on how to use the products, the cost, the business relationship. Nokia, in turn, could study the satisfaction of Bell Canada people who sell the Nokia phones. Nokia may also want to know how satisfied the end-users are with their phones. Bell Canada, in turn, will study the end-user satisfaction of customers who actually use their cellular services.

The ultimate objective is to understand what customers want, and how that relates to what they pay. This provides an image of the perceived net value of their purchase. Not only does the value tree articulate what the customer values and how the business delivers on that value, it creates a comparison to competitive alternatives. This comparison can then be linked back to business processes so the business can continually reprioritize their finite time, energy, and financial resources.

Capturing Customer Value Data

An important decision is to determine who and what to survey to create the necessary customer value data to create the "worth what paid for" value tree. Two types of data must be collected. The first type of data to collect is related to the actual buying decision-makers of the business's customers and competitors' customers with the full spectrum of costs and benefits of products and services. This data should be non-event-driven, which means it should not be connected to "feelings" about any particular purchase.

✦   Market perceptions.

   —Decision-maker.

   —Your customers and competitors' customers.

   —Full spectrum of benefits and costs.

   —Non-event-driven.

A second type of data to collect is relative to specific transactions completed by the customers who are actually using the products and services, i.e. the business's customers. This type of data should be limited to feelings about the specific experience and related to a recent event, e.g. purchase, usage.

✦   Transactions.

   —Customer using the product or service.

   —Your customers.

   —Limited to a specific experience.

   —Recent-event-driven.

The market perception data, which is focused on the feelings of the decision-makers, should take the value tree structure shown in Figure 7.3. The tree branch of "quality" should be divided into products and services and the tree branch of "price" should be divided into initial costs and lifecycle costs. The product tree branch should list features that are important to the customers. The service tree branch should list the different interactions with the customers.

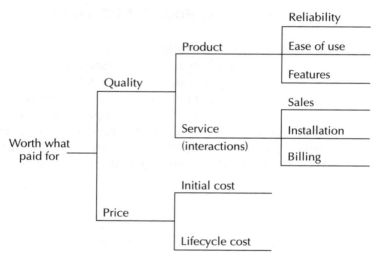

Figure 7.3   Market perception/decision-maker
(reproduced by permission of Ray Kordupleski)

The feelings of the customer involved in the actual transaction should be mapped out in the billing branch of the quality/service branch and disaggregated into the physical attributes of the service and the actual interaction attributes. These attributes should represent what is most important to the customer. The attributes and branches listed in these value trees are only examples but will serve as a good starting point for most businesses. (See Figure 7.4.)

Figure 7.5 shows an example of a financial institution's market perception/decision-maker value tree. The decision-makers in these markets judged stability, variety, and particular features and options as important for the bank's products. The customers judged

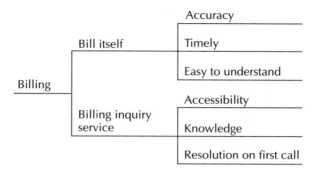

Figure 7.4   Transaction/customer surveys
(reproduced by permission of Ray Kordupleski)

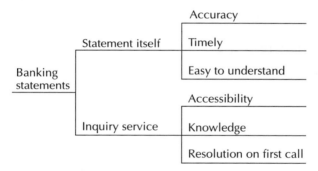

Figure 7.5   Banking example – transaction/customer surveys
(reproduced by permission of Ray Kordupleski)

how well they feel the financial institution did on account initiation, servicing, and statements as most important to them.

Survey Management Standards

The sample sizes of the surveys should be at least at a 95% confidence level with plus or minus 5% precision of measurement. The survey should ask questions that make up the "worth what paid for" value tree along with overall questions about the satisfaction of products and services. It should also capture relative satisfaction with the product and service prices. Other responses should be on a 10-point scale with bipolar anchors. Professionals who understand the dynamics of surveying and the data collection should do the surveys.

+ Sample size.

  —95% confidence.

  —+ or −5% precision.

+ Required questions.

  —Worth what paid for.

  —Overall satisfaction with products and services.

  —Satisfaction with prices.

+ Scales and responses.

  —10-point.

  —Bipolar anchors.

  —Professional personnel.

Derive the Hierarchy of Needs and Their Importance Weights

The next important step is to use the product and service attributes to create a hierarchy of needs with the respective weights of importance to the customers. Table 7.1 is a fairly good representation of the balance between the importance of product features and the importance of service or "interaction" attributes. Early research

Table 7.1 Attributes – impact weight

Attributes	Impact weight
Product quality	30
Sales interactions	15
Repair interactions	30
Installation interactions	10
Billing interactions	15

indicates that most customers will rank the more human attributes of interaction as most important in this hierarchy of needs.

Human Touch ... Attributes of a Highly Human Interaction

Early research has shown that the majority of a customer's perception of a business is linked to a distinct set of human interaction attributes. There are nine specific core human interaction attributes that are most important to customers. These nine human interaction attributes will vary slightly by industry and market but are generally consistent. They support the three primary human needs for buying cited in the previous chapters – acknowledgement, respect, and trust.

These nine distinct human interaction attributes are as follows:

Interaction attributes		*Human buying need*
1	Being accessible	Acknowledgement
2	Responsiveness	Acknowledgement
3	Follow up	Acknowledgement
4	Doing things promptly	Respect
5	Keeping people informed	Respect
6	Keeping your promise	Trust building
7	Knowledgeable	Trust building
8	No surprises	Trust building
9	Doing it right the first time	Trust building

These nine human attributes, provided by Ray Kordupleski, have proven to be more important than the product features or price of the product. They create the majority of how the customer forms their opinion (perception) of the value of the product or service they are purchasing. They are largely interaction attributes that either fulfill or don't fulfill the human needs of customers during interactions with the business. The more integrated these nine attributes are in each of the businesses interactions, the more the customer "feels" valued, acknowledged, and respected. These nine human interaction attributes can be referred to as a business's "human touch".

Impact of a simple human touch

Table 7.2 illustrates just how significant an impact just one of these nine human touch attributes, "keeping people informed", can have on the customer's feeling about the business. This particular example is a telecommunications repair scenario. The average excellence rating for this type of repair is 51%. If the repair is accomplished within two hours of notification, the customer rates the business at an 81% excellence rating. If the repair takes longer than two hours, the customer gives the business a 74% excellence rating. If the repair takes longer than one day, the customer gives the business the 46% excellence rating. If the problem is fixed within two hours and the business communicates to the customer that the problem is being addressed, the customer's excellence rating jumps to 84%. If the repair is done within two hours and the business calls the customer during the repair letting them know that they are currently working on a problem and it will be fixed shortly, the customer gives the business a 90% excellence rating. The difference between the 81% and 90% in a competitive market is significant. This difference was achieved simply with the human touch of a courtesy phone call that created the feeling of acknowledgement and respect within the customer.

Table 7.2   Resolve problems – excellence rating

Resolve problems	Excellence rating
Average excellence ratings	51%
Fix within two hours	81%
Takes longer than two hours	74%
Takes longer than a day	46%
Fix within two hours, tell customer	84%
Fix within two hours, tell during service	90%

Human needs are consistent

While there has been considerable debate as to whether these human touch attributes and the corresponding human "needs" they fulfill have changed over time, research has shown that the factors that drive a customer's perception of value are less related to being a "consumer" and more related to being a "human being". As such, the essence of being human has not changed over time despite what many businesses seem to believe. From Maslow's early days of studying the hierarchy of needs, starting with food, shelter, and other things such as physical health, humans have had a similar set of consistent and predictable human needs when they consume products and services.

These nine "you're a real person and we care" interaction attributes can be translated as follows:

1   Accessibility

- Customer needs help when they want help.

2   Responsiveness

- Responsiveness doesn't necessarily translate into helping the customer quickly but rather into showing a genuine caring for the customer's personal needs. The fact that a retail store decides to be "more responsive" to its customers by opening earlier every day has little value if, when a customer walks in the door, no one shows any genuine interest in responding to them.

3   Knowledgeable

- Knowledgeable doesn't necessarily mean having knowledge about products or services, but instead knowing what a human being really needs. A business cannot acquire this type of knowledge until it understands the customer as a person.

4   Prompt

- Being prompt means delivering a product or service when the customer expects it.

5   Keep informed

- Keeping the customer informed means providing information to counter any potential human anxiety from uncertainty surrounding the purchase or consumption of a product or service.

  —An example would be, if a customer orders a product over the Internet that the business has promised to deliver in three days, but after the third day, the customer sees no sign of the product and so becomes anxious, wondering what has happened. If the business had the systems in place to be notified that they could not keep their delivery promise, a service rep could call the customer prior to the delivery date and provide comforting information about what was happening and when the package would actually be delivered. The customer's anxiety would be dissipated with this simple human touch. The customer would then remain informed and relaxed.

6   Keep your promise

- Delivering on any promise the business makes to a customer.

7   No surprises

- No surprises unless it's a well-thought-out good surprise, because no human being likes bad surprises.

8   Follow-up

- Follow-up is showing the customer simple courtesies such as thanking them, making sure certain activities happened, checking for closure.

9 Do it right the first time

- Making sure that the product or service was done right the first time to avoid rework and failure costs.

The "nine" doesn't change significantly, but environments do

While these nine human interaction attributes show up in almost every survey, the aspect that does change is the degree to which the weightings change in a particular situation, sequence, or industry. Another changeable aspect to these human factors is how proficient a business must be at any one of these interaction attributes relative to their competitors. Ten years ago, customers may have asked themselves: Where is the bank branch? What are their hours? How long is the wait in the teller line? Today, the customer may want to know: Where is the ATM and is it working? What is their website? How slow is it? In order for the business to truly understand how well they can satisfy these nine attributes, they must first understand what the customer perceives as "excellence in service" in any one of these attributes compared to the business's competitors. It is these attributes that are the primary building blocks of a relationship.

Cascading Waterfalls of Highly Human Interactions

In most businesses, these nine human attributes have a cascading effect starting with a business which is selling and marketing to the customer and ultimately interacts with them during follow-on activities such as delivery, installation, service, repair, and billing. Each subsequent interaction stage has a cascading effect, based on the customer's perception, from each previous interaction stage, i.e. marketing interactions affect sales interactions, which in turn affect installation interactions which influence service interactions. For example, if the sales efforts are highly human and personal and the follow-on service activities are cold and impersonal, the previous sales efforts as well as the perception of the entire company will be negatively affected. Therefore, these nine attributes need to be satisfied in every interaction that takes place. The cascading waterfall of satisfying interactions produces the customer's perception of value received. The dynamics of this cascading waterfall of interactions can be divided into "what they get" and "how they get it". The "what they get" portion is derived from tangible product attributes ranging from such consumables as financial services to washing machines. The "how they get it" portion is derived from the actual interactions of such activities ranging from sales, delivery, installation, repair, hotlines, training, websites. When the products are more customer-oriented and less interaction-oriented, the interactions become less important to the perceived relative value of the product. In the case of more customer-oriented products, the perceived value is more weighted toward such things as brand image (i.e. Is this a reliable and trustworthy brand?), and how the customer's image changes when they use the product. There are also the factors and processes that drive the customer's perception of price, such as the negotiation process, the engineering and design process, the process of information gathering (comparison shopping), payment terms and conditions, fees, and rates. These different attributes, perceived quality of product and service, image, price, can all be mapped, along with other dynamics, to create "waterfalls of interactions" that will represent the customer experience through their entire lifecycle with the business. The most common waterfalls are:

+ Product.

+ Service.

+ Prices.

+ Brand image.

In most cases, a business cannot reach excellence unless the business satisfies customer needs across all four waterfalls. Waterfalls can also be created to determine employee fulfillment. It is also important to realize that no one organization or employee in any business can totally satisfy the customer in any one of those waterfalls as the interactions are interdependent.

Under each one of the steps in the waterfall, there are certain specific attributes that must be done right. For instance, under the billing step, the company must be able to get certain attributes correct, such as:

1   No surprises.

2   One-call inquiries, service, and corrections.

3   Timely billing.

These distinct human interaction attributes created from specific activities can be thought of as the "you're a real person and we care" actions. One of the particularly interesting dynamics of how strongly customers react to these simple activities can be seen in skyrocketing fulfillment and value perception scores after such actions as a simple courtesy call is made to let the customer know that the business cares. This is most evident in service-related industries that have regular repair and service activities, e.g. banking, telecommunications, retail.

One Dehumanizing Interaction Affects the Entire "Waterfall"

The damage done when customers are treated poorly during one interaction in one area of the business is difficult to erase by another favorable interaction in another area of the business. For example, most businesses don't realize that how "human" a customer is treated during a product return or repair has a "spider effect" on the perception of other aspects of the actual quality of the product, fairness of price, and brand image. This is why seemingly small improvements in the humanness of interactions have exponential impacts on revenue and profit, e.g. a 2% increase in how human a business treats its customers yields a 0.5% increase in revenue. For example, one step of the waterfall might be sales. It would be erroneous to assume that the Vice President of Sales is totally responsible for satisfying the customer during the sales activity. The Vice President of Sales cannot totally satisfy the customer in the sales process because he or she relies on other departments such as engineering, legal, finance, billing, and installation. A salesperson may have done an exemplary job with the customer but numerous mistakes were made during billing which now taint the salesperson's efforts. In order to measure the success of fulfilling the customer's aggregate experience, the experience must be measured on a cross-functional basis.

Figure 7.6 shows a representative cascading waterfall of "you're a real person and we care" with the most important human interaction attributes to customers.

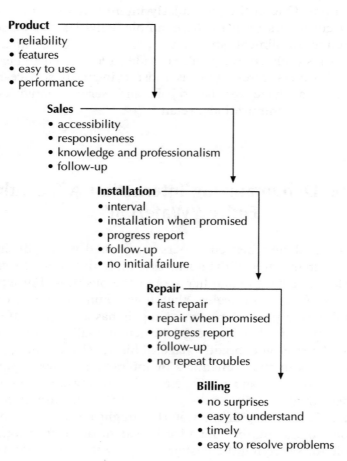

Figure 7.6   The waterfall process
(reproduced by permission of Ray Kordupleski)

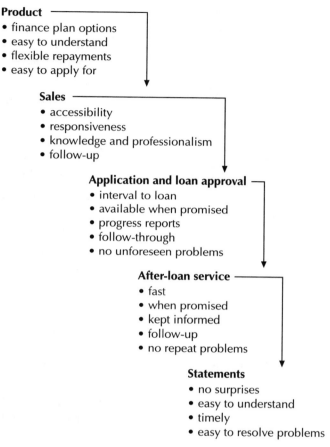

Product
- finance plan options
- easy to understand
- flexible repayments
- easy to apply for

Sales
- accessibility
- responsiveness
- knowledge and professionalism
- follow-up

Application and loan approval
- interval to loan
- available when promised
- progress reports
- follow-through
- no unforeseen problems

After-loan service
- fast
- when promised
- kept informed
- follow-up
- no repeat problems

Statements
- no surprises
- easy to understand
- timely
- easy to resolve problems

Figure 7.7   Example home loan waterfall process
(reproduced by permission of Ray Kordupleski)

Figure 7.7 shows an actual banking industry cascading waterfall for a home loan product with the most important human interaction attributes to customers.

Connecting Human Interaction Attributes in a Series of Human Interactions

The next important step is to take the cascading waterfalls of human interaction attributes or customer needs (weighted for importance)

Business process	Customer need		Internal metric
30% Product	Reliability	40%	% Repair call
	Easy to use	20%	% Calls for help
	Features/Functions	30%	Functional performance tes
30% Sales	Knowledge	30%	Supervisor operations
	Responsive	25%	% Proposal made on time
	Follow-up	10%	% Follow-up made
10% Installation	Delivery interval meet needs	30%	Average order interval
	Does not break	25%	% Repair reports
	Installed when promised	10%	% Installed on due date
15% Repair	No repeat trouble	30%	% Repeat reports
	Fixed fast	25%	Average speed of repairs
	Kept informed	10%	% Customers informed
15% Billing	Accuracy, no surprise	45%	% Billing inquiries
	Resolve on first call	35%	% Resolved first call
	Easy to understand	10%	% Billing inquiries

Value perception drivers

Figure 7.8   Business process – customer needs – internal metrics
(many of the smaller internal metrics were purposefully left out to avoid creating an overly complex table. Therefore, the internal metric percentages in the figure do not add up to 100%; reproduced by permission of Ray Kordupleski)

and connect them with the supporting business processes (weighted by interaction importance) with their respective internal metrics. (See Figure 7.8.)

Connecting the Price Component to the Human Interaction Attributes

The next important step is to map out the pricing component, i.e. price perception drivers, in the cascading waterfalls of human interaction attributes or customer needs. Costs and their relative importance should cover such costs as initial outlay, monthly maintenance, operating, savings, and the scrap value or disposal costs. These cost categories should be weighted in order of importance, and so should the subcategories of each category of cost. (See Figure 7.9.)

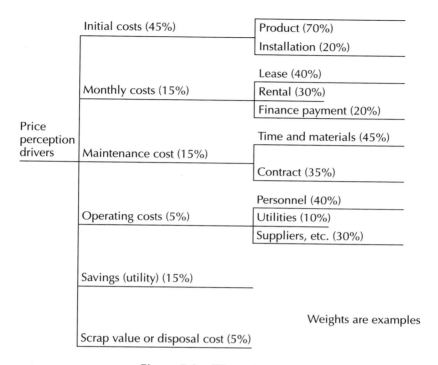

Figure 7.9   The price tree

(many of the smaller internal metrics were purposefully left out to avoid creating an overly complex figure. Therefore, the internal metric percentages in the figure do not add up to 100%; reproduced by permission of Ray Kordupleski)

Making It All Relative to Competitors

The next important step is to map the comparison of the human interaction attributes, product and service features, and pricing components to that of the business's competitor. Table 7.3 is an actual example of a bank's relative perceived customer value profile, including the key purchase criteria with their respective weightings and the ratio comparing its business with its competitors.

Table 7.4 gives the key purchase criteria for the bank's bill and billing services.

Table 7.5 illustrates how a telecommunications business's relative perceived customer value profile with the key purchase criteria would be mapped.

Table 7.3   Key purchase criteria – importance weight % – your company – competition – ratio

Key purchase criteria	Importance weight (%)	Your company	Competition	Ratio
Products				
Stability	16	8.6	8.0	1.08
Features/options	14	8.0	7.8	1.03
Variety	5	9.0	8.6	1.05
Sub-total	35			
Service				
Account initiation	29	8.3	8.1	1.03
Financial consulting	6	8.3	8.3	1.00
Account servicing	15	7.9	8.1	0.98
Statements	15	7.0	8.0	0.88
Sub-total	65			

Table 7.4   Key purchase criteria – importance weighting % – business – competitors – ratio

Key purchase criteria	Importance weight (%)	Business	Competitors	Ratio
No surprise	45	7.9	8.9	0.88
Call only once	35	8.2	8.2	1.00
Easy to understand	10	8.7	8.2	10.6

Good Is Not Good Enough

In order for a company to receive an excellent overall customer satisfaction rating, the company must be able to successfully execute three of the five most important attributes to the "excellent" level, and the two remaining to the "good" level. The reason why businesses experience such a large customer improvement when a simple follow-up phone call is placed in the customer interaction process is that most businesses don't take the time to properly resource their human touch. These human touch activities distinguish one business's interaction from another's because

Table 7.5   Key purchase criteria – importance weight % – your company –
competition – ratio

Key purchase criteria	Importance weight (%)	Your company	Competition	Ratio
Products				
Reliability	16	8.6	8.0	1.08
Features	14	8.0	7.8	1.03
Durability	5	9.0	8.6	1.05
Sub-total	35			
Service				
Sales	29	8.3	8.1	1.03
Installation	6	8.3	8.3	1.00
Repair	15	7.9	8.1	0.98
Billing	15	7.0	8.0	0.88
Sub-total	65			

these activities are largely ignored and the lack of "humanness" stands out in the customer's mind. A business still must execute successfully on the other operational activities for its human touch to make the business stand out in the customers' eyes relative to competitors.

The Slippery Slope

The slippery slope concept refers to the CVA concept that illustrates how dramatically a customer's loyalty degrades when a business scores below an 8 out of 10 on the "worth what paid for" score. If the business does not do an excellent job on its human touch activities for each interaction, customer loyalty degrades precipitously. Once the business scores an 8 or above, improvements in customer loyalty are worthwhile but don't represent dramatic changes in customer loyalty.

Figure 7.10 depicts the slippery slope for the customers' perception of total quality.

Figure 7.11 illustrates the slippery slope for a particular bank.

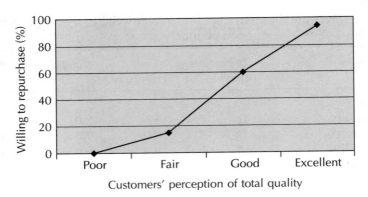

Figure 7.10   Good isn't good enough
(reproduced by permission of Ray Kordupleski)

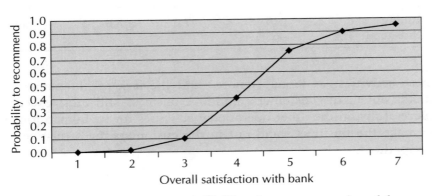

Figure 7.11   Actual bank likelihood to recommend model
(reproduced by permission of Ray Kordupleski)

Continuing the Art of CVA

Casting the right players

Making the change of improving the humanness of customer interactions involves casting the right players, such as a sponsoring
executive champion, change agent, marketing research, and
project administrator, and the business units themselves, with
process-oriented people. While most of the project activities for
these project participants center around understanding the business's current situation and improvements, it is equally important
to understand not only which individuals would best suit these role

requirements but also what would constitute personal wins for each individual during the project.

Executive champion

The executive champion should have high-level clout, a good sense of the human interplay of employee needs in a project, an appreciation of customers as people, and a clear vision and mission. This executive doesn't have to be the one with a vision but must feel that the change agent's vision is valid and sound. The executive champion takes on the role of the "strong protector". This "strong protector" role must protect the program and its agents of change from attack during initial proving periods. This executive must also manage important cultural issues, such as how this new information makes people look, good or bad. If one person looks bad, then they may attack the concept or project because they are in competition with a person that the information made look good. Other reactions that should be guarded against are: "That's not the way we do things around here", or "It's somebody else's baby, and I don't want any part of it". The executive champion is the one who pulls the arrows out of people's backs, and then reinvigorates the team with a pep talk, "Go out there and hit them again". The executive also provides high-level guidance to the people working on the project. The executive must make sure that priorities are managed, not simply "added" to create more work for an already fully engaged staff. The most important priorities should not center on "What should we do?" but should center on "What should we not do?" The inability to create an effective triage of priorities will only fuel "attacks" during this type of project. The executive champion also needs to emotionally engage the business units so they will believe that spending time and resource on this project will ultimately be the best chance of achieving their business objectives. Any changes occurring in the business units will not be lasting unless process changes take place. This is why it is important to have "process" support to make these changes systemic. The champion will also need to emotionally engage the business units not only so that they will understand the new information but also so that people will accept the importance of the subject and the information revealed.

Change agent

The change agent is an individual who is typically not striving to become the next senior officer in the business but who is dedicated toward making positive change happen in the company. This person must also understand how the company works with all its major processes. They also must understand "who's who" in the organization, i.e. someone may hold a particular position of responsibility but is predominantly influenced by another individual in making decisions. They must also understand the vision, and be able to communicate that vision, and how this vision relates to the business's major processes and political framework. Also, this person must be sensitive to the timing of change as well as to the steps required for positive change. The change agent can be from almost any role within the business, e.g. sales, research, operations, or marketing. In some cases, the change agent comes out of the research organization, but more than 50% of the time they come from another organization. In some situations, a non-executive change agent or market research person can see the full vision of what needs to happen but doesn't have enough authority or budget to make that vision happen. They also may be naive in their understanding of what it would take to actually bring sweeping corporate change to fruition. They may not have "lived through" a major change in a corporation and as a result don't fully understand how long it will take, what effort is necessary to make it happen, and the effective timing of events. They may also be tempted to promise more than can be delivered based on the time and resources available to them.

Marketing research

The marketing research organization should be able to manage the research efforts and capture the data. Not only should marketing research people be able to understand and manage market research, they should ensure that whatever data is collected is "meaningful". This means that marketing research collect the right data from the right markets. They also ensure that the data is believable and reliable, has precision and confidence, and can be understood by people who are not professional market researchers. An additional role for the research organization is that they need to monitor how clean the data is. The data must be as flawless as possible because any flaws in the customer data could possibly change the answers to what "we should do" and what "we shouldn't do", which may create inappropriate project priorities. In addition, flaws in the data will fuel the appearance of "political blunders" within the organization. Any flaws or errors will also give power to the nay-sayers who are resisting this change. In many cases, one major data flaw can taint support for the whole project. If these flaws require that reports be continually updated in the early stages of the project, the project credibility may be irreparably damaged. If the organization does not have sufficiently strong marketing research, external market researchers may be brought in who will be able not only to effectively design the appropriate surveys for the marketplace but also to manage the administration of the survey as well, e.g. Internet, phone, mail, face-to-face.

Ideally, the most rigorous and professional way to create the underpinnings of the change program is to gather hard data from the marketplace. In some situations, executive opinion can be used to create a "picture" of the marketplace. In most cases, the best approach is to utilize a market research organization to gather information from customers in order to best understand the dynamics of customer perception and value. In some cases, a firm may be large enough to have its own market research organization where there are several individuals who manage and outsource the majority of market research activities.

Econometricians

Econometricians are also very helpful in applying various statistical analysis techniques. These econometricians should be keen on understanding the economic and business impact of the statistics and how those statistics relate to the business. They can also provide the statistical analysis outputs to the value trees and maps.

Project administrator

The project administrator should have solid administrative and people skills. This person should have the skills to manage the numerous meetings involved, manage the flow of information and work requests, coordinate e-mails, record meetings, manage conferences, manage the project data, the workshops, the logistics, and the series of project reports. Neither the executive champion nor the change agent will probably have much desire or time to handle this type of administrative role. While the change agent may have good solid project management skills, the change agent still relies on the administrator for administrative details. In some cases, the administrator is simply any dedicated project manager. One of the understaffed skills required for an effective project is the ability to make the project presentation look "pretty". Many projects have failed, though they exhibited good work, because of ineffective sales and marketing of that project.

An Implementation Story – CVA at Suncorp

To make a practical and meaningful difference, any approach such as CVA needs to quickly translate into specific and focused action. The end goal is to achieve a positive impact on the business, in order for the investment of time and resources to be justified. Suncorp's investments in CVA have already been rewarded. Many of the specific elements which their analysis of CVA data revealed to be the most important to customers can be grouped together under the overall umbrella of meeting the basic human expectations of a healthy relationship or social interaction. The following section presents some of the action-oriented results of the leading-edge work of Ilmar Taimre, Project Director for Suncorp's Customer Satisfaction Initiative, and his team. Ilmar's CVA work is supported by the visionary leadership of Steve Jones, Suncorp's CEO.

While they are not the largest bank or insurance company in Australia, Suncorp believe that they can make significant strides with a goal of world-class service encounters with customers, i.e. treating each of their customers as human beings. Suncorp is currently Australia's sixth-largest bank and second-largest insurance company, with assets of over $31 billion. There are over 3.5 million customers and approximately 8,400 staff. Suncorp have 193 retail and business banking outlets and 81 insurance branches and sole agencies. Their main businesses are banking, insurance, investment and superannuation products, with a focus on retail customers and small- to medium-size businesses. Suncorp also recently acquired a large insurance company – GIO, one of the larger insurance companies in Australia.

Suncorp have the highest cross-sell rates in the Australian financial services sector – 3.6 products per customer, of those people surveyed who nominated Suncorp as their main financial institution. Currently, 63% of customer households have two or more products and 40% of households have three or more products. They are currently on a trajectory to improve these performance metrics even further with the progression of their CVA work.

From a strategy perspective, Suncorp's CVA program supports each of their four primary goals:

1   Grow revenue faster than the industry in each line of business.

2   #1 in customer satisfaction in each LOB (line of business).

3   Improve productivity faster than inflation.

4   World-class employee satisfaction.

Suncorp believe that if they execute all four goals, their investors will experience returns in the top 15–20% of alternative investments. The end goal of these strategies is to double (plus) value to Suncorp shareholders within five years.

At the core of all of these strategies is to be No. 1 in customer satisfaction. While there are many individual initiatives aimed at driving towards this common goal, almost all of them can be thought of as a conscious effort to treat customers as individual human beings in every interaction. Inside the company, this goal is described as consistently delivering "world-class" services.

Suncorp have chosen to focus specifically on world-class service rather than price satisfaction because they do not have the same economies of scale as their largest competitors and therefore could not compete as effectively on price. Another rationale is that competing on product (as opposed to service) features would generally allow competitors to replicate most new product features in a relatively short time. However, service competencies typically require a longer time to develop and often involve end-to-end process changes which most large organizations find difficult to implement quickly. Thus, a strategy that aims to compete on service made the most sense as a way of building a sustainable competitive edge for Suncorp.

Support for this strategy was strengthened when Suncorp researched their marketplace and found that none of their competitors is considered exceptional in delivering customer service. In effect, the competitive positioning labeled "top notch services" was vacant.

One of the main factors behind the widespread perception of lower service levels in the Australian financial services marketplace is that in the mid-1980s, Suncorp's large bank competitors were faced with downsizing their extensive branch infrastructure to reduce the unacceptable expense burden. In doing this, the major banks undertook large-scale branch closures, which directly impacted many small towns and suburban centers. At these locations, branches were replaced by automated service options such as ATMs and telephone banking. This created tremendous animosity with customers, to the point that derogatory comments about the eroding quality of bank services became commonplace, both in the media and in political circles. At the same time, most of Suncorp's competitors implemented aggressive "fee for service" initiatives because of increasing expense pressures. In the previous regulated banking era, service levels had been cross-subsidized by other profitable segments of the business. After de-regulation, as margins were squeezed, those very profitable segments dwindled, and the big banks seemed to have little choice but to reduce levels of service to their customers.

Customers have reacted negatively to this "death by a thousand cuts" approach to reducing levels of customer service and a range of new or increasing fees. In this context, Suncorp have had the advantage of being perceived as a "regional" bank rather than one of the "big four". Suncorp have not needed to embark on a widespread program of branch closures. This has given them an added perception of having a friendlier, human face. This perception is also fueled by local press publicizing issues of social responsibility for banks in small towns and suburban locations.

Suncorp started implementing their "worth what paid for" approach by bringing together all the "stakeholders" of all the seven major lines of business. These seven lines of business are broadly grouped into one of four areas – consumer banking, investments, insurance, and business banking.

Consumer banking includes transaction banking and home lending. Business banking includes owner-managed businesses, and small-to medium-sized businesses. Insurance includes home insurance and motor insurance. These seven main lines of business account for over 80% of Suncorp's revenue. This made it critically important for Suncorp to undertake specific service initiatives in each of these areas to differentiate their levels of service from their competitors. Internally, they refer to these specific service initiatives as their "Blue Ribbon" service initiatives.

"Blue Ribbon" service initiatives

In November 2001, Suncorp launched five Blue Ribbon service initiatives as the first installment derived from their CVA activities. These Blue Ribbon initiatives have each passed through the three essential stages of executing a value-based competitive strategy:

1   Choose value.

2   Deliver value.

3   Communicate value.

First, a business must choose the value it wishes to deliver based on the needs discovered from its customers. Second, the business must develop a competency to effectively deliver that value. Third, a business must effectively communicate that value in order for it to truly exist in the minds of its customers.

To ensure that the company's scarce resources are deployed to maximum positive effect, Suncorp kicked off their portfolio of Blue Ribbon service initiatives in those areas where they knew from the data that:

✦   Customers highly value a particular aspect of service.

✦   Other competitors are struggling to deliver this same aspect of service.

By tightly focusing their energies in this way, making sure they could consistently deliver on some high-impact service promises, and then actively publicizing these to the market through advertising and other service channel promotions, Suncorp were consciously aiming to touch some "hot buttons" in the market:

+ positively with customers;

+ negatively with their competitors.

Each "Blue Ribbon" service initiative has been carefully crafted to respond – in non-bureaucratic and straightforward human terms – to one or more of the key dimensions which define the overall quality of the service experiences most often encountered by their customers.

They identified the most important service dimensions by applying statistical analysis to their CVA survey results and then creating "Blue Ribbon" service initiatives specifically focused on the specific attributes which were revealed to be the most important of all. Not surprisingly, almost all of these most important service dimensions can be readily mapped back into the fundamental checklists of what it takes to:

1   Build and nurture any human relationship.

2   Participate in an effective human interaction or "value exchange".

At the end of the day, being good at running a service business is essentially the same thing as being good at treating people exactly how we would like to be treated ourselves.

Of course, the business world is also highly competitive. That's one reason why Suncorp prioritized the implementation of their first wave of Blue Ribbon service initiatives to focus on specific service attributes that are important to customers but at which competitors are widely perceived to be falling well short of matching customer expectations. For example, unacceptably long queues in bank branches or excessive call-center "hold times" were identified as common areas of complaint across all competitors. These two examples are discussed in more detail below.

Much of the success of the Blue Ribbon service processes can be attributed to the careful addition of a "human touch" in the small details which convey acknowledgement, respect, and trust to customers. The tools used to implement these human touch details took the form of such aids as service scripts, checklists, and standard operating procedures. These supporting tools are specifically aimed at responding to the "human" needs of customers during the different stages of a service encounter. Much of this has to do with simply reducing anxiety/uncertainty about the "unknown":

+ What the customer needs to do right now?

+ What the customer will need to do next?

+ What can go wrong?

Reducing this uncertainty is accomplished by proactively providing the customer information about questions that they typically asked during specific interactions. Another area where Suncorp invested special effort was always aiming to talk to their customers about these service pledges in everyday customer language, not in "corporate speak". Each of the Blue Ribbon service promises was tested in a variety of wordings, in an attempt to come up with the words that resonated most clearly with the majority of customers. In some cases, the words customers found to be most believable and straightforward were not the first choice of internal managers, even though the underlying service standard was identical.

Several Blue Ribbon service initiatives are focused around the three main ways customers interact with the company:

1 Call-center.

2 Branch.

3 Internet.

More recently, in their second wave of Blue Ribbon service initiatives, Suncorp introduced specific service promises for their mobile lenders and intermediary agents.

While these are all important customer interaction points, the call-center is considered to hold the main "pulse" of how the customer views Suncorp.

Suncorp's first wave of Blue Ribbon initiatives

Suncorp launched their first group of five Blue Ribbon initiatives:

+ Home loans – qualified approvals by phone in less than 15 minutes.

+ Call-center hold-time 60 seconds or less.

+ Motor insurance repairs within five days.

+ Business loan approval within five days.

+ Branch-teller-queue wait-times five minutes or less.

A second wave of Blue Ribbon initiatives was launched several months later. It is Suncorp's strategy to continue introducing additional new service promises to build an overwhelmingly commanding "world-class" service position, especially wherever there is particular weakness of their competitors in the marketplace. The common tag line across their ads is "Remember service"? "We do".

Home loans – qualified approvals by phone in less than 15 minutes

Suncorp's Blue Ribbon initiative for home loans promises that if a customer calls Suncorp on the phone about a home loan, they will confirm how much the customer can borrow within 15 minutes. Suncorp also will provide a personal home loan consultant to personally meet with the customer at the customer's convenience to help design the ideal home loan solution. The promise reads as follows: "Call Suncorp for a home loan and we'll confirm how much you can borrow within 15 minutes. We'll also provide your own personal home loan consultant who'll meet with you on your terms to help design the ideal home loan solution".

Call-center hold-time 60 seconds or less

Suncorp's research revealed that Australian banks – as well as many other large organizations – had unwittingly fomented a deep undercurrent of resentment among customers by introducing "automated" phone services that downplayed or discouraged the human factor. These phone systems are often designed so that customers are forced to step through numerous menu options before being able to choose to speak to a real human. Even after selecting the option to talk to a human being, customers are often placed on "hold" while waiting to speak to the next available consultant. Typically, the hold-time is filled with automated recordings repeating messages along the lines of "Your call is very important to us ..." What most companies don't realize is that poorly worded messages such as "Your call is very important to us ..." can have opposite to the intended effect. The poorly worded message creates distrust because the company itself is proving – by its action – that the customer is not especially important to them since the customer is forced to languish on hold while listening through many iterations of these recordings. Essentially, actions speak louder than words. When there is a contradiction between words and actions, customers see the company as hypocritical and not truthful. Unfortunately, organisations often fall into the trap of promising levels of service – either implicitly or explicitly – which they do not have the processes in place to support.

When Suncorp analyzed the key drivers of the overall telephone banking experience, the negative consequences of forcing customers to navigate voice response systems (VRS) without any immediate option to talk to a real human became clear. The analysis also revealed that most customers in this day and age are reasonably willing to accept that sometimes a short wait on hold may be needed. But, when hold-times exceed a maximum threshold, customers' acceptance drops away dramatically, as their sensation of feeling like "just another account number" in a dehumanized process overshadows the rest of the service encounter. The result is a customer who is dissatisfied with the overall experience. When the dehumanization of the voice response systems is coupled with other partially dehumanizing interactions (e.g. "Can you please tell me your 10-digit account number?"), the cumulative build-up creates a lasting negative image in the customer's mind that is not easily overcome. In order for a firm to overcome a series of negative human interactions, it would have to perfectly execute at least four largely positive humanizing interactions sequentially to change a negative overall impression.

Suncorp found that they could accurately predict their customer satisfaction score based on the average hold-times experienced by their customers. They also could quantify how long a customer was willing to wait on hold without significantly impacting the satisfaction of the call. They found that the customer's tolerance for waiting on hold dramatically falls after roughly 60 seconds. From this analysis, Suncorp set a target of answering nine out of ten customers (90%) who wanted to talk to a real human in 60 seconds or less. Once they consistently achieved this level of competency, they began a public advertising campaign based on this service standard. In addition, the remaining one out of ten customers does not wait much longer than 60 seconds. Operationally, implementing this type of competency required certain shifts in staffing as well as the appropriate training for the staff and the right tools, e.g. scripts. This "60 seconds or less" Blue Ribbon initiative was advertised along with four similar Blue Ribbon initiatives. Suncorp's promise reads as follows: "We aim to ensure most telephone calls to our call-center are answered in under one minute. Already, we answer 90% of calls in under 60 seconds".

Motor insurance repairs within five days

From their CVA research, Suncorp realized that the reputation of many car insurers was quite poor when it came to the process of actually lodging a claim and getting a damaged vehicle repaired quickly and competently. This offered a tremendous opportunity to differentiate themselves in service levels. Suncorp began by instituting their own assessment centers, which created a foundation for removing many of the dehumanizing elements from the auto claims process. Suncorp discovered that much of the human anxiety that plagues customers who need to process auto claims comes in the form of the following uncertainties:

✦   How long is my car going to be off the road?

+ What hassles do I have to go through to get my car fixed?

+ Do I have to get three different written quotes from three different repairers?

+ How do I know that the repairer is going to give me a quality job?

In addition, most customers only have a minimal understanding of how automobiles function, and have no real desire to ever learn – they simply want their car to work. To be thrust into a situation where an unknown party (repairer) is dealing with their automobile, the level of uncertainty and human anxiety climbs to an even higher level. From these human behavioral discoveries, Suncorp have created a Blue Ribbon initiative promising their customer that if their car is still drivable after an accident (80% still are drivable), the customer only needs to drive their car to any one of Suncorp's assessment centers. Suncorp have assessment centers located in every major city in Queensland as well as in Sydney and Melbourne. Suncorp will then arrange the car repair through their network of authorized repairers and guarantee the repairs for life. These repairs are promised to be completed within seven days once the car is dropped off. If, for whatever reason, the repairs take longer than seven days, they will provide the customer a courtesy car at no charge. Suncorp found from their survey research that one of the factors that underlies much of the stress associated with the auto claims process is the customers' anxiety – due to their unfamiliarity with the claims process and with motor repairs generally – that they are somehow going to get "screwed" by the insurer or repair facility.

Recognizing this, Suncorp have designed their ads to address the common anxieties and cynicism of customers going through the auto claims process.

Looking at their consolidated research across a range of service encounters and market sectors, they concluded that a constantly recurring factor causing the build-up of human anxiety in any service encounter is driven by the time pressure placed on most customer's lives. This is why many of Suncorp's service initiatives are linked to giving back time to the customer. They are careful to communicate that customers can confidently expect quite specific and predictable time-savings when they choose to interact with

Suncorp. More importantly, before any advertising of the time-savings occurs, they make sure they can operationally deliver on their promise consistently. Thus, for the car repair initiative, their promise reads as follows: "If you're able to drive your Suncorp-insured car into one of our assessment centers after an approved claim, we'll have you back on the road within a week. All repair work will be guaranteed for life. And if for some reason we can't fix your car within seven days we'll arrange a free courtesy car for you until your car is repaired".

When Suncorp initially investigated the emotional dimensions in a typical customer's insurance claim, they discovered that most customers were under growing time constraints in their normal lives. For these customers, any event or activity placing increased potential pressure – imagined or real – on this time constraint caused a significant increase in their anxiety level. From this early information, Suncorp began focusing on the cycle time of the end-to-end insurance claim process. As they investigated further into the emotional aspects of the customer's perception of the overall experience, they found that there was a series of activities, or lack of activities, beyond the time issue that left customers with "nagging" doubts as to whether they were truly being taken care of by Suncorp. Much of this customer anxiety seemed to form the spontaneous starting point for each individual, sometimes fed by a general market sentiment of negative word-of-mouth about banks and insurance companies, and their impersonal services. The result is an ambient background noise or legacy of customer distrust, which functions as a fertile breeding ground for suspicion and fears of being tricked somehow. For example, a customer's lack of trust could easily lead to thoughts such as: "There must be some tiny loophole that they are going to use to cheat me". This nagging sense of distrust in the marketplace, along with the customers' time constraints, led Suncorp to focus on providing a quick turnaround for the customers' auto claims while leaving the customer in no doubt that their car would be properly repaired with high-quality parts and craftsmanship. An important lesson for Suncorp to learn was that even though they had operationally already addressed the question of customers' confidence by providing a lifetime guarantee on the repairs, they had not adequately communicated this to their customers, so that many customers did not realize that this guarantee applied. A promise inadequately communicated to the customer doesn't exist in the minds of the customer. Suncorp discovered this communications issue after it applied high-level statistical analysis to its CVA surveys. They analyzed several of the statistical patterns and delved into the statistical suggestions of this problem with additional focus groups. They also investigated how to best communicate this guarantee to the customer. Suncorp found that until they effectively communicated this quality of work guarantee, the customer continued to have doubts as to whether their insurer would really stand behind the repair work.

Another important human need which emerged from additional qualitative work around accident claims was the fact that customers ideally just wanted their insurance company to handle all the "hassles" from the minute the accident happened to when they picked up the car. An auto accident can be a dramatic event. Any entity that can lessen some of the burden arising from that event will garner favor with the customer. As with the lifetime guarantee of quality work, Suncorp had already operationally set up processes to handle the many "hassles" of the claims process for the customer. But, in previous years, they had not adequately communicated this competency and its value to the customers and to the overall marketplace. This prompted Suncorp to be more explicit in communicating how they handle "all the little details" of the claim process and how that benefits the customer emotionally, i.e. "Yes, you will get your car back in seven days, and yes, your repairs will be guaranteed for life, and yes – the actual process is hassle-free because all you do is drop your car off at one of our assessment centers and everything else is taken care of by us – you don't have to even think about it until you get your car back". One of the key aspects of this communication is that it was accomplished with everyday language for real, genuine, ordinary people as opposed to business jargon. While it is very important to use more advanced statistical analysis and survey techniques, many of the clues to the importance of using everyday language came from qualitative focus group observation and from unsolicited customer letters. For example, Suncorp received one letter describing exactly how the customer emotionally felt about each part of their motor claims insurance process. Letters such as these were used to form the communication scripts to describe the total experience of their offerings in this marketplace. Suncorp experimented with alternative wordings to communicate the same basic content. The aim was not to distort or manipulate the truth, Suncorp's focus was to clearly articulate the value of its product and services to its customers.

Another important issue in communicating Suncorp's value to customers and the marketplace was striving to differentiate their very specific market offerings from their competitors' offerings, which could easily sound very similar. They found that a powerful way to achieve this was to use a certain level of specificity clearly delineating their quantifiable service offering from their competitors' "feel good" promises. By being "up front" and specific, and quoting a numeric measure that customers can easily relate to, they could achieve measurable differentiation in the mind of the customer, e.g. seven-day turnaround, 60-second response time.

Business loan approval within 5 days

Suncorp have applied these principles across all their main lines of business, including business banking. For business banking customers, their promise reads as follows: "Call Suncorp for a business loan and we'll give you an answer, in writing, within five working days". This is based on their CVA survey and focus group research confirming that customers in the business sector do value a quick turnaround period for business loans. While it is by no means the only important factor, it is definately one important driver of overall satisfaction with the business loan process.

The following example is for the commercial lending market. Figure 7.12 illustrates that customers who experience acceptable turnarounds give higher overall satisfaction ratings.

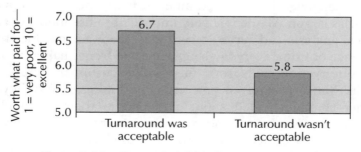

Figure 7.12   Commercial lending – all customers
(reproduced by permission of Suncorp)

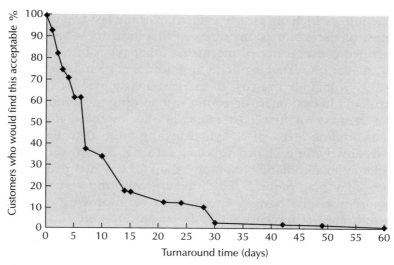

Figure 7.13   Acceptable turnaround times – commercial lending
(reproduced by permission of Suncorp)

Figure 7.13 illustrates that acceptability of turnaround time drops quickly beyond a five-day turnaround period.

Branch-teller-queue wait-times five minutes or less

In their bank branches, Suncorp have published a service promise whereby a customer will not have to wait more than five minutes in a queue before being served by a consultant. This is referred to as Suncorp's "five-minute" guarantee. They have chosen this service attribute because their analysis revealed that this was by far the worst-performing attribute of a customer's branch service encounter, for all competitors in the industry. In effect, it was a customer "hot button". Across the banking sector, "cost-saving" initiatives over many years have either implicitly or explicitly "pushed" customers away from "expensive" real human beings and toward machine-oriented interactions, e.g. telephone banking, ATMs. While high-level measures of productivity and cost, such as cost-to-income ratios have been trending downwards for most competitors throughout this same timeframe, the overall gains in productivity have arguably not been as dramatic as might have been expected. One possible reason is that eroding levels of customer satisfaction – which are clearly evident over the last five to ten years for most of the major competitors in this industry – have had the unintended consequence of increasing other types of costs that are rarely, if ever, captured explicitly in traditional accounting systems. These costs include the cost of increased customer attrition – the "churn" of old customers defecting and needing to be replaced by a similar number of new customers, or the lowering efficiency of sales, as eroding levels of customer loyalty mean that more people shop separately for each new product, rather than view their current provider as an automatic "one stop" shop for any new products and services they may require. Traditional accounting systems simply do not capture the bottom-line impacts of improving or eroding cross-sell rates, repurchase rates, defection rates, etc.

Suncorp also realize that there are substantial lead times involved in making the process improvements needed to deliver consistently and cost-effectively while maintaining exceptionally high service standards. This type of competitive differentiator can take a long time to replicate, unlike many product-based innovations that can be imitated relatively quickly.

Currently, approximately 95% of Suncorp's customers are served within the five-minute queue waiting time. Their promise reads as follows: "We aim to serve customers who visit our branches within five minutes. Already, 95% of customers are served within this time".

Discovering the Subtleties of the Human Touch

It is important to note that many of the points of human fulfillment are very subtle and require quantitative techniques beyond sophisticated quantitative information-gathering and analysis. almost always simple and careful listening during customer focus group exercises will yield small but very important nuances of human customer interaction. In many cases it is best to use quantitative approaches to build a simple framework as a starting point. Once the framework is built, then the human subtleties drawn from careful observation of customer focus groups can be layered on top of the framework. For example, Suncorp's quantitative framework for building this foundation is based on their customer value added (CVA) approach. The CVA framework is then overlaid with the subtle nuances of human needs and behaviors, i.e. the "meat on the bones".

Taking the Value of Common Courtesies for Granted

Suncorp believe it is important to create service scripts for their customer service representatives. While they feel service scripts are an important tool for their service reps, they do not insist the service reps follow the scripts verbatim. They believe that following service scripts verbatim creates a mechanical approach, which the customers can sense is impersonal. Therefore, while Suncorp do ensure that the service reps follow a logical sequence of specific steps covering the emotional and practical operational needs of the customer situation, service representatives also have some "room to move" within the scripts, to adapt them to their own personality or vary them depending on the individual customer interaction. This approach allows Suncorp to achieve their business brand objective of creating a genuinely "friendly" approach to customers, while not overlooking the key stages essential to a high-quality service interaction. To fully realize this brand objective, Suncorp found that it was necessary to explicitly train and encourage their service reps to consistently interject simple elements of common courtesy into each step in the interaction process, e.g. warm greeting, addressing customers by name, thank you. This need to explicitly direct their service reps to interject common courtesies came from the discovery that the value and use of common courtesies, used with balance and genuine sincerity, was not necessarily always immediately apparent to all new trainees. Many businesses make the common mistake of assuming that their customer-facing employees automatically know exactly what they ought to do.

The Human Need for Closure

As we have discussed in other parts of this book, "closure" is a critical aspect of every satisfying human interaction and is pivotal to ensuring the customer's anxiety is kept at a minimum. This is a basic and deep-seated human need. In business situations, this means that the customer wants to feel that in each step of a process, there is a sense of completion and finality. Internally, in their process design teams, Suncorp sometimes refer to this as building an explicit "rite of passage" into the key "handover" stages in an end-to-end process. Most businesses prematurely assume that customers feel closure before they actually do. The feeling of closure is not only important in emotionally progressing a customer onto the next required step of a process but also to create closure for an entire scenario, e.g. completing a loan, resolving a billing problem, returning a defective product. In Suncorp, this is accomplished by ensuring that key points in their service processes have explicit events to clearly indicate to the customer that they have moved from one stage of the process to the next stage of the process. Suncorp draw "lines of visibility" on their process maps to understand when these key transitions, or "moments of truth", occur from the customer's perspective. For example, Suncorp send out a customer letter confirming that they have acquired all the information necessary to make a decision on a business loan application. The simple letter also signals that it is their intention to treat this customer as an individual human being, not simply as a faceless business loan applicant. Suncorp also differentiate their human treatment of customers by ensuring that the employee who handles the initial loan enquiry is the same employee who replies back to the customer with the decision. This ensures a consistent human interaction element for the customer.

Suncorp found the assumption of closure to be an issue in their process once they started investigating the subtle emotional nuances of how the customer perceived issues or problems were handled. They found that their former approach too often created situations in which a disconnect occurred between what the service rep felt in terms of closure and what the customer felt in terms of closure. When they dug into these issues, Suncorp found that, even when the issue was "properly" resolved and closed in terms of the internal company policy, a significant percentage of their customers harbored doubts that the process step was completed and that it could still be perceived to be an "open" issue pending further uncertain actions. From this insight, they introduced an explicit step in key points on their processes to check that the customer understands what next steps either Suncorp or the customer must take in order to bring the problem to closure. Being explicit and proactive about ensuring closure also significantly reduces many potential bad surprises. The assurance of acceptable closure at the intermediate stages of a process is also important in setting positive expectations for the process of final closure. An important aspect of each intermediate closure step is to implement an explicit follow-up step to ensure that each intermediate step required for final closure is believed to have taken place by the customer. Of course, there needs to be a balance maintained in adding the additional steps to a process – it is also important to avoid "overkill" with this type of thing, which can end up irritating the customer and add unnecessary overheads to the cost of completing these processes. As so often with this type of process design, piloting one or more alternative approaches with real customers and staff can pay big dividends in uncovering what works best in practice.

In addition to lack of closure reducing customer satisfaction, closure issues also create productivity and efficiency issues. When a service rep fails to create closure with a customer, many times a customer will contact the business multiple times because of the unresolved questions that a lack of closure creates. Lack of adequate closure significantly increases follow-on calls to the call-center or visits to the branch where the customer's anxiety is still plagued by two major questions:

1   "What am I supposed to do next? ...Because I'm no expert in this ...".

2   "Am I all done now?"

Alleviating these two important questions, which arise from a natural need to know where you stand, can be accomplished by establishing a simple standard operating procedure similar to that of a checklist, e.g. Did you tell the customer what will happen next? Or tell them: "Here are some of the likely things that could happen next". Suncorp discovered that by focusing proactively on creating adequate closure, productivity and efficiency benefits also occurred, which supported another of their strategic goals.

The customer views a business as a series of interactions. And what they remember about the business is how human those interactions were. It only makes sense that a business should view themselves in the same manner. Approaching business in this manner requires an understanding of both the art of human behavior and the science of implementing it consistently across multiple interactions. The art of human behavior is as much about understanding how to enable a team of employees to create the changes necessary within an organization to implement the science of the human touch as it is about understanding and addressing the objective – customers' needs as human beings. The journey begins with an honest self-assessment of the business and its markets. It then enters into a phase of selecting the right players to create the necessary organizational and behavioral changes internally. The business then collects hard customer data that these players utilize to help the business begin to better address customers across a series of different interactions. One of the keys is to consistently embed specific human interaction attributes, such as being accessible, responsive, prompt, attentive, and knowledgeable, into each interaction. This human interaction ability must be measured against their competitors' in order to have any relevance and will only make significant impact if customers rate it as excellent. Merely being good at the human touch has little impact. Implementing the art and science of the human touch consistently across all interactions would create a marketplace competency against which few businesses could compete.

8

Human Touch as a Process

THIS CHAPTER IS A COMPELLING ILLUSTRATION OF HOW ONE BUSI-
ness was able to take its founding principles of genuine caring
and respect for both customers and employees and embed these
attributes into their core business processes. These processes were
then rigorously measured and continuously improved upon to
create one of the world's most caring and respected businesses –
Ritz-Carlton.

This is the story of Ritz-Carlton's visionary and pragmatic founder,
Horst Schulze, and his journey from an innate belief in genuine
caring for both customers and employees as the foundation for
long-term profitability and market leadership business success to
developing the science of the human touch through applying the
process-oriented disciplines of total quality management (TQM).
Other material contained in this chapter was taken from Ritz-
Carlton's 1999 Application Summary for the Malcolm Baldrige
National Quality Award.

The Beginnings

Eyes of a child

The spark of Ritz-Carlton's human touch began with its founder
Horst Schulze's early discovery that the essence of business success
was simply genuine caring. Horst Schulze began his career in the
hotel and travel business at the age of 14. He can recall his mother's
first words of advice when he began working in a restaurant. She
would say, "All of the people who come into this hotel are very

important". From then on, Horst recalls treating all his customers with the respect of "gods".

Horst also observed that the most successful workers at restaurants had an enduring sense of self-respect as well as a genuine caring nature for their customers. He recalls observing that when the restaurant's best maître d' entered the room, he carried with him a tremendous aura of self-respect that was immediately felt by every customer in the room. This maître d' extended this sense of self-respect to every customer he spoke with and they returned the same respect to him. In essence, he "gave" the customers respect from his own self-respect while at the same time showing genuine caring and concern for them. This caused customers to gravitate toward him, want to be served and acknowledged by him. In doing so, the customers felt their own self-respect grow. Horst observed that it was the qualities of respect, importance, and caring that created the near-perfect interaction between employee and customer in a business environment. These early observations were the beginning of Horst's founding principles on which he based his strategies for future business success. For the ensuing decades, his future business success would focus on one simple fact – guests and staff are human beings.

Birth of Ritz-Carlton

When Horst Schulze came into a position of influence, he could bring his earlier observations of genuine caring and respect for both customer and employees to bear on creating one of the world's most well-respected luxury hotels – Ritz-Carlton.

When Horst finally took his place at the head of Ritz-Carlton, these early impressions drove him as well as haunted him. The ultimate challenge would be how to initiate and sustain this degree of caring and respect on an international scale. Intuitively, Horst used his sense of the "art" of the human touch to earn Ritz-Carlton hotels the accolade of being voted the finest hotels in the world with only five properties. However, they still lacked the science to make it consistent and efficient.

We were the best of a lousy lot

Ritz-Carlton had every reason to be complacent. Many hotel groups consistently voted them No. 1 in customer service and satisfaction among their peers. Despite these accolades, early implementations of customer comment cards indicated that a certain portion of their guests were dissatisfied with at least one aspect of their stay. Beyond their performance of genuine caring being inconsistent, the costs of meeting their customer needs were becoming excessive because of unnecessary chronic costs. Most hotels remained profitable despite these quality deficiencies because competitors had similar problems. Horst joked: "We were the best of a lousy lot". They concluded that the only vote that really counted was the customer's vote and, clearly, there was still work to be done.

He believed that to continue this performance for the long term, they must study what they had done to better understand the science behind the "magic" of genuine caring they had created. From the first analysis, it was clear that the heart of their success was truly caring for customers as human beings.

More than "three hots and a cot"

As Ritz-Carlton began to explore their intuitive human caring and the respective human needs that they fulfilled, they found that their customers wanted more than just well-prepared meals and a nice bed to sleep in – they wanted to "feel" certain feelings. Horst states that people did not stay at a luxury hotel such as Ritz-Carlton simply to have any well-appointed room for the night but to make themselves "feel well" as a human being. It is this understanding that drives the view of their entire product as a product existing solely to make the customer "feel well". This led them to begin studying the underlying behavioral science for their foundation principle of human caring.

Make me feel like I'm home

Through various interviews and customer feedback cards, Ritz-Carlton found that customers wanted to "feel at home" when staying at the Ritz-Carlton hotel. Ritz-Carlton then began to

delve further into the psychological underpinnings of what customers meant by "feeling at home". This analysis yielded psychological evidence that the customers actually wanted to feel as if they
were a "member of a family staying at their mother's home". They
wanted to feel the same "secure and comforting" feeling as they
experienced in their own mother's home. As in most homes where
children grow up, few things could go wrong that couldn't be fixed
very quickly by mom or dad. Parents have a natural instinct to keep
children happy and well taken care of. If a child has a problem, they
bring it to their parents with perfect assurance that it will be fixed.
They won't receive a busy signal, won't be forced to navigate a
voice response system, won't be delegated to another department,
won't be met with apathy or irritation – they will see the caring eyes
of their parents and know that everything will be taken care of for
them.

Horst observed early in his career that the reason most people eat at
restaurants is not to satisfy physical needs of nourishment but to
boost their sense of well-being as a person. To bolster his point, he
points out that the foods people consume in restaurants are available
at any grocery store and can be prepared and eaten at home. The
same behavioral mechanics apply to why people enjoy a pint of beer
at the local pub or a mixed drink at their town's local "watering
hole" rather than purchasing the alcohol in a store and consuming it
in the privacy of their home. They enjoy a drink at the local pub
because it is an emotional escape from pressures of the day, or
because of a need to commiserate with others. The desire to social-
ize or feel a sense of camaraderie is more powerful than the simple
physical act of consumption.

Making the art of caring … a science

The bigger question loomed – could they sustain this genuine
caring for customers with further growth and expansion? In addition, how could they extend this founding principle of genuine
caring to every aspect of their business? Horst realized that the
hotel chain could not exist without understanding the processes
that support this human approach.

The decision was made to start looking at "best in class" companies outside the hotel industry. More specifically, they were looking for firms that focus on managing and improving their processes, with the overall objective of high customer service and satisfaction. They began with a list of companies determined by the Secretary for the Department of Commerce to be exceptionally managed companies. Examining these companies led Ritz-Carlton down the road of quality to explore the disciplines of quality management, continuous improvement, and process management.

Defining the magic

One of the most significant activities that their early quality work led them to was the need to create an explicit definition of how they were going to achieve their long-term business goals. The essence of these definitions is captured on the Ritz-Carlton pocket guide for employees. Most of the sentiments in these definitions center around respect and genuine caring for both the employees and guests. The pocket guide includes:

+ Three Steps of Service.

+ "We Are Ladies and Gentlemen ..." statement of self-respect.

+ The Employee Promise.

+ The Ritz-Carlton Credo.

+ The Ritz-Carlton Basics.

The "Three Steps of Service" (Figure 8.1) defined distinct common courtesies at the beginning and end to each guest interaction with guests' needs being fulfilled "in the middle".

The next statement on the pocket guide (Figure 8.2) reflects Horst's earlier observations about the value of self-respect. This statement is meant to send a clear message to employees that they should be proud and respectful of themselves and their guests.

The next statement on the pocket guide (Figure 8.3) communicates the importance of Ritz-Carlton employees and the principles and values by which they should conduct themselves.

Three Steps of Service

1   A warm and sincere greeting. Use the guest name, if and when possible.
2   Anticipation and compliance with guests needs.
3   Fond farewell. Give them a warm good-bye and use their names, if and when possible.

Figure 8.1   Three Steps of Service
(reproduced by permission of Ritz-Carlton)

"We Are
Ladies and
Gentlemen
Serving
Ladies and
Gentlemen"

Figure 8.2   We Are Ladies and Gentlemen ...
(reproduced by permission of Ritz-Carlton)

The Employee Promise

At the Ritz-Carlton, our Ladies and Gentlemen are the most important resource in our service commitment to our guests.

By applying the principles of trust, honesty, respect, integrity and commitment, we nurture and maximize talent to the benefit of each individual and the company.

The Ritz-Carlton fosters a work environment where diversity is valued, quality of life is enhanced, individual aspirations are fulfilled, and the Ritz-Carlton mystique is strengthened.

Figure 8.3   The Employee Promise
(reproduced by permission of Ritz-Carlton)

The Ritz-Carlton CREDO

The Ritz-Carlton Hotel is a place where the genuine care and comfort of our guests is our highest mission.

We pledge to provide the finest personal service and facilities for our guests who will always enjoy a warm, relaxed yet refined ambience.

The Ritz-Carlton experience enlivens the senses, instills well-being, and fulfills even the unexpressed wishes and needs of our guests.

Figure 8.4   The Ritz-Carlton CREDO
(reproduced by permission of Ritz-Carlton)

The next statement on the pocket guide (Figure 8.4) is the Ritz-Carlton Credo, which emphasizes genuine human caring toward guests as well as the emotional environment guests can expect.

The essence of all of these statements reflects the intention to deliver humanness to guests, not sleeping facilities.

On the reverse side of the pocket guide, the Ritz-Carlton Basics are written out to clarify and reinforce "how" such an environment is created for employees and guests.

The Ritz-Carlton Basics

1   The Credo is the principal belief of our Company. It must be known, owned and energized by all.

2   Our Motto is: "We Are Ladies and Gentlemen Serving Ladies and Gentlemen". As service professionals, we treat our guests and each other with respect and dignity.

3   The Three Steps of Service are the foundation of Ritz-Carlton hospitality. These steps must be used in every interaction to ensure satisfaction, retention, and loyalty.

4   The Employee Promise is the basis for our Ritz-Carlton work environment. It will be honored by all employees.

5   All employees will successfully complete annual training certification for their position.

6   Company Objectives are communicated to all employees. It is everyone's responsibility to support them.

7   To create pride and joy in the workplace, all employees have the right to be involved in the planning of the work that affects them.

8   Each employee will continuously identify defects (using MRBIV: mistakes, rework, break down, inefficiencies, variance) throughout the Hotel.

9   It is the responsibility of each employee to create a work environment of teamwork and lateral service so that the needs of our guests and each other are met.

10 Each employee is empowered. For example, when a guest has a problem or needs something special, you should break away from your regular duties to address and resolve the issue.

11 Uncompromising levels of cleanliness are the responsibility of every employee.

12 To provide the finest personal service for our guests, each employee is responsible for identifying and recording individual guest preferences.

13 Never lose a guest. Instant guest pacification is the responsibility of each employee. Whoever receives a complaint will own it, resolve it to the guest's satisfaction, and record it.

14 "Smile – we are on stage." Always maintain positive eye contact. Use the proper vocabulary with our guests and each other. (Use words like – "Good morning", "Certainly", "I'll be happy to", and "My pleasure".)

15 Be an ambassador of your Hotel in and outside of the workplace. Always speak positively. Communicate any concerns to the appropriate person.

16 Escort guests rather than pointing out directions to another area of the Hotel.

17 Use Ritz-Carlton telephone etiquette. Answer within three rings with a "smile". Use the guest's name when possible. When necessary, ask the caller, "May I place you on hold?" Do not screen calls. Eliminate call transfers whenever possible. Adhere to voicemail standards.

18 Take pride in and care of your personal appearance. Everyone is responsible for conveying a professional image by adhering to Ritz-Carlton clothing and grooming standards.

19 Think safety first. Each employee is responsible for creating a safe, secure, and accident-free environment for all guests and each other. Be aware of all fire and safety emergency procedures and report any security risks immediately.

20 Protecting the assets of a Ritz-Carlton hotel is the responsibility of every employee. Conserve energy, properly maintain our Hotels, and protect the environment.

Baldrige Award as a Means, not an End

There was a growing realization with Ritz-Carlton that their quality work needed a more structured approach to take their performance to the next level. They then adopted the selection criteria for the Malcolm Baldrige National Quality Award (MBNQA), which provided such an approach. They also began their quest for continuous quality improvement just four short years after they opened their first hotel. Horst admits that their first initiatives had limited success because they attempted to create a revolution, dictating that every quality initiative be done at lightning speed rather than evolve into a quality framework. After a three-year learning experience, they began a more mature quality approach in 1991. In spite of the early 1990s recession and the purchase of Ritz-Carlton by Marriot International, which slowed their initial progress, Horst remained inspired by the two words "continuous improvement". He realized that two competitive companies who respectively scored a four and seven out of ten could have their competitive positions reversed if the company who scored a four continuously improves and the company who scored a seven does not. Horst has observed that most companies do not continuously improve their products and services or focus on the root drivers of long-term costs, but instead concentrate on managing short-term costs. Today, every hotel that Ritz-Carlton owns has a quality manager.

The quest was structured by the selection criteria for the MBNQA, which provided an excellent assessment tool to develop a comprehensive roadmap to achieve their vision (see Table 8.1). Ritz-Carlton developed their roadmap to cover the seven award criteria of the MBNQA.

1   Leadership.

2   Strategic planning.

3   Customer and market focus.

4   Information and analysis.

5   Human resources development and management.

6   Process management.

7   Business results.

The seven award criteria each have a section for:

+ Approach "Plan".
+ Deployment "Do".
+ Results "Check".
+ Improvement "Act".

Each area of the roadmap influences Ritz-Carlton's ability to improve the humanness of customer interactions and the supporting employee environment.

1. Leadership

Under the Leadership criteria, the approach "Plan" phase includes the plan for leadership to provide a basic empowerment process for employees to ensure that they have both the responsibility and authority to fulfill guests' needs regardless of job function (see Figure 8.5).

Ritz-Carlton employees are trained to accept responsibility of a customer request regardless of whether it is normally assigned to them as a job function or area. For example, if a customer tells a waiter at the restaurant that the toilet in their room is not flushing, that particular waiter "owns" that customer's problem. Ritz-Carlton has empowered employees to do "whatever it takes" to solve the customer's problem.

For example, if a customer asks a Ritz-Carlton bellman for directions to the restaurant or men's room, the bellman is encouraged to physically guide the customer to their desired location. Ritz-Carlton measures responsiveness along three specific response attributes:

1   Defect-free.

2   Timeliness.

3   Caring fashion.

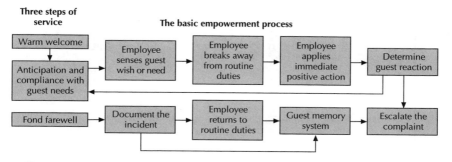

Figure 8.5   Three steps of service – the basic empowerment process
(reproduced by permission of Ritz-Carlton)

Table 8.1 MBNQA matrix
(reproduced by permission of Ritz-Carlton)

MBNQA	Approach "Plan"	Deployment "Do"	Results "Check"	Improvement "Act"
1. Leadership	A passion for excellence The seven pyramid decisions Basic empowerment process	Senior leaders "Start-up" new hotels Distribution of "the pyramid" Daily reinforcements of the gold standards	Performance evaluations	Development/training plants Leadership center Developmental job assignments
2. Strategic planning	Fact-based strategic objectives Fact-based key process identification	Divide/subdivide objectives Select process owners Develop processes Provide necessary resources	Actual versus planned performance compared quarterly by upper managers at the corporate and hotel level Daily operations review by the workforce	Act on the differences Evaluate/improve planning process
3. Customer and market focus	Market research that concentrates on the quality of the hotel facility and operations	6P's concept Operation of the "CLASS" database Standard performance measurement	Daily hotel measurement • SQI • RevPAR • Market segment Monthly measurement • Advance bookings • Customer satisfaction • RevPAR • P&L	Evaluate/improve annually

4. Information and analysis	Selecting performance measurements for: • Upper managers • Daily operations Comparative benchmarking	Individual process owners select performance measurement for: • Upper managers • Daily operations Share/replicate best practice performance, on-going	Statistically trained employees, consulting specialists	Continuous improvement
5. Human resources development and management	Jobs are designed so our people: • Know what to do • Know how well they are doing • Can regulate the process or their own personal conduct	Employee education, training and development	QSP Day 21/365 Training certification review Performance appraisal evaluations Analysis of employee surveys	Site visits by senior HR leaders Analysis of employee surveys
6. Process management	Manage key production and support processes	Incorporate changing customer requirements The GreenBook Process owners modify Processes for each new hotel	PQI SQI Process audits	Major changes that require project management Incremental day-to-day improvements
7. Business results	Strategic objectives define long-term targets Tactical processes set annual targets	Lead people Manage processes Standard performance measures	Actual versus planned performance compared quarterly by senior leaders at the corporate and hotel level Daily operations review by the workforce	Continuously and forever improvement

Acronyms: P&L = Profit and Loss. PQI = product quality indicator. QSP = Quality Selection Process. RevPAR = Revenue per available room. SQI = service quality indicator

In the first measurement attribute, Ritz-Carlton direct that each customer response should be defect-free, i.e. done correctly. The second is timeliness. The measurement of timeliness has less to do with the passage of time and more to do with how the customer perceives the timeliness. If the customer perceives timeliness as a one-hour response an employee response of five minutes may be as inappropriate as five hours. Both would be considered inefficient. The third attribute is responsiveness in a caring fashion. Under Ritz-Carlton's current system, if a restaurant guest communicates to the waiter in the restaurant that their toilet does not flush, the waiter will communicate to the concierge who is the liaison to Engineering. Engineering is obligated to respond to the customer within ten minutes as well as keeping the customer informed about the solutions.

In addition, each employee has the authority to spend up to $2000 to alleviate any problem for any customer. Typically, in most businesses, if a customer approaches an employee with a problem outside their normal job responsibility, the employee will respond by saying, "I'll tell someone about it". The customer responds with the feeling that the employee doesn't care about him or his problem because it was delegated to someone else, and he often believes that nothing will ever be done about the problem.

A simple example of taking responsibility and initiative is when a member of a handicapped-racing team was staying at the Buckhead hotel in Atlanta for a big race and needed special assistance. Before the race, he had told the bellman that he needed his regular wheelchair available at the end of the race. The bellman met him at the finish line with his regular wheelchair. The bellman was empowered to leave the hotel to help the guest. Another example is a guest staying at a Ritz-Carlton in Naples lost a brand-new ring on the beach and an employee took the time to rent a metal detector and scan the beach until the ring was found. The employee was empowered with both the responsibility and the authority to rent the metal detector to find the guest's ring. In most organizations, these exceptionally human gestures will occur once in a while because of the individual human attributes of individual employees. To consistently have these exceptional acts of caring occur, the organization must empower all employees with the responsibility and authority to provide genuine human caring. Ritz-Carlton's reputation for responsibility and initiative in genuine caring prompted a married couple with one partner recuperating from surgery to stay in the Ritz-Carlton rather than in a hospital and they attribute much of their healing to the respect and caring received from the Ritz-Carlton staff. This couple emphasized that they felt the staff truly cared about their well-being during their recovery.

The directive to respond to customers overrides all other directives regardless of role. At first glance, this directive could possibly cause immediate bedlam if there are not set processes or rules that have less of a chance to be misinterpreted. Ritz-Carlton have made this a functional model by mapping out each employee's job function and process with the added process of deviating from their assigned task when asked by a customer for help or assistance. Each employee has been trained as to their flowchart of processes and is expected to respond and return to their original function numerous times during the course of a day. The actual flowchart indicates that the employee should break away to "fill the customer need" and then "return to their original job". This is specifically mapped out in their job roles (see Figure 8.5).

Write down what's right and do what you write

An important step in communicating and reinforcing more human-oriented values is to publish them in an easily referenced form. Ritz-Carlton have referenced their primary values, philosophies, and credos in a handy pocket guide.

In any questionable situation every Ritz-Carlton employee, from the most experienced to the most recently hired, has an easily available guide to enable them to make the best possible response. The pocket guide is a reminder of the expected "Ritz-Carlton" attitude, behaviors, courtesies, and goals. Because these values and expectations are actually written down and in the possession of every employee it becomes possible to accomplish the "human touch" consistently throughout the business.

"Ritz-Carlton is a place where the genuine care and comfort of our guests is our highest mission." There is an important distinction on exactly what entity actually delivers this genuine caring and comfort. The business itself never can deliver genuine caring and comfort but its employees can, i.e. the business itself is not human but the employees are. Having said that, employees need emotional leadership and guidance. An important part of this emotional leadership is having clearly stated values and philosophies. A helpful mechanism to communicate this both to employees and customers is establishing a credo, i.e. a succinct statement representing the principal beliefs of a company.

Ritz-Carlton's Credo is rich in humanity

"The Ritz-Carlton Hotel is a place where the genuine care and comfort of our guests is our highest mission. We pledge to provide the finest personal service and facilities for our guests who will always enjoy a warm, relaxed yet refined ambience. The Ritz-Carlton experience enlivens the senses, instills well-being, and fulfills even the unexpressed wishes and needs of our guests."

When contrasting Ritz-Carlton's Credo to other corporate credos, Ritz-Carlton's use of human relationship terms is ever apparent, e.g. genuine care, comfort, warm, relaxed, enlivens, well-being, unexpressed wishes. These words are not simply words chosen to create an impression but are truly meant to be executed to the fullest extent possible. Ritz-Carlton want to deeply affect its customers emotionally by touching as many appropriate human senses as possible in order for the customer to "feel well". The senses that contribute to the sense of well-being are both physical and emotional. The physical senses are sight, smell, hearing, touch, and taste. The emotional senses are such things as sense of self, sense of self-worth, respect, abatement of fear, and sense of well-being. Creating an environment to achieve the stimulation of the senses requires the desire by both management and employees to do so. This desire must be innate in both management and employees. Credos can help sustain the focus and importance of these objectives but will never replace the necessity for management and employees to truly desire the end state of the customer's emotional need fulfillment. In support of this desire there must be an infra-structure of process and enabling technologies.

Avoid blaming employee performance for poor job match

Matching employee emotional predisposition with customer emotional needs is critical. There is a common destructive spiral from management when firms have not done this emotional need matching. In the cases where management has not had sufficient understanding to focus hiring practices toward this type of emotional needs matching, management will chastise employees for their resulting poor job performance and customer ratings when, in fact, it is the management's failure that has created the problem.

Let guests determine role importance

Horst made it a practice of introducing himself to the hotel employees as President of Ritz-Carlton. He used to tell them that he was a very important person but only equally as important as every other employee at Ritz-Carlton. He made the case that, if he did not show up for work one day, the customers probably would not notice. He then said that if the other employees did not show up for work, the customers would notice.

Another way to demonstrate to employees how important they are is to allow them to participate in the decision-making process of continuous improvement activities. From a human perspective, this creates a sense of belonging as well as pride in their work and the joy of achievement.

Avoiding the three-month fix, i.e. the Wall Street shuffle, the major underlying challenge to all of Ritz-Carlton's work on improving their genuine human caring was to justify the work's time and funding. As in any business, there was the temptation to create the proverbial "three-month fix" to their customer satisfaction challenges. Ritz-Carlton's efforts not only created an environment in which employees created service excellence for their customers, but also, for the long-term proposition, an environment where employees "want" to create a warm, human sense of well-being for their customers. Keeping this long-term focus in the face of the obligatory three-month reports to Wall Street made staying this course of action difficult throughout the early stages.

Horst firmly believed that the creation of true long-term revenue and profit transcended what Wall Street was waiting to hear during these reports. Horst comments that "most businesses focus more on control and expenses rather than the mechanics of how the money is made long-term". Horst maintains that more revenue and profit can be generated from investing in genuine caring for guests than any other investment, regardless of the industry.

2. Strategic Planning

Strategic planning is what enables executives at Ritz-Carlton to make specific decisions that set the direction for business excellence. Examples of this would be identifying key production processes based on the following three criteria:

1   Work that ranks as very important to customers.

2   Work that is rising in importance to customers.

3   Work that is poor in comparison to competitors; these processes must then be developed and deployed.

An important aspect of this leadership objective is to involve the "Ladies and Gentlemen" of Ritz-Carlton in developing these strategic plans. First, leadership communicates the measures and objectives to the different organizations within Ritz-Carlton. These organizations then identify the deeds that will collectively meet the objectives. These different organizations also submit the suggested budget to perform these deeds. Activities that have been agreed upon are then tied to financial planning and budget processes.

Upper management then checks the results monthly. The framework depicted in Table 8.2 represents a typical review process of key performance measures. This information enables continuous improvement and benchmark comparisons.

Table 8.2   Focus – indicators – what's reviewed – process owner
(reproduced by permission of Ritz-Carlton)

Focus	Indicators	What's reviewed	Process owner
Employee pride & joy	Key survey questions Turnovers	Actual versus plan/ trends	Human Resource Director
Customer loyalty	Overall customer satisfaction Customer difficulties	Actual versus plan/ foremost competitor, trends	Operations Director Quality Director
RevPAR/P&L	Advance bookings Market/business performance	Actual versus plan/ industry trends	Marketing Director Finance Director
Key processes	Key production and support processes	Actual versus plan/ trends	Funtional leaders

3. Customer and Market Focus

Ritz-Carlton's customer and market focus is supported by the understanding that their guests are unique human beings with human needs.

Different people need different things

Another important discovery for Ritz-Carlton was the need to not only understand the emotional needs of their guests but also to segment how Ritz-Carlton actually fulfilled those emotional needs in order to appropriately staff personnel. A good example of this was the discovery that the human needs of regular hotel guests and the human needs of meeting planners were distinctly different. The meeting planners are another segment of Ritz-Carlton's customers whose interest is in planning meetings to be held at Ritz-Carlton properties by external groups. In order to assist Ritz-Carlton, J.D. Powers was hired to study the expectations of this customer segment. J.D. Powers mapped out the meeting planners' expectations. Once their expectations were mapped out, Ritz-Carlton created specific processes to satisfy the meeting planners' expectations. They then put a measuring mechanism in place to measure how Ritz-Carlton could fulfill the specific expectations and needs of the meeting planners. The measuring mechanism itself then was used to provide the basis upon which Ritz-Carlton could create a continuous improvement mechanism in each area for satisfying the meeting planners' needs and expectations. Keeping the guests informed is not as big an issue as keeping the meeting planners informed. One of the biggest potential problems involving meeting planners is that different meetings are scheduled in two adjacent rooms but the activities of each meeting are totally incompatible. For example, if one meeting requires a quiet atmosphere for study and the adjacent room is hosting a loud, boisterous party, there will be tremendous dissatisfaction caused for those who need quiet.

Focus on humanness, not just the task

A study of Ritz-Carlton's checkout process revealed the necessity of focusing on humanness. They found that their guests felt slightly dissatisfied with the Ritz-Carlton experience at checkout. Upon investigation, they found that customers felt the checkout staff were not listening with enough empathy about concerns they had had during their stay. There was too much focus on employees executing an efficient checkout process and not enough focus on the importance of being empathetic or compassionate with the guests during checkout. Psychologically, guests simply wanted to feel they would be "heard" when communicating simple concerns about their stay. Ritz-Carlton's research revealed that their guests didn't necessarily want the front desk staff to "fix" any particular problem, they simply wanted to feel validated, that their observations were legitimate and that the front desk staff genuinely cared about their concern. Ritz-Carlton responded by modifying their hiring process for front desk people to include a high degree of empathy to match the guests' emotional needs.

Self-respect generates self-respect

Ritz-Carlton's motto, "We Are Ladies and Gentlemen Serving Ladies and Gentlemen", comes from the profound observation that in order for most guests to feel respected, the employees serving them must have a sense of self-respect.

The desire to create this customer end state is critical but it must be coupled with the competency to create it. The mechanics of behavioral psychology suggest that there is a higher likelihood that a person who has already achieved self-respect will be more capable of creating this result in another human being. If a person truly feels a high sense of self-esteem, during an interaction they are more likely to transfer that feeling to others. An example of this is found in Horst's story of the maître d' entering the room and immediately attracting the attention of guests. Therefore, if a certain segment of a firm's customers has the predominate desire to feel important and respected, the firm should focus on hiring people who already have a sense of importance and self-respect. Ritz-Carlton's motto, "We Are Ladies and Gentlemen Serving Ladies and Gentlemen", creates a powerful self-generating cycle of need fulfillment for both employee and customer. The mechanics are as follows:

1 Firm determines customer segment has high need for self-respect.

2 Firm hires employees with high degree of self-respect.

3 Firm trains and rewards employees to enhance their transfer of self-respect to customers.

4 Employees interact with customers transferring a high degree of self-respect.

5 Customer's need for self-respect is filled.

6 Customers reflect back to employees the customer's mutual respect.

7 Management rewards employees.

When people experience Ritz-Carlton's service, they feel the respect the employees have for themselves and in turn feel the respect they generate for their guests.

This cycle of respect is self-perpetuating and nourishing for both guests and staff.

Information supports customer and market understanding

Ritz-Carlton's customer and market focus is supported by the information needed for hotel development in operations. Market research concentrates on the quality of hotel development in operations. In addition, formal discussions occur between:

1   Support and operations people.

2   Internal and external customers to identify administrative and support processes which impact hotel products and Ritz-Carlton's mission.

The sources for market research are divided into the following categories:

+   Customer information.

+   Brought to our attention.

+   Readily available but requires analysis.

+   Must be created by a special study.

The needs for market research are divided into the following categories:

+   Determination of market segments.

+   Identifying potential customers.

+   Relative priorities of customers.

+   Demand forecast.

+   Individual dissatisfaction of customers.

+   Widespread customer dissatisfaction.

+   Competitive quality status.

+   Opportunities for improving RevPAR (Revenue Per Available Room) rapport through quality.

These measurements produced operational and guest data to enhance ongoing operational efficiency and effectiveness.

Table 8.3   Needs and sources of market research at the Ritz-Carlton
(reproduced by permission of Ritz-Carlton)

Needs for market segments/ customer information	Brought to our attention	Readily available but requires analysis	Must be created by a special study
Determination of market segments			Alliances with travel partners (airlines, credit card companies, convention bureaus, etc.)
Identifying potential customers		Sales and marketing function ranks potential and current customers by volume, geography, and profit	Same as above
Relative priorities of customers	"Automated memory system" that links returning guests to their preferences	Analysis of "CLASS" database	Focus groups Customer satisfaction results
Demand forecast		Use of information technology DFS	
Individual dissatisfaction of customers	Complaints, claims, client alerts, feedback from the sales force, summarized in the SQI/PQI		
Widespread customer dissatisfaction		Pareto analysis of the SQI and PQI	Interviews with customers
Competitive quality status	Criteria, rating and awards from travel industry publications	Ratings from customers, star report, sales force reports Summary of above analysis	World-class customer and employee satisfaction data
Opportunities for improving RevPAR through quality	Pareto analysis to identify major causes of customer dissatisfaction	Summary of above	Special psychological studies to understand: 1. What customers mean, not what they say 2. How to appeal to the customer in the language they most understand

Acronyms: CLASS = an automated "memory system" that links returning guests to their preferences. DFS = demand forecast system. PQI = product quality indicator. SQI = service quality indicator.

The six Ps concept

After Ritz-Carlton completed research on their market segments, customers and their relative priorities, they developed their six Ps concept. Ritz-Carlson's six Ps concept enables the feelings of well-being to be delivered to guests through genuine caring, comfort, and prestige. This is accomplished by defining and answering the following six questions:

1   Problem or need of the customer?

2   Product (what is it?).

3   Promises (what can it do for the customer?).

4   Personal advantage (what can the customer do because of it?)

5   Positioning (what is the benefit of it versus the competition?).

6   Price/value (what must customers give up in time or money to get it?).

The answers to these six questions are the first stages in designing the processes to deliver the vision of well-being to their guests. Delivering genuine care, comfort, and prestige creates well-being.

Technology enables genuine caring – CLASS database

The use of technology and information is a valuable tool in aiding Ritz-Carlton's ability to treat customers as human beings. Ritz-Carlton created their CLASS (Customer Loyalty Anticipation Satisfaction System), which is a guest recognition database that anticipates repeat customers' preferences and requirements (see Figure 8.6). For example, when a customer visits the Buckhead hotel in Atlanta and is identified as a repeat customer, their preferences can be easily viewed on Ritz-Carlton's database. If the customer communicated on the previous visit that he wants four pillows on the bed, this request will be automatically fulfilled prior to the guest entering the room. If the customer flies to

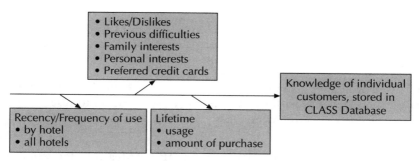

Figure 8.6   Operation of the CLASS database
(reproduced by permission of Ritz-Carlton)

Hong Kong, when he checks in two days later there will be four pillows on the bed. Beyond individual guest preferences, Ritz-Carlton management can glance at customer satisfaction results and employee surveys in any city in the world from Chicago to Shanghai. These customer and employee surveys are supported by detailed information on financials and accurate sales forecasts. In a prior age, Horst could have only hoped that his hotel in Chicago or Shanghai was doing well; now he knows.

"A major challenge faced by The Ritz-Carlton is to remember each of its 800 000-plus customers. In response, a special organization exists in each of our hotels called Guest Recognition. This special function uses the CLASS database to remember returning guests and generate essential preference and schedule information to all concerned. In this way, the Ladies and Gentlemen of the Ritz-Carlton and our suppliers understand what is 'new or different' about each individual customer or event."

4. Information and Analysis

Measurement and the information that it yields is key to understanding and improving the quality of human caring in this very human environment.

There are two basic types of measurements used at Ritz-Carlton:

1   Operational organizational measurements for upper management at both the corporate and hotel levels.

Table 8.4 Before operations measures
(reproduced by permission of Ritz-Carlton)

Subject	Unit to measure	Use
Macro-environment analysis	Summaries of performance, money, ratios, indexes	Annual input for senior leaders to reset organizational and operational measures
New hotel development	Defect points (i.e. PQI)	Measures for senior leaders to plan, assess, and improve each new hotel development
Daily variable demand	Production/hours worked ratio	Plan daily operations and pricing

2   Operational (i.e. process) measurements for planning, assessing, and improving daily operations.

A further distinction in measurement is made as to whether the information is applied:

+ Before operations (see Table 8.4).

+ During operations (see Table 8.5).

+ After operations (see Table 8.6).

PQIs are the product quality indicators, which consist of the ten most serious defects that can occur in the development phase of a new, rich profit hotel.

Table 8.5 During operations measures
(reproduced by permission of Ritz-Carlton)

Subject	Unit to measure	Use
The gold standards	Taste, sight, smell, sound, touch	Operational measures for the individual employee to plan, assess, and improve their work

Table 8.6 After operations measures
(reproduced by permission of Ritz-Carlton)

Subject	Unit of measure	Use
Vital few objectives	Organizational performance indicators, money, 1–5 scale, percentages	Improve organizational performance
Key production and support processes	Weighted defect points, production/hours worked ratio, revenue per available room	Improve daily operations Improve pricing policies

PQI defects:

1   Substandard management contract.

2   Missing/wrong concepts.

3   Late feasibility study.

4   Wrong/late schematic design.

5   Detailed design changes.

6   High-risk facility suppliers.

7   Late construction days.

8   Missing/inadequate key production and support processes.

9   Inadequate presales results.

10   Inadequate caring mindset of employees.

SQIs are the service quality indicators, which consist of the 12 most serious defects that can occur during the regular operation of a rich profit hotel. The seriousness of these defects is weighted by a value point.

SQI defects:

		Points
1	Missing guest preferences	10
2	Unresolved difficulties	50
3	Inadequate guestroom housekeeping	1
4	Abandoned reservation calls	5
5	Guestroom changes	5
6	Inoperable guestroom equipment	5
7	Unready guestroom	10
8	Inappropriate hotel appearance	5
9	Meeting event difficulties	5
10	Inadequate food/beverage	1
11	Missing/damaged guest property/ accidents	50
12	Invoice adjustment	3

The total is multiplied by the weight, totaled and divided by the number of working days applicable to obtain an average daily point value. The average daily point value is disseminated to the workforce daily.

Help from outside research

Ritz-Carlton buy syndicated surveys to help them understand how they measure up to the competition. Ritz-Carlton are also a member of the Mayfair group, which is 50 of the top companies in the world. The Mayfair group is a very exclusive club of best-in-class companies that share the results of consistent measurements across companies and industries. Ritz-Carlton hired J.D. Powers to survey their meeting planners every four weeks to measure customer survey results against customer expectations as well as to attempt to discover any new customer expectations which may arise. Ritz-Carlton also take a scientific cross-section from each hotel in conjunction with J.D. Powers to measure customer expectations and the degree to which they are met as well as monitoring whether new customer expectations are developing.

Ritz-Carlton use SQIs (service quality indicators) and PQIs (product quality indicators) to track and communicate their quality performance to employees. SQIs are displayed in each hotel, allowing the departments to monitor important production and guest service performance. This allows them to quickly address any challenges as soon as they happen.

5. Human Resources Development and Management

The main objective is to increase both the meaning and satisfaction the employees derive from their work. This approach consists of three basic components:

+ The Ladies and Gentlemen know what they are supposed to do

   (a) Learn and use the goal standards.

   (b) Master the procedures of their job (training certification).

   (c) Generate ideas to improve products, services, and processes.

+ They know how well they are doing

   (a) Keep the Ladies and Gentlemen informed on how well they are doing in many forms.

   (b) They receive coaching from managers and peers on individual tasks throughout the day.

   (c) They receive daily information from the SQI report.

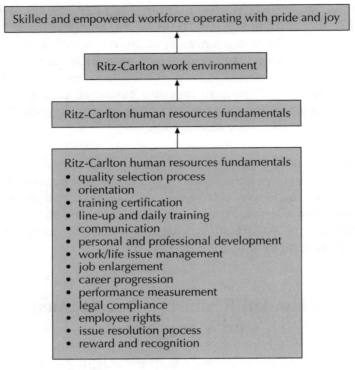

Figure 8.7   Human resource approach
(reproduced by permission of Ritz-Carlton)

(d)   They receive semi-annual performance appraisals on their general performance.

✦   They have the authority to make changes in the process under their authority or their own personal conduct

(a)   The ability of our Ladies and Gentlemen to regulate how work gets done is assured through basic standards set out in a credo card.

(b)   'People have the right to be involved in the planning of the work that affects them.''

To achieve these objectives, Ritz-Carlton employ a proven model that supports their human resource philosophies (see Figure 8.7). The model covers the Human Resources Fundamentals used in the work environment to ultimately achieve a skilled and empowered workforce operating with pride and joy.

Caring people care better

Ritz-Carlton do not just hire people, but carefully selects people. These carefully selected people are oriented to the heart and soul of Ritz-Carlton as well as the body of knowledge that Ritz-Carlton have gained over the years. Ritz-Carlton explore every possible avenue of what their guests truly need as human beings, as well as what type of human beings are the best employees to satisfy the guest's needs. Ritz-Carlton strive to match specific human attributes of employees to specific human needs of customers. This relatively unique but intriguing idea came from Ritz-Carlton studying their guest's specific human needs. They realized that they would have to focus their hiring practices toward patterning specific human characteristics of employees with specific human needs of customers. This can be contrasted to most businesses hiring their employees based on skill sets rather than selecting employees for the specific needs of their guests.

Use your best to train, and pay, them

The problem of just hiring as opposed to carefully selecting is compounded by poor training practices. It is not uncommon for the first training session in the hotel industry to be: "... Bill the new waiter follows John the old waiter (who himself has only worked there one year) and John's first lesson to Bill is "this job sucks!"" Ritz-Carlton avoid this scenario by carefully selecting people using a customer needs job profile for each job category. The employee then attends a two-day orientation program, beginning with the hotel's general manager, to orient the employee to the Ritz-Carlton human caring philosophy, direction, beliefs, and values. They also learn that Ritz-Carlton are not there to sell rooms but to sell caring. The employees are then moved on to training. The people who are chosen to train are the best in each of their respective departments, e.g. the best room serviceperson, the best concierge, or the best waiter. The employees who are training the new employees are paid a premium for their training activities above and beyond their normal activities. The new employees are then put through a test as to whether they have learned every aspect of their job. If they do not score 100% on their training, they must go through the training again. Staff who must recycle through training are not seen as failures but simply as on the journey to successful guest service.

Train every day

Once they have scored 100%, the training does not stop. Every day for the rest of their career, there is 15 minutes set aside for training. This occurs in every Ritz-Carlton around the world, on every shift, for every person. Ten minutes of the 15 minutes consists of reinforcement of the original training, which originates from the corporate office, whereas the other five minutes for new training originates from each individual hotel. This causes a very strong alignment of employees not only to their tasks at hand but also to the original Ritz-Carlton credo that they are taught to live by. Horst did not allow one meeting to take place without the employee promise being displayed on the wall. This constant written reminder is just another physical remembrance of why they come to work every day.

Caring employees need special care

As mentioned in an earlier chapter, Ritz-Carlton employ highly empathetic people as front desk staff. They found highly empathetic employees became overtaxed emotionally more quickly than the previous personality types hired for front desk staff simply by virtue of their highly empathetic nature. This created a higher turnover rate for front desk staff and prompted Ritz-Carlton to increase the frequency of rotation in these positions to other less emotionally taxing positions. This need to rotate front desk personnel more frequently as well as the increased level of turnover is a calculated cost of fulfilling the objective of truly delivering Ritz-Carlton's guests a sense of caring and well-being. Ritz-Carlton's philosophy is that investments in caring are as important, if not more important, than investments in the physical attributes of the property. They believe that the overriding determinant of excellent service is human caring.

6. Process Management

Ritz-Carlton are a process-focused organization with many standard process procedures. Ritz-Carlton understand that, in order to achieve a high degree of genuine caring, processes must be thoroughly planned so the "Ladies and Gentlemen" are provided with the means to meet standards, create a market, and thereby generate income efficiently.

Trace poor service to its root cause

Approaching a business's lack of humanness as "defects" is an effective approach to ultimately discovering the root cause of the lack of humanness within a process. It also serves as an effective approach to systemically addressing the problem rather than temporarily removing it. Another way of looking at defects is to regard them as "inhibitors", which act as a barrier for human treatment. The process of discovering defects and their root causes begins with the establishment of quality teams that are dedicated to the disaggregating processes that influence behavior. In doing this, most positive or negative interactions with customers can be traced through processes.

A good example of the tracing poor service to its root cause was how Ritz-Carlton evolved their approach to addressing their number one complaint of "slow in room service" at their first hotel. When guests experience slow room service, they feel a host of dehumanizing emotions ranging from feeling unimportant, anxious, inconvenienced, uncared for, and a lack of control.

Initial attempts to apply traditional management techniques of reprimanding staff to improve the service proved ineffective as the root cause of the problem remained untouched. Using traditional management techniques, local managers chastised the room service managers, in turn prompting the room service managers to chastise the waiters creating a more pronounced room service problem. After Ritz-Carlton became disciples of the quality management process, they approached the problem complaint of "slow in room service" in a totally different manner. Ritz-Carlton began by forming a quality team to proactively and meticulously understand all processes linking the room service chain of processes. After the processes were mapped, the root causes of slow room service could be identified and addressed. The quality team created included representatives from the waiters, cooks, order takers, and room service manager. Every quality team that is created to address these types of issues will always include the manager of the process. An important prerequisite for the formation of these quality teams is to teach the members how to optimize the dynamics of the working "team". As the quality team began to analyze the process, they found that the initial steps of the process required that the order taker, cook, and waiter perform efficiently. The team then traced the steps of the actual room service delivery. They found that the elevator seemed to be causing the delays in the room service process. At this point, the team involved the engineering people. The engineering people then involved the elevator manufacturer's technicians. The elevator technicians checked the functionality of the elevator and found that it was working properly. The team then decided to actually ride up and down in the elevator to analyze why the elevators seemed slow. They began to time the average elapsed time for the elevator to travel from the main floor (where the kitchen was) to the top floor and back to the main floor. Their analysis revealed that most of these round-trip elevator rides were 15–20 minutes. During these test rides, the team made notes as to what caused the elevator to stop at different floors during the round-trip test run.

This prompted the team to involve housekeeping in the process analysis. Housekeeping revealed that because of a shortage of linen, the maids needed the housemen who supplied the maids with room supplies (linens, shampoo, and soap) to constantly run between floors "stealing" linen from one floor to supply another floor. This constant running between floors by the housemen tied up the elevators. This caused the room service staff to have long waits for the elevator that resulted in slow room service. In normal housekeeping operations, a hotel needs at least three "parrs" – (100 beds' worth of linen) – one set of linens is on the bed, the second set is dirty, and the third set is being washed. Housekeeping was attempting to operate with only two parrs, which caused problems elsewhere in the Ritz-Carlton service chain.

Upon further investigation, the team discovered that when the hotel was initially opened, funds were stretched thin. As a result, management made the decision to order one less parr of bed linens to save on laundry costs. This shortage of linens continued for many years after the need to cut costs disappeared. After the quality team discovered the root cause of the complaint "slow room service", they instructed housekeeping to add one parr of linen to their linen supply. As a result, customer room service complaints dropped by 48%. Ironically, it was Horst himself who actually made the initial decision to cut the initial number of parrs from three to two to save on opening costs for their first hotel.

Little defects cause big delays

Ritz-Carlton was also faced with a customer service issue of how to speed up the room preparation process in order to make the rooms available for guests more quickly. The quality team found that housekeeping was spending an inordinate amount of time refolding towels because the towel-folding machine folded the towels incorrectly obscuring a portion of the Ritz-Carlton logo. Housekeeping also commented that if the towels were not folded with the Ritz-Carlton logo exactly centered, management would criticize their job performance. The manufacturer who developed the towel-folding machines was asked to make a minor adjustment allowing the machine to fold the towels correctly the first time. This problem seems inconsequential, until they calculated the additional time housekeeping spent refolding each towel. For this one hotel, the calculation was the number of towels per room multiplied by 150,000 room changes per year.

Strive for perfection ... zero defects

At the heart of a business focused on quality management is a commitment to continuous improvement. The underlying belief of continuous improvement is that in any activity, e.g. customer interaction, there is always room to improve. The goal of a quality culture is theoretical perfection or "zero defects". At a zero defect level, no bad surprises occur when all defects have been removed and all promises are kept. The zero defect principle can be effectively applied to any industry. Ritz-Carlton applied the zero defect principle to customer complaints emanating from mechanical problems in rooms. Most of these problems appeared relatively minor at first glance but actually dominated the guests' perception of Ritz-Carlton's ability to fulfill their human needs. Mechanical issues such as these elicited feelings ranging from disappointment to disgust, anger, and fear − all of these powerful emotions prompted by seemingly minor defects such as a bad battery or light bulb.

Most of the mechanical issues, such as light bulbs being burned out, dead batteries in television remote controls, keys not fitting, or even spots on bedspreads were all very "fixable" separately but the difficulty is in coordinating the proactive management of them over several hundred rooms. A quality team was then created to strive for "zero defects" in mechanical issues for every room. The first attempt at creating "zero" mechanical room problems was piloted with no success.

Several years later a new team with a new approach made a second attempt and succeeded. This new team developed a system called CARE (Clean And Repair Everything) to reach their goal of defect-free guestrooms. This team suggested that each hotel take four rooms out of circulation each day and have these four rooms totally refurbished by the maintenance team to zero defect status. The following day, a different four rooms would be set aside for maintenance until the maintenance team reached the initial four rooms. From there, the cycle would be repeated. It required three months to fully cycle through all the hotel rooms. After this program was instituted, Ritz-Carlton moved from an average of 50 "defects" (complaints about mechanical problems) per thousand occupied rooms to one "defect" per thousand occupied rooms. Ritz-Carlton also merged the deep cleaning housekeeping processes with the engineering preventative maintenance schedule ensuring that all guestrooms are guaranteed to be defect-free every 90 days.

Horst's goal was to bring Ritz-Carlton to the level of one defect per hundred thousand rooms and ultimately one defect per one million rooms. This level of quality is a "six sigma" level of quality. Six sigma is a system using the principles of quality management for improving the quality of organizational processes and products to a level of three defects per million. The level of six sigma is unheard of in the hotel business. Horst believed that if Ritz-Carlton continued to focus on continuous improvement, they will continue their market leadership. Those hotel chains that do not focus on continuous improvement will be destined for a lower market segment. They may achieve short-term profitable quarters but will not be able to sustain long-term profitability.

Ritz-Carlton aim for exceptionally high quality standards in every area of their business. Some businesses can have exceptionally high quality standards in one aspect of the business and be almost devoid in another aspect of the business. For example, the airline industry's safety standards are of the six-sigma level whereas their quality standards for customer service are widely recognized as substandard. It may appear that the industry views their business as the transportation of inanimate objects rather than human beings.

Make experiences more human, not more perfect

One cautionary observation is that efforts to gain process efficiency have sometimes unknowingly engineered important elements of humanness out of a process. An example of this taken from outside the Ritz-Carlton story unfolded at an annual motorcycle rally where enthusiasts get together to share the joys and experiences of riding their favorite brands of motorcycles. Motorcycle manufacturers attend these rallies to help promote their products. It is a common practice for manufacturers to offer "test rides" on their latest models. Anyone who is interested can sign up for a test ride and expect a long wait in line for a short ride. The more popular motorcycle manufacturers have longer lines with sometimes hundreds of people waiting for hours just to ride a new model. One manufacturer decided to improve the test ride experience by fixing the inefficiencies of the long wait in the test ride process. They implemented a procedure to schedule all rides by appointment only. They believed that eliminating the long wait in line would dramatically improve the experience for potential customers. What they did not realize was one of the most pleasurable aspects of the test ride experience was the long wait in line. During these long waits, prospective customers took great pleasure in talking with fellow enthusiasts about their shared experiences and love of motorcycles. The valuable lesson learned was that the attempt to make a human experience more perfect and efficient could destroy the most valued aspects of the experience.

Defects don't dissatisfy, missed expectations do

The existence of defects in a process does not necessarily create dissatisfaction. Defects only create dissatisfaction when they are tied to a customer expectation. A good example of this situation occurs when Ritz-Carlton take a room reservation a week in advance with certain requested room attributes, e.g. king-size bed on the west side of the hotel. Fulfilling this request would not be difficult if no current guests extended their stay. A complication arises when a certain percentage of guests decide to extend their stay beyond their original reservation. It is almost impossible to remove a guest from their room without causing hard feelings. The defect of not being able to provide a guest with a particular room when they have no reservation causes little problem because the guest doesn't fully expect to secure the room of their preference. On the other hand, the guest who arrives at the hotel expecting that their reserved room will be ready for them will react quite strongly with emotions such as aggravation, annoyance, confusion, and feeling defeated. The defect is now linked to an expectation and as a result is dehumanizing.

7. Business Results

Genuine caring and the bottom-line

Horst Schulze of Ritz-Carlton conducted a profitability impact analysis as to what would happen if customer satisfaction scores were moved from 92% to 97% over a four-year period. This analysis assumed that the remaining 3% of their customers would have needs that were inconsistent with a majority of the 97% of Ritz-Carlton customers. Using the existing statistics of Ritz-Carlton's four million room nights a year, the premise was that if those 5% of previously dissatisfied customers (200 000 guests) did not leave the hotel unfulfilled and not tell others they were dissatisfied, it would equate to 8% additional occupancy in a comparable economic year. This added 8% occupancy rate would add $300 million in profit to the bottom-line. This $300 million could never be achieved by cost cutting without significantly affecting customer satisfaction. However small and insignificant pure cost-cutting measures appear to management, customers will invariably notice and will likely be less satisfied and experience more dehumanization as a result. On the other hand, process improvement measures cut costs while at the same time improving customer satisfaction. Many times, the companies that focus on pure cost cutting are responding to Wall Street's insatiable desire to hear about cost-cutting initiatives. This creates a perpetual cycle of harmful cost-cutting initiatives that affect both the customer and long-term profitability.

Other Ritz-Carlton process improvement efforts made quantifiable improvements such as their meeting planner satisfaction, which is measured both internally and externally. Externally, they use J.D. Powers and associates to measure their customer satisfaction versus their foremost competitor. Figure 8.8 shows level and trend superiority. These percentages represent extreme satisfaction.

Ritz-Carlton internal guest satisfaction is also measured both internally and externally. Externally, they use nationwide surveys to measure their customer satisfaction versus their foremost competitor for frequent leisure travelers (Table 8.7) and frequent business travelers (Table 8.8).

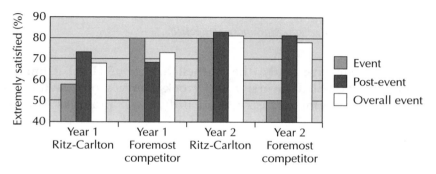

Figure 8.8   Meeting planner satisfaction
(data from Ritz-Carlton's MBNQA Application Summary; source: J.D. Powers Associates)

Table 8.7 Frequent leisure traveler – 1999 key comparisons
(reproduced by permission of Ritz-Carlton)

	Top two boxes		Top box	
	RC	FC	RC	FC
Overall satisfaction	91%	80%	70%	52%
Cleanliness of room and facilities	90%	77%	64%	48%
Adequate security	83%	64%	57%	38%
Value for the money	42%	32%	19%	10%
Staff knowledgeable and helpful	67%	54%	41%	28%

RC = Ritz-Carlton; FC = foremost competitor.

Table 8.8 Frequent business traveler – 1999 key comparisons
(reproduced by permission of Ritz-Carlton)

	Top two boxes		Top box	
	RC	FC	RC	FC
Overall satisfaction	91%	84%	68%	57%
Quality of facilities from location to location	85%	68%	62%	39%
Quality of services	88%	67%	61%	37%
Has alert and helpful staff, responsive to my needs	83%	62%	52%	34%
Provides excellent business class floors	70%	49%	43%	23%
Has very clean and well maintained facilities	96%	93%	74%	60%
Provides full range of business services	77%	58%	48%	26%

RC = Ritz-Carlton; FC = foremost competitor.

In a comprehensive study, the Cornell School of Hotel Administration and McGill University undertook a survey of 13 400 managers in the lodging industry to identify "best practices" in the lodging industry. The study named Ritz-Carlton as the overall best-practice champion.

Ritz-Carlton's measures of financial performance fall into a number of different categories. EBITDA (earnings before income taxes,

Table 8.9   Pretax ROI summary – actual
(reproduced by permission of Ritz-Carlton)

	1995	1996	1997	1998	1999
Total fees ($m)	21 036	36 786	39 930	46 831	58 478
Sales Proceeds ($m)					
EBITDA ($m)	11 951	20 882	21 284	29 668	39 103
Pretax ROI	5.3%	9.3%	9.5%	9.8%	12.9%

Pretax IRR = 24.4%

Table 8.10   Administrative cost summary – actual
(reproduced by permission of Ritz-Carlton)

	1995	1996	1997	1998	1999
Total fees ($m)	21 036	36 786	39 930	46 831	58 478
Admin. costs ($m)	9 084	15 903	18 646	17 163	19 375
Admin. costs % total fees	43.2	43.2	46.7	36.4	33.1

Less = Good.

depreciation and amortization) and pretax ROI (return on investment) are shown in Table 8.9.

The administrative costs (see Table 8.10) are shown as a percentage of total fees, profit, and revenue.

Four hotels by individual owner that were out of compliance with Ritz-Carlton standards were negotiated to another hotel managment company and the costs associated with that transition.

Figure 8.9 illustrates the percentage profit for the Ritz-Carlton compared with their major competitor and all other luxury hotels for 1996 to 1998.

Table 8.11 represents employee well-being and satisfaction, which is measured through their employee satisfaction survey. The table illustrates the key drivers of overall employee morale and their respective responses for 1998 (excellent, very good, good).

Figure 8.10 shows Ritz-Carlton's decreasing employee turnover rate from 77% in 1989 to 30% in 1999. This trend is a direct

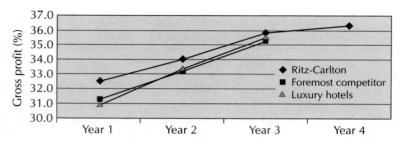

Figure 8.9   Percentage gross profit vs. main competitor
(data from Ritz-Carlton's MBNQA Application Summary; source: PKF Consulting)

result of better selection processes and training as well as drivers of employee satisfaction.

Ritz-Carlton's goal of pride and joy in the workplace and full participation of as many employees as feasible is improved through employees being involved in the planning process (see Figure 8.11).

Ritz-Carlton must ensure that the performance of their suppliers meet specific performance criteria. These performance criteria are measured using a supplier compliance and quality survey form that measures the most important aspects of supplier quality.

Table 8.11   1998 employee satisfaction data – percentage positive
(reproduced by permission of Ritz-Carlton)

Issue	Ritz-Carlton	Service Co. norms
Decision-making authority	83%	55%
Teamwork	83%	70%
Department coordination of efforts	80%	40%
Communication index	87%	57%
Empowerment	85%	67%
Understanding departmental goals	86%	86%
Management		
Constructive feedback	73%	45%
Verbal recognition for job well done	69%	41%
Monetary recognition for job well done	50%	28%

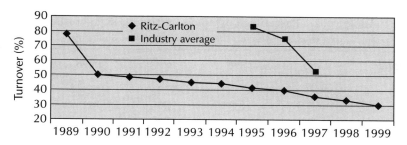

Figure 8.10   Percentage of turnover
(data from Ritz-Carlton's MBNQA Application Summary; source: RCHC/Kaznova
Consultants)

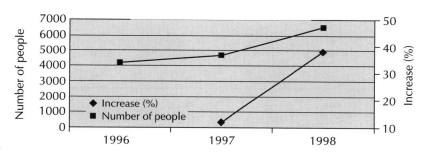

Figure 8.11   Population involved in planning
(data from Ritz-Carlton's MBNQA Application Summary; source: Kasnova Consultants)

Every six months, the purchasing personnel at every hotel complete
the survey, which rates key issues (e.g. fit for use, accuracy, on-
time, defect-free, cycle time, service, etc.).

Ritz-Carlton's goal is to increase the number and percentage of:

1   Hotels that certify their key suppliers (through robust pro-
     cesses) semi-annually.

2   Key suppliers who achieve an 80% or better rating on all
     attributes of their supplier certification survey.

Table 8.12 and Figure 8.12 demonstrate positive gains toward
achieving Ritz-Carlton's objectives over a three-year period.

Table 8.12   Percentage of hotels certifying key suppliers
(data from Ritz-Carlton's MBNQA Application Summary)

Supplier	1995	1996	1997	1998	1999
A	43%	52%	52%	95%	100%
B		12%	82%	100%	
C	8%	21%	47%	95%	87%
D	34%	51%	56%	95%	96%
E	13%	39%	43%	100%	100%
F	39%	47%	52%	95%	100%
G	39%	52%	56%	100%	100%
H	21%	43%	47%	95%	83%
I	43%	52%	56%	100%	96%
J	43%	52%	56%	100%	87%
K	43%	52%	56%	95%	87%
L	43%	52%	56%	95%	100%
M	43%	47%	56%	100%	96%
Total	34%	47%	50%	96%	96%

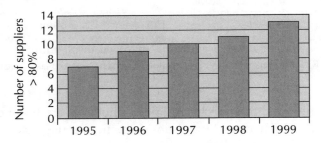

Figure 8.12   Number of key suppliers achieving 80% or better on
supplier certification
(data from Ritz-Carlton's MBNQA Application Summary; source: RCHC)

Figure 8.13 reflects Ritz-Carlton's improvements in operating maintenance. Ritz-Carlton's CARE program of systematic preventive maintenance, which occurs four times year, has kept their property and equipment at world-class functionality while minimizing maintenance costs.

Figure 8.14 shows Ritz-Carlton's improvements in revenue per hours worked.

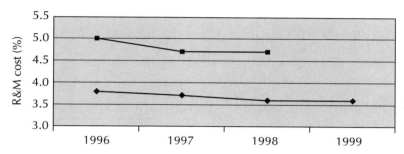

Figure 8.13   Percentage repair and maintenance costs to total revenue vs. luxury segment
(data from Ritz-Carlton's MBNQA Application Summary; source: PKF Consulting)

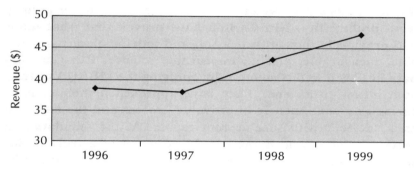

Figure 8.14   Total revenue per hours worked
(data from Ritz-Carlton's MBNQA Application Summary; source: RCHC)

Ritz-Carlton are in a competitive labor market with many competitors competing for the same pool of skilled labor. Therefore, Ritz-Carlton began a program to improve the cycle time for when a potential new employee begins the hiring process to when a job offer is made. Using a rigor quality approach, Ritz-Carlton experienced a 21-fold improvement in this reduction (see Figure 8.15).

To implement the human touch in a business with the certainty, conviction, and depth of a passionately courteous individual, a business will need strong leadership and the rigors of process management to evolve the intuitive art of the human touch into a repeatable and reliable discipline. Through the strong leadership of Horst Schulze, Ritz-Carlton was able to make important

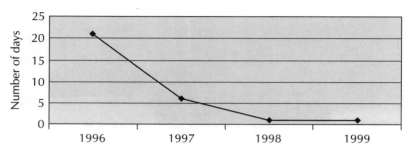

Figure 8.15   Time to process new hire from walk-in to job offer
(data from Ritz-Carlton's MBNQA Application Summary; source: RCHC)

strides in proving that genuine caring can be successfully implemented as a process and the most important driver of long-
term profitability. Ritz-Carlton have proven that what many
had previously thought was a soft and indefinable art is definable, measurable, and an improvable science. Ritz-Carlton's
path has been well structured by applying the MBNQA criteria
as a means to an end. They have approached their genuine
caring as a continuously improvable process and the lack of it
as a "defect" with specific root causes. At the foundation of
their genuine caring is the careful selection of a truly caring
staff that are trained by the best, respected by all, and fully
empowered. From their three steps of service, that includes a
warm and sincere greeting, anticipating and complying with
guest needs, and a fond farewell, to the declaration that "We
Are Ladies and Gentlemen Serving Ladies and Gentlemen",
Ritz-Carlton has shown that, when both staff and guests are
treated with acknowledgement, respect, and trust, extraordinary levels of service can be achieved and sustained.

9

Implementing Technology to Humanize (not Dehumanize)

TECHNOLOGY CONTINUES TO PLAY AN INCREASINGLY IMPORTANT role in how businesses sell to and service customers. Despite the blizzard of technological advances and massive investments, only $0.50 of every $1.00 improves the humanness of customer interactions while the other $0.50 dehumanizes interactions with customers.

There are four basic approaches for implementing technology. The goal is to implement technology to increase the human quality of customer interactions and decrease the probability of dehumanizing interactions.

These approaches:

1   Enable acknowledgement of "you know me".

2   Free employees from task execution to focus on human elements of interaction.

3   Simplify the customer's life.

4   Give control back to the customer.

Technology that Enables Acknowledgement of "You Know Me"

Acknowledging that a business knows and understands its customer, by having information for such things as their basic identity, interaction history, characteristics, and preferences, ultimately serves to acknowledge their existence and worth as a customer and human being. Applying information to acknowledge the customer can be as simple as name recognition or can extend to the more sophisticated acknowledgements of knowing the customer's purchase and interaction history, communication preferences, demographics, psychographics, lifestyle, and market-basket propensities. The business's ability to apply its customer information is a central part of being able to provide that technology. Applying this information using database technology and modeling capabilities is a central enabler for not only providing a single informational view of the customer but also being able to dynamically interact with them regardless of which distribution channel they choose.

Beyond acknowledgement is the ability for a business to enable its employees to provide the customer with sufficient knowledge to direct the customers to what they need, which may differ from what they want, e.g. sometimes customers don't fully understand the risks of a certain product or service.

While the use of sophisticated analysis and modeling techniques can serve the acknowledgement function well, basic transfer of information with customers can also fulfill these acknowledgement needs.

The following is a very basic example of how using customer information in conjunction with a "retail club" not only acknowledges the customer themselves, but also the customer's worth to the business.

Dorothy Lane Market implemented a "Club DLM", as many other retailers have, which provides their best customers with even greater customer service and savings. Club DLM's top 30% receive higher-value coupons as well as the DLM newsletter. In addition, these customers get a free turkey during Thanksgiving and their next-door neighbor receives a turkey coupon for $15 off, the next-door neighbor's "next-door neighbor" receives $10 off, and so on. Club DLM also institute product-specific mailings each month for certain customers who show an interest in specific products. For example, Dorothy Lane's top French cheese customers may receive a coupon for a new French cheese they have recently purchased. Another example would be sending the same top French cheese customers an offer to buy crystal stemware for $40 that normally retails for $100.

Technology that Sets the Business's Human Element Free

Most of what the customer remembers is the human element of face-to-face interactions. That is why it is important to implement technology that will take the burden of task execution away from the employee and free them to focus on the quality of their personal interactions. This means implementing technology to either automate certain tasks that are unnecessary for the employee during a customer interaction or to increase the efficiency of task execution so the employee can focus on the more memorable human portions of the interaction. Implementing technologies that provide better information about the customer and help predict what the customer will probably need begin to accomplish this goal. When technology frees an employee from mundane informational issues, their energies can be better focused on the human elements of acknowledgement, respect, and trust building messages.

When employees have more time to give of themselves as people, customer interaction is improved on two levels. First, the customer feels more acknowledged and respected because conversation is more personable, with enhanced nonverbal communication, including more smiles and good eye contact. On the second level, the customer believes the employee is more effective at his or her task because strong nonverbal communication signals to the customer that the employee really cares about doing the job well are sent, through actively acknowledging the customer during the interaction. This furthers the customer's trust that the employee "did a good job" for them, e.g. accuracy, thoroughness, completeness.

Focus Employees on Non-verbal Communications and Task Fulfillment

The ability of an employee to give of themselves as a human being to a customer is just as important to an interaction as the skillful mechanics of executing the task itself. There should be a balance between the speed at which the task is accomplished and the personal responsiveness of the employee completing the task for the customer. The element of personal responsiveness is inextricably linked to the quality of performance in the eyes of the customer. For example, a teller in a financial institution will be perceived as not being as accurate with a customer's account if the teller does not demonstrate strong interpersonal communication behaviors, e.g. eye contact, smile. The underlying emotional reason for this is that if there is little or no eye contact with the teller, the customer may feel that he was not fully acknowledged as a human being and, therefore, the teller probably did not really care enough to administer their account with the highest degree of accuracy. In this scenario, a strong-minded customer might choose to ask to deal with a different employee; however, many customers would simply leave with a sense of dissatisfaction or distrust already established in their mind before a problem ever occurs. A similar scenario can occur when using a call-center. A customer can perceive by the tone of voice a call-center rep uses that they don't really care or don't have the appropriate information. Some may hang up in the middle of the call, then call back looking for a person who "sounds" as if they care and therefore will do a more diligent job of handling their request. Other customers may finish the original call but after hanging up call back again until they feel satisfied that they have been listened to and their problem solved. Any call-monitoring devices in this case would not reveal the dissatisfaction felt by the customer. Many hidden costs are added to the operational costs of firms simply because they have not hired empathetic people or have not sufficiently trained their employees in the importance of giving of themselves as human beings in a kind and empathetic manner while still successfully completing the task at hand. These inherent challenges are perpetuated by the propensity for business to measure the nonhuman elements of customer interaction because they are easier to quantify, and yet human interactions are often the most important factors in revealing the true customer response.

Technology that Simplifies the Customer Life

As often as technology simplifies customer interaction, technology makes customer interaction more complex. The most notorious example is voice-response systems for adding unnecessary complexity to a customer's life. Another well-known example is complex websites, whether the complexity be in just navigating them or actually performing e-commerce on them, i.e. ordering, tracking.

Most firms ultimately find that simplifying websites for customers is not a trivial matter. Even more complex are web processes, such as ordering products. Ease of ordering should be approached with constant usability testing. Before Barnes & Noble.com created their very efficient Web-based ordering process, they found that even the most obvious ordering setup could be confusing. One of their early attempts asked the customer to choose between three ordering choices (conditions):

1   If you are a returning customer, sign in here, or . . .

2   If you are giving this item as a gift, sign in here, or . . .

3   If you are using a coupon, sign in here.

In this scenario, a customer could be all three, i.e. I am a former customer who is using a coupon to buy a gift. The fundamentals of customer transactions – anything that is going to confuse a customer will ultimately slow them down and many times even stop them from ordering. Alleviating these complexities as well as performance issues, such as the ability to load pages quickly in the customer ordering sequence, is critical to an efficient ordering path that will encourage customers to complete a transaction.

Another interesting behavioral dynamic that Barnes & Noble.com found was that having a graphical representation of the product simplified how customers processed product information in their minds as well as raising their comfort level with actually buying the product. It became quite evident that unless the product was made real and tangible to the customer by some form of graphical representation of the item, e.g. book, customers often would not opt to purchase the item. This is due to the fact that customers are mostly visual processors when making buying decisions. Behavioral science has shown that 75% of the human brain is dedicated to visual processing. Barnes & Noble.com found visual processing such a critical issue, even for used books to sell effectively, that they installed scanners at their receiving desks and loading docks. For new books, Barnes & Noble.com requested that publishers provide a high-quality image of each book (the publisher usually has each book professionally photographed) to be displayed on the website to facilitate maximum sales. For featured books and items, Barnes & Noble.com have their own graphics studio to ensure that there is a compelling visual image of the item to be sold online. For some online concerns a strong visual representation is less critical because of the less physical nature of the product or service. However, for the majority, the bottom-line is: "If people are going to buy, they need a picture".

Another good example of the importance of simplicity is how two well-known ISPs, AOL and WorldNet, approached the same marketplace. While both AOL and WorldNet currently offer world-class software that is very simple and easy to use, WorldNet's initial software was not. When WorldNet first entered the marketplace, they underestimated how critical simplicity and ease-of-use was to attract and support customers. In comparison, AOL invested a tremendous amount of time and resource into making their interface extremely easy to use. This was extremely important when going after customers new to the Internet because, typically, they were a very unsophisticated segment and required the browser to be painfully simple. Although AOL's initial ultra-simple install and use approach constrained some of the flexibility of using AOL, simplicity won the day and won the market. In order to install AOL, the CD slides into the computer, the reference number is input, and it works. In contrast, WorldNet employed AT&T Labs to start with a version of Internet Explorer and attempt to make it easy to use. AT&T Labs was convinced that WorldNet needed to be somewhat easy to use but not too easy, because they assumed more sophisticated people would be using the Internet. The importance of simplicity became readily apparent when each customer who was not computer savvy attempted to load WorldNet's initial software for the first time and invariably had a question or problem. The inordinate amount of customer care calls translated into tremendous expense. AT&T Labs reaction to this deluge of customer care calls was "... well, maybe they shouldn't be on the Internet". AOL understood the financial impacts of making the ease-of-use attributes absolutely bulletproof. This included everything from the initial installation to how the dialer operated during the first hookup. Again, AT&T Labs took the internal perspective rather than the customer-centric approach to creating a product for WorldNet. This ease-of-use problem persisted for almost three years. What AT&T learned from the WorldNet experience was that the customer's tolerance for technical difficulties is extremely low. The critical question became "What is our customer's willingness and capability to handle a single technical problem?" On a scale of 1 to 10, their customer's tolerance level was only 1 or 2 for technical endurance. Beyond just the endurance to handle a problem, there was the cost to the customer of all the time it took to work on installing the software. In reality, WorldNet's new customers would spend a month attempting to get their browser and mail to function with an average of four calls within the first 30 days for minor technical advice and problem-solving. This first month totaled an average care cost per customer of $30–$40 with a significant portion of customers leaving for AOL. AOL's simplicity enabled them to acquire as many customers in one month as World-Net could in a full year.

Give Control

The two most effective ways to give customers control through technology is to enable:

1 Anonymity.

2 Choice and convenience.

Enable anonymity

In many self-service interactions, it is important to allow customers to retain as much anonymity as possible for as long as possible in the interaction process. Allow them to control the amount of anonymity at their comfort level until they choose not to be anonymous. From an emotional perspective, anonymity is desirable because customers withhold trust in initial interactions until they feel the company has earned their trust. After a certain level of interaction is reached, a customer's knowledge and interest will have increased and provisional trust will be granted to the company. A financial institution in the United States found that its customers were more apt to complete the scenario planning process of obtaining a mortgage when their website enabled the customers to initially run through simple scenarios with only minimal personal data. An initial period of anonymity reduces anxiety about revealing personal details, enables the customer to determine whether they are interested in the product and price prior to revealing personal information, and reduces the fear that information given early in the process will be used to make unsolicited and unwanted product offerings to the customer.

Maximize anonymity by minimizing the questions asked

While InsWeb do not sell insurance, their strategy is to "provide the best experience for online insurance shopping for both the person and the carrier". This strategy manifests itself successfully when a person can go online and quickly and easily navigate through their site without any questions about the requested information and then receive multiple high-quality options for quality insurance carriers. One of the current challenges in executing this strategy is that it still takes 15 to 20 minutes for a person to successfully navigate through all the questions and receive the recommendations. One of the main reasons there are so many questions is that when InsWeb first set up their site, they were required to include all the questions that their partner carriers requested as part of their informational needs in order to produce good insurance quotes. While analyzing the amount of time questions took to answer, InsWeb found that their partner carriers had included many questions that were unnecessary and not being used at all. The entire process was disenfranchising people because they wanted more anonymity for a longer time period and they were overwhelmed by the time it took to answer so many questions. As a result, InsWeb eliminated the unnecessary questions. They were caught between a "rock and a hard place" because the initial carriers would not agree to partner with InsWeb unless they included these very specific questions.

To reassure potential customers, InsWeb communicate to them that their personal information is securely stored on their servers for the customer's convenience. When the customer requests a quote from one or more of the participating insurance companies, their information is sent only to those companies. Information is never sent out without express permission. InsWeb never resell, trade, lease, or rent the personal information supplied by customers. Strongly communicating this policy to customers allows them to feel not only belief in their anonymity but also their control over it.

Enable convenience and choice

The proliferation of new technologies to serve customers continues and is accelerating. These technologies can be implemented to provide information for customers to help themselves as well as information to help employees serve customers more effectively.

Two significant ways that technology enables convenience and choice are:

1   Enabling customer control of how and when to interact with one firm.

2   Enabling control of how and when to shop across multiple firms.

Enabling customer control of how and when to interact with one firm

Table 9.1 is a simple example of how both humans and technology are used to support the interactions between customer and business.

Technology should give customers convenience and choice. Many banks currently implement technology to drive people away from a

Table 9.1   Customer-initiated – business-initiated

Customer-initiated	Business-initiated
In person	**In person**
Visit to a bank branch	Sales rep call
Shopping in a retail store	Service rep call
Telephone	**Telephone**
Calling a particular salesperson	Returning specific customer calls
Escalating a problem	Information gathering
	Problem resolution
Machine with option for personal	**Machine with option for personal**
Inbound sales and service, e.g. technical support through call-centers with IVRs and agent options or websites with call back or switch to video options	Outbound sales and service through call-centers
Machine only	**Machine only**
Cash withdrawal from bank machine	Posted information or marketing on website, on ABM, on kiosk
Gas purchase with payment at the pump	"Pushed" marketing messages and sales and service information to customers' e-mail, faxes, wireless
Following stock movements on wireless	
Check in for airline at kiosk	
Mail	**Mail**
Letters of instructions	Marketing solicitation
Letters of complaint	Service information
Application forms for product, service or employment	

Source: Wendy Eggleton.

particular distribution channel. Technology should primarily be used to give customers a choice as to how and at what speed the customer interacts with the bank. This increases their control and therefore reduces anxiety. First, a business must understand what truly drives customer convenience today, not necessarily what has historically driven convenience. For example, historically convenience was a bank branch on every corner but today ATMs and online banking mean convenience. Another example: decades ago most customers defined true convenience as having a gas station attendant fill up their car; today, customers would rather fill the car up themselves without waiting for an attendant. Ultimately, the Internet will give control to customers far beyond its use today.

Enable control of how and when to shop across multiple firms

InsWeb is a pure play (Internet only) insurance service that helps customers compare insurance quotes from leading insurance companies to find the best rates available. InsWeb based its strategy on simplifying the customer's life by compressing the time people need to spend to shop and secure insurance.

InsWeb's process is very simple. After a person fills out the quote request form, they will be presented with a number of brand-name companies, each of which will offer the person an insurance quote. Some companies present their quotes instantly; others respond within several days. The quotes the person receives are not rough estimates. They reflect the specific customer profile derived from information provided on the request form. Once the person has received the quotes, they may request coverage from the insurance company of choice. However, the person is never under any obligation to buy. If the customer chooses to buy from an instant quoting company, they select it, enter their contact information and their request will be submitted to the company. The company will contact them to complete the purchase. If the customer wishes to purchase from an offline company, they simply follow the purchase instructions that accompany the quote.

From a human side, InsWeb replace the time-consuming, inefficient, confusing, and cumbersome process of shopping for insurance. Typically, people wanting to shop for insurance would first have to pick up the phone and find several prospective insurance carriers. They would then have to go visit an agent for each company and fill out many redundant insurance forms. So if they investigate five different carriers they would have to fill out five relatively redundant insurance forms and probably only qualify for two or three of the five carriers. In contrast, people using the

InsWeb site fill out one application and can view all of the prospective carriers with quotes. Although this is a compelling story for both carrier and customer, still some people prefer physical interaction with an insurance agent, i.e. a real person. This may stem from the fact that a certain segment of the population inherently don't trust insurance companies but may trust a personal representative or agent from an insurance company. This is the case even though they realize that they can get a lower price online.

Not only do InsWeb give people tremendous convenience and control, they bring tremendous efficiencies to insurance carriers. InsWeb enable the traditional insurance carrier to be more effective in their marketing, underwriting, and new business acquisition process. InsWeb fix some of the cumbersome customer acquisition process and then focuses on underwriting strengths through technology. In the online world, InsWeb can encapsulate much of the underwriting process within their website and have this process be immediately scalable so it can service one or one thousand customers with the same efficiency. This is done through a sophisticated set of rule-based technological filters. These rules come from the carriers; included are such constraints as people under 25, only married individuals, safe automobile drivers, or individuals with multiple accidents or DUI (driving under the influence) convictions. The compelling aspect of this is that the carriers' business models become simplified as well because they never see any potential customer that they do not want because all of their requirements have been met during the rules-based web session. This provides an incredibly efficient way to deal with prospective customers because there is no cost expended on customers who do not qualify. Acquisition costs are reduced by one-half. Only a certain number of customers will respond, and of those who respond, only a certain percentage will qualify and of those who qualify, only a small percentage will actually accept a carrier's offer. In essence, InsWeb's technology handles all of those screening steps before the carrier even sees one prospective customer. When the carrier does first see the customer, they are already prequalified and are ready to buy the product. In the brick and mortar world of insurance companies, sending out one million pieces of direct mail will, in optimal circumstances, produce a 2% response. Those 2% will actually call the company to inquire about the offer. Of those, 70% will actually qualify for the carrier's offer. Of that 70% who qualify, only 25%

will buy the carrier's product. Using InsWeb, an interested customer logs on to the website, invests 20 minutes inputting their
information and at the end of the process they can see which carriers
are willing to write insurance for them. Customers can gauge the
brand and the price and then buy the insurance product. InsWeb
are seeing a typical close rate of roughly 50%, which is extraordinary for the insurance industry.

Insult to Injury – Voice-response Systems (VRSs)

Most VRSs break all the humanizing rules of technology. VRSs
offer no acknowledgement, further complicate a customer's life,
and take control away from the customer. Yet, voice-response
systems are a permanent fixture in customers' lives. If the voice-
response system is simple and respectful of the customer's emotions, effort, and time, they will not only provide efficiencies to
both the customer and the business but also a humanized interaction. Proportionally, many VRSs still create a dehumanizing experience for a customer because they don't take into consideration the
customer's emotional state and they waste the customer's time.
Both effects create negative value for customers (see Figure 9.1).
In many cases, what begins as a simple query from a satisfied
customer becomes an escalating chain of powerful, long-lasting
negative emotions that ultimately leaves a completely dissatisfied
customer.

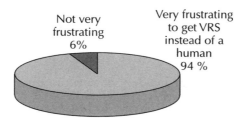

Figure 9.1   Voice-response systems are very frustrating
(data from *Aggravating Circumstances*, 2002 Public Agenda, used with kind permission)

Many VRSs create the following emotional chain:

1   Customer calls business for simple product/service question.

2   Complexity and futility of VRS demeans customer's intelligence, i.e. five minutes of complex VRS navigation ultimately places customer on hold.

3   Length of hold time aggravates customer for "wasting their time".

4   Business lies to demeaned and aggravated customer, i.e. "Your call is very important to us", but hasn't staffed sufficiently for timely customer response.

5   Business insults demeaned, aggravated, and "lied to" customer by attempting to sell new products while on hold.

6   Insulted, demeaned, aggravated, and "lied to" customer takes business elsewhere.

In order to alleviate most of these shortcomings, the following guidelines should be followed when designing a VRS.

✦   Give the customer control

　　— Always give the customer the option of talking to a real human being anywhere in the sequence.

✦   Reduced uncertainty (anxiety)

　　— Tell the customer how long the expected wait time is.

✦   Be honest

　　— Don't tell the customer, "Your call is very important to us", unless the business can back the promise with response times under five minutes.

✦   Design for customer needs, not corporate needs

　　— Limit the VRS complexity to less than three or four levels. Continually test the VRS design phases for usability issues.

✦   Sell only if you can provide timely service

— Advertise during wait times only if the wait time is less than five minutes.

We're going to "sell" you more products while we "aggravate" you while on hold

A common practice of businesses is not only to force customers to navigate through a complex set of questions in a VRS and then place them on hold, but also to play a series of advertising messages with musical background as they hold "for the next available service representative". These messages are designed under the assumption that the customer will be waiting only a short period of time. Because many businesses' call-centers are understaffed, customers are often subjected to listening to the same message or advertisement for an extended period of time. In this scenario, just when the customer is feeling neglected and unimportant, the company is boasting how important this customer is to them and the wonderful array of products they have in addition to the product the customer has called to complain about.

In many situations, interacting with a business is just as intolerable for the employees of the business as it is for the customer. Simply put, many businesses don't regularly test their interaction environments as "real people". Most notable are large business voice-response systems. The automated phone systems and the processes that support them, as employed by large businesses, continue to frustrate and anger customers. Here is an example of how a "sophisticated" major financial institution with six million customers and an explicit "stated" customer focus can, through lack of attention, wind up delivering very dehumanizing interactions. This bank's mission statement begins by promising: "At Bank X, we help customers reach their financial goals by listening carefully, anticipating needs ...". This bank employs intelligent people and has the financial resources (over $250 billion in assets) to create the most human interaction possible using a VRS. The example used here is an actual account of one customer's interactions with this financial institution. What is important to note is that an entire series of pleasant and well-executed customer interactions was destroyed at the end by the bank not having the proper processes and communications in place. This customer wanted to return his leased car when the lease was ended. Not only did this simple task turn out to be time-consuming but also extremely dehumanizing and humiliating. In anticipation of the end of the lease, the customer assumed he would receive notification about the process needed to return the car and complete the necessary paperwork. When it came to within 30 days of the end of his five-year lease and there was no notification, he became concerned. He didn't want to incur any penalties because of not following the correct procedure. He decided to make a phone call to Bank X. The phone call began with navigating through the multiple levels (four) in their voice-response system in an attempt to be connected with a real human being. Once he made his final selection to be connected to a real human being, the phone rang roughly six times and then entered a message system saying that this person was unavailable and by pressing 1, the customer could leave a message. When he attempted to leave a message, there was an additional message saying that this person's voice mailbox was full. There was another message saying that there was an alternate person who could be reached at another number. He called the other number and found out that this second person's voice mailbox was full as well. There was another alternate number given at this person's mailbox, which connected to another full mailbox. At this point another choice offered connection with the bank operator. When he pressed this number he was immediately disconnected. The customer went through this same scenario several times, understandably feeling frustrated and held hostage by Bank X because during the time he was trying to communicate with them his lease expired and he received a bill with financial penalties. He decided to try a new strategy and pressed zero at the first opportunity. Finally, he was connected with an operator who, when he expressed his frustration with their dysfunctional phone system, explained that because of a bug in the system if one mailbox was full, they all registered as full. The operator gave him a number to call, which turned out to be the wrong number, but this person did give him the correct customer service number. When he called this number he was asked, "How did you get this number?" After telling his horrific VRS experience he asked the customer service rep, "If this number is a secret, how are people supposed to get customer service from Bank X?" The customer service rep responded, "I don't know, but we get a lot of calls". At this point, our disgusted, annoyed customer was finally able to complete the appropriate paperwork to solve the problem. While some of these communication problems were circumstantial, many of the broken processes were systemic in the bank's communication process. Very simply, the bank could have avoided this scenario by putting themselves in their customer's place and attempting to use the voice-response system they expect their customers to use.

Dynamics of People Interacting with Technology versus Humans

Businesses must also be aware that there are certain behavioral dynamics that are distinct to technology interfaces but do not exist with human-to-human interactions. These differences in behavioral dynamics between interacting with humans and interacting with technology relate to:

+ Differences in expectation levels.

+ Which interactions are most memorable.

+ Special considerations for how people interact with technology.

Despite these differences, many human needs still exist at varying degrees between human interactions and technology that many firms neglect, e.g. a customer's need for acknowledgement and respect does not go away at the ATM or Internet site.

Differences in expectation levels

Studies have shown that human beings' expectations are five times higher with technology-based interactions than with human-based interactions. For example, when people log on to a company's website, their expectations for attributes such as accuracy, working right the first time, and speed will be five times higher than they are when interacting with a real human being face-to-face. Similar dynamics occur with telephone equipment as well. The lesson to be learned is that when applying technology, there will be little tolerance for even minor functionality issues. The impression made by technology that is not 100% functional will reflect on the entire business. One of the underlying reasons for this is that people expect other people to be "human" whereas they expect a machine to be a machine and work flawlessly.

Therefore, it is important to segment expectation levels and performance goals along the continuum of man and machine interactions. The varying levels of customer expectations should set operational standards or goals. Customer expectations of responsiveness when dealing with a real human being, e.g. call-center rep versus an electronic channel, are significantly different. Given the criteria of response time, efficiency, and accuracy, interaction with an employee can be slower and less efficient than interaction with a website. A good analogy to use is, if customers are standing in line waiting for the customer service representative to find a sales record customers will wait much longer with a lower level of frustration and a higher degree of patience than they would if they had entered in a tracking number on the same company's website and were waiting for a reply from the Internet system. The underlying behavior or reasoning is that the customer can visually observe that the customer service rep is "working" diligently on the problem or request whereas there is no explicit evidence that an Internet site is working on a request. Therefore, the customer's patience or tolerance for the timeframe is much less. Expectation levels for employees over the phone is slightly higher than an in-person interaction because there are only verbal cues from the customer service reps that they are working on the problem diligently, rather than visual cues. This heightened visual orientation is due to the fact that 75% of a human being's brain is dedicated toward processing visual stimulus. Therefore, setting operational standards for response based on how many visual clues are inherent within the given interaction type is a high priority. "Dead time" will seem longest while waiting for a PC to respond to a request versus waiting for a response over the telephone, versus waiting for a response during a face-to-face interaction. It is possible to modify the inherent visual cues of each interaction type by creating more explicit signs that there is attentive work being done on the customer's behalf. Face-to-face interactions contain sufficient explicit clues of attentiveness and caring. Telephone interactions can be helped by service reps continuing to pursue personal verbal interactions while they are trying to retrieve or analyze a customer's request. The nonhuman interaction types, such as the Internet or an ATM, need to build in explicit visual signals that emulate human visual cues of actual face-to-face interactions. For example, instead of ATMs just displaying the words "processing your request", they may have a cartoon visualization of a teller going to retrieve the money and handing the money to the customer. In addition, human customers expect changes to occur more quickly using electronic channels versus human channels of interaction. If customers have requested a change to occur on a PC, their expectations are that it will be executed very quickly. If a similar request for change is asked of a human being, the expectation of response time is significantly lower. This human behavior extends to operational failures. Customers have only partial tolerance for nonhuman interaction channels being unavailable or dysfunctional, e.g. a busy signal on the telephone, an ATM being without cash, a PC being down.

Which interactions are most memorable?

Customers form the majority of their impressions of a business on the human contact they have with a business. Interactions with technology or machines are usually of minimal importance. Customers, who conduct almost all of their interactions using a business's electronic channels and automated machines, still form their strongest impression of the business during the isolated cases in which they interact with human employees. For example, one large bank found that customers who predominantly used PC banking or telephone banking formed their impressions of the bank during the rare occasions they physically visited a branch.

Sometimes technology attempts to create an impression of caring or acknowledgement using methods such as recognizing website visitor by their first name. People will almost completely discount that type of machine recognition. People will remember another human being's recognition of their name but a machine's recognition is almost meaningless and forgettable.

The real risk of implementing technology without considering the implications of this dynamic of human behavior can lead businesses into a high-risk environment in which technology actually reduces the probability of creating and sustaining a relationship rather than enhancing it by adding further convenience to the customer.

The fact that people predominantly remember human interactions explains the inherent weakness of making this fatal decision: "We'll increase profits by pushing our customers away from face-to-face contacts and toward less expensive technology interfaces with little effect on long-term customer behavior". What happens, generally, is that short-term profits are affected because of the short-term cost reductions of using technology instead of a real human to interact with customers. What is not taken into account regarding the long-term profit equation is the effects of losing the human feelings of acknowledgement, respect, and trust that human interactions are highly effective at delivering to customers. Businesses have found that while they may have saved expense, they have lost an important human relationship element, which has cost the business more in loyalty than they have saved in expense reduction. There currently is a concerted effort to re-establish this lost human link.

It interesting to note that in a 1913 training document for businesses, there was a cautionary note stating:

> It is worth it to say that the weak spoke of modern business is the telephone.

Special considerations for how people interact with technology

Human needs don't change when customers choose to use technology. Most human needs have not fundamentally changed over time. The common mistake of businesses when implementing technology is to assume that somehow human beings put their needs for acknowledgement, respect, and trust on hold when interacting with technology. When implementing any type of self-service options, business must remember that each customer still needs to feel respected, wanted, and valuable to the business. For example, if an ATM machine runs out of money, the customer feels dejected and insulted.

This fact was one of the essential items overlooked in the years of Internet hype that believed Internet technology held a universal new promise for business. Many people believed the Internet represented an entirely new business model, not simply a support system for existing industries. In addition, the assumption that people would forgo the social intercourse of shopping for sitting behind a computer screen was misjudged. These calculations, which ignored the human element of shopping, created radically inaccurate retail forecasts.

People have always been and still are very much visual processors, highly biased toward graphics and pictures rather than plain text. This fact is often overlooked when firms implement their website without having a sufficient display of graphic representations of products and services displayed. The methods people use to satisfy these needs will differ with moods that alter from one day to the next; being happy with surfing the Web for a book title may change another day to wanting to hold a physical book in a bookstore. People are driven by multisensory characteristics and react emotionally to all of their senses. For example, a customer goes to a local bookstore to buy a book, enters a store smelling of freshly brewed coffee, opens a smooth new book and feels the printed pages, enjoys the colors on an artistic book cover, listens to peaceful, relaxing music floating in the background and revels in the experience of that multisensory physical environment. The next day, the same person may want to sit in front of a PC at home and be able to search through 15 million titles in one second in an online environment.

The same dynamics of desiring both human and machine interfaces at different times is reflected in the online financial community with firms such as Charles Schwab. Charles Schwab are best known for their active customers who trade multiple times a day (more than a thousand trades a year), yet 25% of their trades are done over the phone by real human beings. Their best customers want to do both. For certain trades to feel comfortable, customers must fulfill the human need for acknowledgement and trust, whereas for other types of trades, they are completely comfortable with the online interface. It is almost as if some companies believe that the customers who use e-commerce interfaces are distinctly different customers than the ones who use human interfaces. Granted, there are some customers who exclusively use only one particular customer-facing infrastructure, but for the most part people use multiple customer-facing infrastructures on a regular basis. A good parallel to this is the family that has two different types of vehicles for various family activities. On one occasion, the family piles into the minivan to go swimming at the local park because it can carry the kids, pets and lots of water toys. On the other hand, when the family goes to church on Sunday, they may opt to take the family sedan for basic transportation. The family is the same family in both cases but requires different utility at different times from its vehicles. In the business world, the criteria a customer uses to make a shopping decision will change according to the situation. Possible criteria for choosing a web interface would be lowest price, large selection, or convenience.

It is important to segment implemented technology in terms of what the emotional content of the interactions are along a continuum of high to low interaction content. A simple way to segment emotional levels is to determine what levels of trust, acknowledgement, and respect are required to satisfy the human needs in any type of interaction and segment those interactions along a range using face-to-face interactions for the highest emotional level and pure technology for the lowest emotional level.

A good example of this is applying self-service technology such as ATM transactions. The product is very measurable and quantifiable and the interaction is quick and simple. It is a common mistake for firms to implement technology in areas where customers need human interaction rather than an automated process. In many cases, the implementation of technology in inappropriate areas only serves to aggravate emotions rather than calm them. Therefore, technology is best applied to activities that have little emotional involvement. Such activities are more transaction-oriented and can be characterized as "at a distance" communications.

Medium- to high-level emotional scenarios require real human involvement because no technology can satisfy deep emotional needs in a human being. Using real human beings for non-transactional activities is critical, not only to address the emotional needs of customers but also to avoid the escalation of those negative emotions that occur when an already upset customer is forced into dealing with frustrating, ineffectual technologies, e.g. voice-response systems, poorly designed web interfaces. The underlying emotional need in these scenarios is to validate customer concerns, either through a sympathetic voice or a kind facial expression. These irreplaceable human interactions communicate to the customer that what he or she is feeling is valid and understood.

The incredible opportunity for technology to support more human interactions is as often a *curse as it is caring* when naive implementations attack the very dignity of customers. The silent damage done to human customers from implementations driven by cost reduction without consideration of human factors inflicts wounds far exceeding any short-term cost savings. Damage becomes even greater because customers' expectations are five times higher when interacting with technology than when face-to-face with employees. Therefore it is important to implement technology judiciously by understanding and then segmenting implementation by the emotional content of interaction types. Business can start to reverse the trend of dehumanization by focusing on four traditionally weak areas in which technology has not enhanced but diminished humanness. These four areas directly support the three primary buying needs – acknowledgement, respect, and trust. The first area of focus is providing a single informational view as well as real-time modeling capabilities creating the feeling "you know me". The second area to focus on is applying technology to free employees from task execution enabling them to focus on the human elements of interaction. The third area is to apply technologies to truly simplify (not complicate) the customer's life. The fourth area of focus is using technology to increase (not decrease) the customer's sense of control through convenience and choice. An increased sense of control can be created through choices ranging from how and when to interact with a firm to the timing and level of autonomy and privacy. Technology is and will be a central enabler for creating humanness across an entire business when it is focused on a customer's sense of dignity and self-worth.

Conclusion – Releasing Your Business's Humanity

RELEASING YOUR FIRM'S HUMANITY IS TO PROFITABLY DELIVER THE best products for customers and do it in a way that acknowledges and respects their dignity and worth as people. The journey to accomplish this begins with the simplest of actions by any single person in the business. It could start with the checkout clerk who uses more eye contact and smiles more often at customers, the customer service rep who tries to deal with his customer's service issues as if they were his own, the manager who takes extra care in making sure his small group of employees clearly knows the objectives and has fun accomplishing them, or the business unit leader who increases the level at which her organization couples responsibility with authority to fulfill customer's needs.

For leaders, actions focused on creating a vision and culture to actively develop their carefully selected employees will have the bigger impact on customers as people. Operating within a strong human culture, employees can efficiently concentrate on fulfilling the primary buying determinants of customers: acknowledgement, respect, and trust. The areas of focus for acknowledgement should be a customer's existence, importance, feelings, and characteristics. In the area of respect, objectives should be focused on respecting the customer's dignity as a person. Communicating respect begins with simple actions such as using common courtesies and should extend into other areas such as respect for a customer's time, personal space, privacy, home, and diversity.

Focus on trust is critical because people don't buy without trust. Trust in customers is built on a foundation of product quality and operational excellence with supporting actions building trust in how human the business will treat them during interactions. Other supporting actions should promote integrity, openness, and the continuous education of customers as to the business's relative value. Equally, if not more important, is eliminating the causes of distrust. Effectively creating feelings of trust, acknowledgement and respect requires specific skills centered on communicating clear signals of humanness and caring and being an even better listener – both verbally and nonverbally. These actions should be implemented consistently across all interactions with an under-standing of the hierarchy of human needs, their relative importance, and their supporting business processes. Each one of these distinct interactions in each area of the business should be viewed as one step in a sequence of interdependent steps that make up an entire process. This will enhance the business's ability to ensure consistency and effectiveness in their human touch process as well as help identify the steps or root causes of actions that dehumanize.

Supporting these processes are the enabling technologies and the degree to which they increase or decrease the humanness of customer interactions. Businesses should focus on the areas in which they have traditionally been weak in enhancing the humanness of interactions. These areas are enabling convenience and control, anonymity, simplicity of life, and the sense that the business truly "knows" them. Technology should also set employees free from task execution to focus on the human elements of the interaction.

To accomplish these objectives is to create competitive competencies for the new era of customer fulfillment, as well as creating a deeper meaning for business success ... significance.

Index